Why
INDIA
Matters

Maya Chadda

LYNNE
RIENNER
PUBLISHERS

BOULDER
LONDON

D0191772

Published in the United States of America in 2014 by
Lynne Rienner Publishers, Inc.
1800 30th Street, Boulder, Colorado 80301
www.rienner.com

and in the United Kingdom by
Lynne Rienner Publishers, Inc.
3 Henrietta Street, Covent Garden, London WC2E 8LU

Library of Congress Cataloging-in-Publication Data
A Cataloging-in-Publication record for this book
is available from the Library of Congress.

ISBN 978-1-62637-038-8 (alk. paper)
ISBN 978-1-62637-039-5 (pb : alk. paper)

British Cataloguing in Publication Data
A Cataloguing in Publication record for this book
is available from the British Library.

Printed and bound in the United States of America

The paper used in this publication meets the requirements
of the American National Standard for Permanence of
Paper for Printed Library Materials Z39.48-1992.

5 4 3 2 1

To RB and Jawahira

Why India
Matters

Contents

Acknowledgments

This book has been long in the making and would have seen daylight much sooner had personal tragedy not delayed it. By the time I picked up the threads again, India's rise—the first in a series that I suspect is yet to come—had already peaked. The slide in India's fortunes since 2011 compelled me to accommodate both the upward and downward spirals. Fortuitously, this broadening of the analytical canvas has made the book more enduring than it would have been had I stopped in 2010. India matters in my view because of its successes as well as failures. I hope readers will find it useful to see India's path as one of many that world states can pursue in their quest for power.

The book would not have been written had two individuals in particular not given me their unfailing support and encouragement. Prem Shankar Jha, my friend and intellectual colleague, read painstakingly through many versions of the chapters, made useful suggestions, and provided valuable insights. I am most grateful to him for his time and for sharing his prodigious knowledge of India's politics and economy. The responsibility for the content and analyses, however, is all mine. The second individual is my publisher, Lynne Rienner. She has been the soul of patience and understanding. I am grateful to her for not losing faith in me and encouraging me to continue with the book.

I would also like to thank Rob Sauté, who went through the initial editing of the manuscript; Shena Redmond of Lynne Rienner Publishers, for her guidance throughout the production process; and Jan Kristiansson, whose editorial eye brought greater clarity and precision to the text. Several colleagues at William Paterson University deserve special mention for granting me the time to conduct research and write. Isabel Tirado, Nina Jemmott, Steve Hanh, and Kara Rabbitt all supported me throughout this project. As a member of the Council on Foreign Relations, I participated in task forces and roundtable discussions that contributed immensely to a more measured understanding of changes in India against competing transformations elsewhere in the post–Cold War world. Last but not least, I thank many of my close friends, who remain nameless here but are no less important, for sustaining me through the rough times. I am grateful to them all.

—*Maya Chadda*

Why India
Matters

1

The Puzzle
of India Rising

In 1991, after four decades of painfully slow, inward-looking growth, India's economy was in a crisis: India's balance of payments was heavily in the red, and it was on the verge of defaulting on its foreign debt. Two national elections in quick succession—in 1989 and then in 1991—had ended the dominance of the Congress Party, which had ruled during most of the first forty years following India's independence, and seemingly dealt a crippling blow to the party's capacity to make the hard decisions needed to avoid collapse. As if the nation's cup of woes were not sufficiently full, India had lost its protector in international politics with the disintegration of the Soviet Union at the end of the Cold War. India's brave attempt to combine economic growth with political democracy seemed on the verge of failure. Indeed, many wondered whether the Indian state itself would survive.

So how has India confounded the skeptics? One answer may lie in the unique nature of the Indian state. India is not, and has not even tried to become, a unitary nation-state. Most scholars have had to grapple with this seeming anomaly because their concepts of statehood and state-society relations have been shaped by five hundred years of political evolution in Europe, which transformed loosely bound territorial political formations into absolutist, monarchic states

1

and then into the strongly centralized nation-states of the industrial epoch. Prevailing concepts of the strength and weakness, coherence and incoherence, stability and instability of nation-states, as well as the yardsticks by which these are measured, have arisen from this evolution. The typical paradigm of an ideal state, therefore, defines it as a single coherent entity with all its parts working together to maintain internal stability and project power abroad. The post–World War II literature on state formation repeats this bias for an internally well-integrated, coherent, and strong entity as a precondition for rapid development. The East Asian developmental states are put forward in support of this argument.[1] Yet India does not fit into this paradigm easily. As a result, it defies attempts to explain its achievements and predisposes analysts to magnify the importance of its failures.

These debates about the nature of the state and its relationship to society have been complicated by new international developments since 1991. The end of the twentieth century saw the breakup of the Soviet Union and a rebirth of identity politics across the entire European landmass. It also saw new forms of warfare deployed in which states were waging wars not against other states but against peoples or nonstate groups with access to international bazaars in arms. The effort to cope with these challenges led to the erosion of the fundamental pillars of the Westphalian order, which gave birth to the system of sovereign nation-states some 375 years ago. While all this was happening, the victors of the Cold War, the United States and Western Europe, found themselves having to also cope with a new phase of globalization that seemed to threaten the industrial and financial bases of their power.

Most projections into the future have concluded that the next decades will see the birth of a multipolar world in which the United States will retain its preponderance but economic and military power will shift to Asia Pacific, particularly to China and to a lesser but significant measure to India. Commenting on the emerging world system, David Scott observes, "The international system is now clearly in a state of impending significant structural change, a 'long cycle' perspective. In that sense the 'Asian Century' . . . is the most accurate of the paradigms to have emerged for the 21st century."[2]

Commentary on this "rise of the rest" and its implications for America's global power has become a veritable industry.[3] Almost all these commentaries have focused on China and India not only because of their size, large populations, and rapidly growing economies but also because of the rapid expansion in their military strength and growing strategic ambitions sparked by the acquisition of large amounts of sophisticated weapons.

The emergence of such revisionist new states, whose rise revised the anticipated distribution of international power in the twenty-first century, has frequently threatened international peace. The rise of Nazi Germany and fascist Japan, for instance, plunged the world into war. And even when newly powerful states have not caused war, they have altered the balance of global power decisively. Arrival of the United States on the world stage demonstrated this shift. In the current world situation, India's rise is far less threatening than the emergence of a powerful and rapidly growing China, but observers nonetheless worry that competition between rising China and India might destabilize the region with unpredictable consequences for the rest of the world. In any event, they point out that how these two achieve their rise will force students of international politics to reconsider how culture, power, and economy converge to create a powerful new actor on the world stage.[4]

Until recently, international media commentary characterized India as a poor, underdeveloped country divided from within by ethnic, caste, and religious conflicts and possessing little international power and hardly any capacity to shape the world order. Since the early 1990s, this perception has undergone dramatic change but has also given rise to a fierce controversy about its implications and whether India can and should aspire to be a great power. Opinions have varied depending on the observer's point of view, but there is a fair degree of consensus that the huge market provided by a stable, democratic India will be one of the main drivers of future global growth; that India will act as a stabilizer in the crucial quadrant of the world that lies between Iran and Thailand; and that it will provide an ideological and economic counterweight to China.[5] The key precondition for India's ascent is, however, an active government willing and able to further growth with equity and wield power with restraint.

Popular Perceptions About India's Rise

When India's growth rate began to rise in 2003, many observers questioned whether it could be sustained. Opinions were divided:

some observers were highly optimistic, others felt far less sanguine, and still others conceded that sustained growth was possible only if India bit the bullet, mobilized sufficient political will, and made the required but hard decisions to restructure its economy. Among the commentators, an influential segment of critics on the left believed that India's market-friendly growth strategy was morally bankrupt and virtually unattainable because of deep-rooted structural flaws the current state of India was incapable of correcting. Another segment countered this argument by pointing to East Asia to contend that prosperity, even if it bred inequality initially, was the fastest and surest way to reduce poverty.[6]

Weighing in on the side of optimism, a 2010 article in *Foreign Affairs* characterized India as "dynamic and transforming" and hailed it as "an important economic power on track . . . to become a top-five global economy by 2030. It is a player in global economic decisions as part of both the G20 and the G8+5 (the G8 plus the five leading emerging economies) and may ultimately attain a permanent seat on the United Nations Security Council. India's trajectory has diverged sharply from that of Pakistan."[7]

In 2012, Goldman Sachs, a global firm with worldwide investment and financial interests arrived at a fairly confident assessment of India's growth potential despite dire warnings in the rest of the press of derailed growth.[8] The report cited two favorable conditions for optimism: India had sustained close to 8 percent growth in the previous decade (2002–2011), and it would add almost 110 million young workers to the population in the next two decades, which would increase the nation's gross domestic product (GDP) by 4 percent annually as demand for products and services expanded and savings and investments grew to new levels.[9]

Two reports by leading international institutions further affirmed India's rapid evolution as a world economic power. The first report, by the World Bank in 2006, ranked India as the twelfth-largest economy in terms of GDP. The second report, issued in 2011 by the International Monetary Fund, placed India at number nine.[10]

In four studies since 1997 mapping the future of the world economy and politics, the US National Intelligence Council (NIC) has envisioned India becoming a dominant military power in the region. These studies take particular note of the growing reach of India's navy in the Indian Ocean and surrounding bodies of water.[11] "Over the next 15–20 years," one report observes, the Indian leaders will strive for a multi-polar international system, with New Delhi as one of the poles and serving as a political and cultural bridge between a rising China and the United States. India's growing international confidence, derived primarily from its economic growth and its successful democratic record, now drives New Delhi toward partnerships with many countries. However, these partnerships are aimed at maximizing India's autonomy, not at aligning India with any country or international coalition.[12]

Not everyone agrees with this optimistic assessment of India's rise, however. Another view put forward with passion in some scholarly tracts and the popular press—often by India-born, US-based authors—asserts that the Indian state is basically repressive and exploitative despite the trappings of democracy. India's seeming strength is an illusion, these authors claim, and India is a state destined to be crushed under the weight of its own contradictions. A study conducted by the London School of Economics entitled "India: The Next Superpower?" argues that deep and pervasive fault lines within Indian society "call into doubt India's superpower aspiration." The authors of the study advise that instead of seeking to "expand its influence abroad, India would do well to focus on the fissures within."[13] They go on to say, "As for India's place in the global economy, given the vast developmental challenges that remain domestically, it would be difficult to imagine India asserting its economic dominance in international markets any time soon."[14]

In the popular press, Pankaj Mishra, a leading commentator on India, has most clearly and repeatedly articulated this point of view. In an op-ed piece in the *New York Times* in 2006, Mishra writes that perceptions of India's rising power are based on a narrow business-centric perspective that ignores salient facts.[15] A May 27, 2012, article, which he posted on Bloomberg View, reiterates the negative assessments of the earlier piece.[16] India's market-oriented reforms, he comments, have created "private wealth" but little public access to the basic services essential for the well-being of India's people. The growing gap between rich and poor is leading to dangerous social upheavals, such as tribal uprisings in large swaths of North and Central India under the banner of Maoism.[17] Unable to bridge the income and opportunity gap or stem the violence, the state has simply abdicated responsibility and ceded control, in his view, to entrenched cabals of landlords and police in the violence-prone areas. In short, India is fast-forwarding toward an implosion.[18]

Where Mishra and similarly inclined commentators see a bleak future in India's embrace of market-based growth strategies, others see insurmountable political and institutional obstacles to growth.[19] These observers argue that India's coalition governments are just too weak to make the kind of tough decisions needed to complete the changes that sustained growth would require.[20] These arguments gained added force in 2012 as India's economy slowed and industrial production plummeted while the government was paralyzed. These pessimists point to the abysmal state of India's infrastructure, insufficient investment in research and technology, corruption, and populist pandering to vested interests. These weaknesses, they argue, will prevent India from enacting the kind of reforms necessary to transform the economy at a pace sufficient to reap early benefits and sustain momentum.[21] A failure to grasp this moment of change would prove catastrophic, according to this view; it would consign India to the margins of the global economy and global politics.

The first doubt is grounded in ethics, for it is based on a belief that growth is good only insofar as it benefits the weaker and poorer sections of a society. The second is grounded in comparisons between actual and possible outcomes: between what India has actually achieved and what it could have achieved with more efficient decisionmaking and better timing. Pessimism about India's future arises out of deep misgivings about the social and political consequences of rapid growth and growing concern about India's capacity to address them. The latter critiques have become more pronounced because of a growing opacity in Indian state decisionmaking—an increasing difficulty in identifying chains of command and therefore in ascribing accountability.

These two views of India's future—domestic economic growth and an increasingly assertive role in international affairs or economic failures and dysfunctional democracy—are mutually exclusive. So one of them has to be wrong. Or does it? In this book I show that the conflict between them is more apparent than real. The way that outsiders view India is necessarily different from the way insiders do. The coexistence of growing state power with unresolved internal problems is not peculiar to India, but rather, it is characteristic of almost all societies in the midst of rapid change. The same juxtaposition of wealth and poverty, self-confidence and uncertainty, order and disorder, and the same hodgepodge of impulses toward democratization and authoritarianism, can be found in England in the eighteenth century or in China today. It is in the very nature of transitional societies that they are riddled with contradictions as the old order dies out and the new order struggles to be born. It would be strange indeed if India had proved an exception to this rule.

Foreign governments know that India is beset by internal problems but believe that it has the capacity to meet them.[22] Decisionmakers abroad regard India as a rising power precisely because of its achievements, not because of how they have been generated.[23] For proof, foreign decisionmakers need to look no further than the acceleration of the growth rate after 1991. For thirty years, from 1956 to about 1985, with the exception of two years of national emergency from 1975 to 1977 and non–Congress Party coalition government from 1978 to 1980, India enjoyed strong, stable rule under the Congress Party. But it achieved a growth rate of only about 3.7 percent, one of the dozen slowest in the world.[24] The strength and stability of the government did not translate into stellar performance. In the post-1991 period, this equation reversed. The period following the 1992 elections was characterized by weak and unstable minority governments in New Delhi, but contrary to expectations, the growth rate rose steadily until it exceeded 9 percent annually for five years beginning in 2003. These contrasting outcomes challenge the conventional wisdom that a strong government is necessary for rapid growth.

The two views of India—the one focusing on the results and the other on the way they were achieved—therefore complement each other. Either is misleading if taken in isolation or pushed too far. That India is growing rapidly does not mean that it will continue to do so indefinitely. That rapid growth is creating new inequalities and conflicts does not mean that these will not be resolved.

This book seeks to explain the paradox of steadily improving outcomes and perceptions of steadily deteriorating governmental processes. That is where, it argues, the answer to questions about India's future lies. It seeks to show that India has performed better after the end of dominant-party democracy *because*, not *in spite of,* that end. It argues that the stability that the dominant-party system allegedly gave to the Indian polity was temporary because dominant-party democracy was itself a transitional form of government. By the mid-1970s, it was increasingly clear that the excessive concentration of power in India's central state, which had created the illusion of strength and stability, was counterproductive.[25] Despite that concentration built within the ruling party, the Indira and Rajiv Gandhi governments (1980–1989) postponed hard decisions and were therefore less and less able to combine political stability with economic reform. To get out of the trap of low growth, India needed to carry out structural reforms, but concentration of political power could not automatically deliver economic growth.

The dominant-party model—in which the Congress Party kept winning every election for the first forty years with one interruption—nevertheless bridged the gap between a colonial, centralized form of government and a return to a much older multilayered federal structure of government in a modern, democratic form. In India the multilayered state long antedated the arrival of the British. It evolved out of the search of Indian empire states, from the Mauryas through the Mughals, for ways of controlling a far-flung and ethnically diverse empire with minimum use of coercion. It did this by allowing most of the component elements of the state to more or less govern themselves within guidelines that embodied the unifying ideology of the central authority. In India the outstanding examples were the Hindu-Buddhist ideational amalgam of the Maurya Empire, which persisted for almost a thousand years after the empire's demise, and the Indo-Islamic syncretism, which reached its fullest flowering in the Mughal period.[26] British colonial administrators also retained elements of a multilayered order with differential levels of regional autonomy.

Each of these empire states created a layered political order whose very looseness required a constant dialogue between higher and lower layers of administrative power. In this structure local authorities enjoyed considerable power to interpret edicts they received from above.[27] Such an arrangement for governance is not then an alien idea and has constituted an important element of India's political ethos. India owes the smoothness of its transformation from dominant party to coalition rule to the latter's conformity with a pattern of governance with which people are already comfortable.[28] Coalition rule accommodates contending interests and ethnic groups, and, in fact, the stability of the system has depended largely on how well it has responded to the demands of diverse communities. The price that such an automatically "reflexive" system of government exacts, however, is a loss of valuable time: arriving at a consensus at so many levels of government in so diverse a country is necessarily slow.

Indeed, policymakers have intuitively grasped that the rhythm of change would be slow and tortuous and dependent on the electoral outcomes of state-level elections (held every two years but in a staggered fashion) that may or may not bring proreform parties to power. They saw no choice but to approach change step-by-step and in a piecemeal fashion. Its gradual pace allowed reforms to win larger numbers of converts to its cause as the circle of beneficiaries widened. Montek Singh Ahluwalia, the principal adviser to Prime Minister Manmohan Singh, best captures the logic behind the slow pace of change:

> Gradualism implies a clear definition of the goal and a deliberate choice of extending the time taken to reach it, to ease the pain of transition. This is not what happened in all areas. The goals were often indicated only as a broad direction, with the precise end point and the pace of transition left unstated to minimize opposition—and possibly also to allow room to retreat, if necessary. This reduced politically divisive controversy enabled a consensus of sorts to evolve, but it also meant that the consensus at each point represented a compromise, with many interested groups joining only because they believed that reforms would not go "too far." The result was a process of change that was not so much gradualist as fitful and opportunistic. Progress was made as and when politically feasible, but since the end point was not always clearly indicated, many participants were unclear about how much change would have to be accepted, and this may have led to less adjustment than was otherwise feasible.[29]

The Indo-US civil nuclear deal, commonly known as the 123 Agreement, was initiated in 2005; it provides an example of how "reflexive" change worked in the realm of foreign policy. This agreement was three years in the making and constituted a watershed in US-India relations. It was finalized and signed in October 2008. Before coming to fruition however, the proposal had to go through several complex stages, including amendment to US domestic law, especially the Atomic Energy Act of 1954; an articulation of a civil-military nuclear Separation Plan in India; a safeguards (inspections) agreement between India and the International Atomic Energy Agency; and a grant of an exemption for India by the Nuclear Suppliers Group, an export-control cartel formed mainly in response to India's first nuclear test in 1974. The Manmohan Singh government signed the agreement in July 2005, assuming that it would face little significant opposition within the country. Normally, the Left Front parties would have bitterly opposed any proposal that tied India's

security to the United States, but in 2005 they were a part of the ruling coalition and were therefore expected to support the nuclear deal.
The Left Front, however, refused to even consider the agreement, and
it remained bogged down in Parliament. The ensuing identification of
positions, the sorting of potential allies from opponents, and the
overcoming of resistance by appeal to an ever-widening circle of
actors that finally included virtually the entire country took so long
that the deal almost fell through. It was saved only by the George W.
Bush administration's firm commitment to it and by the Singh government's willingness to put its own survival on the line.

The Indo-US nuclear agreement demonstrated the growing
importance of political consensus-building within India all the more
vividly because domestic policy and foreign policy were becoming
intertwined. Before then, state governments and local communities,
except those hosting transborder ethnic minorities, were little
affected by foreign policy decisions made in New Delhi. Now the
future of India, particularly the role it can play in international
affairs, will depend upon the extent to which its time-consuming patterns of consensus-building can respond to the challenges thrown up
by an ever more rapidly changing world. The pessimistic view is
grounded in the belief that India lacks the capacity to do so.[30]

Scholarly Debate on India's Rise

One reason the debate on India's future remains inconclusive is that
to settle it, an objective measure, or set of measures, of state power is
needed.[31] But there is no consensus among international relations
theorists on what these should be. Students of India are deeply
divided on the issue. The realist school of thought seeks to measure
India's power by quantifying its impact upon global politics. The second school seeks to measure power by the development of capacities
to attain desired outcomes and not by outcome alone.

Baldev Raj Nayar and T. V. Paul's volume *India in the World
Order: Searching for Major-Power Status* belongs to the first category.[32] They explain how the changing distribution of international
power—from the end of the Cold War that left only one great
power to shape international politics, namely, the United States,
and subsequent emergence of several regional powers to challenge
US dominance—has created new space for India, China, Brazil,

South Africa, Turkey, and Indonesia to exert greater influence over international events. "The passing of the bipolar system," they write, "has created new opportunities for India by liberating it from being too closely tied to the apron strings of the Soviet Union."[33] These opportunities have grown further with the passing of "the unipolar moment" (clearly signaled, in their view, by India and Iran's successful defiance of the US-imposed nuclear nonproliferation regime). They argue that a weakening of US hegemony and a resulting search for new alignments have brought India to the attention of the major international players. This shift in the international balance of power, rather than any growth in India's economic or military capabilities, has enabled India to play a more active role in shaping international events.

How has India used these new opportunities? Nayar and Paul identify the specific arenas where India's influence has grown or has the potential to grow: India's relations with its neighbors in South Asia, India's changing role in the world economy as evidenced by its trade investment and financial links, and India's relations with the other major powers. Beyond these immediate geopolitical concerns, they measure India's growing importance through its contribution to the "global commons."[34] On balance, they conclude that India is growing in importance and will become a highly influential actor on the world stage.

To arrive at their conclusions, Nayar and Paul devise a typology of middle powers that delineates hard and soft aspects of power and can be very useful for ranking countries using conventional measures of power. Based on their framework, we can identify the elements of current power, compare an existing with another rising state, or compare a rising state at different points in its history. It enables us, for instance, to compare India's capabilities in 1947 with those of 2000. Here, 1947 becomes the baseline for comparing expansions in the economy, military, demography, and technology. We can also compare India and China in 1978 and then again in 2000. These snapshots taken at different points of time do not, however, tell us how a country got from one point to the next or how we might assess its future potential.

Baldev Raj Nayar and T. V. Paul focus largely on India's power beyond its borders. In contrast, Stephen Cohen represents those who concentrate on internal elements of power to suggest that India's potential is best appreciated on its own terms.[35] In his view, India's role "is primarily to 'be India,' and to address the human security issues that stem from its own imbalances and injustices. By doing that India will make one quarter of the world more secure, not a trivial accomplishment. . . . As India moves ahead into the future," he observes, "its central identity is likely to remain pretty much the same" although the "rate of change both within India and in that larger world . . . *is* accelerating, as are notions of what constitutes a 'great' power."[36]

Cohen makes two important points about India's future. His first point is that these changes in the concept of power have made the Indian experiment far more important than it was during the Cold War. Today, economy and democracy have risen in importance over military hardware and the number of ships a country might possess. In this context, India's rise is a function of changes in the way the world measures power. But his second point is that India is a different kind of power. Unlike many other nation-states past and present, India carries within it the imprint of *a whole civilization acting as a nation-state in the international arena*.[37] The only other contemporary nation to possess that characteristic is China. Cohen argues that India's history, social structure, patterns of culture, and tradition of strategic thought (or lack thereof) are reflected in its responses to both domestic and international challenges. These have produced and reproduced, in his view, a particular conception among the country's elites of India and its role in the world. Whether India will become a great power will depend on how that conception engages the present. India is doing far better than before, he observes, in enlisting its history to solve the challenges presented by shifts in domestic and international environments. For example, he shows how modern India's self-image is derived from a construction of Indian history as that of a single civilization with a core theme of unity and how an identity defined in this way shaped India's choice of nonalignment following independence.

Cohen's analysis has the great advantage of drawing us deeper into the social and historical sources of India's power and in that way compensates for Nayar and Paul's lack of a historically rooted analysis of how and why India might make particular responses to domestic and international challenges in the present century. Neither perspective, however, tells us how India's future will be shaped by how it has met challenges since the end of the Cold War. Cohen's conclusions push us to think about India as a different kind of power, one that will rise in influence because it will have responded to the challenges of the new century in a quintessentially Indian way. What that might be is not, however, very clear; nor do we know how we might apply this idea of a different kind of power to understand the transformation of India's politics and economy in the wake of the dominant-party collapse and the rise of coalition politics in India. For Nayar and Paul, the post–Cold War coalition governments are weak instruments of transformation. They predict India's rise, but we are not told how the contradiction between domestic weakness and international influence will be resolved.

Neither of these explanations of India's growing importance in international affairs helps us to understand why new directions in foreign policy and a measurable acceleration of economic growth have accompanied a decline in the authority of the central government. The fiscal crisis of 1990 ushered in economic reforms that rapidly accelerated growth, while the collapse of the Soviet Union required a redefinition of India's international posture. India's coalition governments responded by forging a strategic partnership with the United States and by vigorously pursuing a "look east" policy to create a whole network of economic and security ties with countries in the Far East and Southeast Asia. These are just two examples of the new directions in policy. We therefore need a conceptual frame that provides a single causal explanation for these seemingly contradictory trends and that therefore helps us identify the key elements of the process by which these responses are institutionalized and conflicts resolved.

Eric Ringman's theoretical writings provide a useful starting point for developing a relevant conceptual framework for India.[38] Ringman is less interested in measuring existing power than in assessing a nation's potential for acquiring power in the future. He identifies three key determinants: a state's ability to reflect or produce a vision of change, a state's ability to create institutions that translate this vision into reality, and a state's ability to resolve conflicts arising from change. In Ringman's view, these three abilities are better clues to assessing potential for power as long as they are not applied mechanically.[39] In simple terms, his approach is akin to that of a bank manager assessing the ability of a client to repay a loan: not only does he examine the applicant's existing bank balance and income, but he also assesses the applicant's capacity to earn, inherit, or otherwise increase assets.

Ringman's model provides a better template for understanding state power in the post–Cold War world than the conventional models discussed above. This is because the old order characterized by competition between capitalism and socialism has passed, but the new order is still struggling to be born. The power to imagine alternative futures is therefore increasingly important in the twenty-first century. The Westphalian state, with its defined boundaries and hard notions of sovereignty backed by military power, has weakened. Attempts are therefore being made to build an alternative international order that can incorporate interdependent economies, porous boundaries, and collective defense.[40] One NIC report warns that "by 2025, nation-states will no longer be the only—and often not the most important—actors on the world stage and the 'international system' will have morphed to accommodate the new reality. But the transformation will be incomplete and uneven. Although states will not disappear from the international scene, the *relative power* of various non-state actors—including businesses, tribes, religious organizations, and even criminal networks—will grow."[41] The cascading impact of the Arab Spring, a veritable people's revolution in 2011, which toppled so many authoritarian regimes in the Middle East, underscores this argument. So did a nationwide nonviolent anticorruption movement in India led in 2011 by activist Anna Hazare, which challenged the entire Indian political class and the preeminent institutions of government.

The importance of Ringman's notion of capabilities is obvious if we consider Mikhail Gorbachev's attempt to change the Soviet Union by implementing perestroika and glasnost. Even though this vision of an alternate future failed in the end, we cannot explain what happened to the Soviet Union without understanding the hopes and failures associated with that vision. Gorbachev did not and perhaps could not muster the requisite entrepreneurial creativity or mechanisms for resolving the contradictions his vision had created. Likewise, the rapid rise of China would not have been possible had Deng Xiaoping not had the courage to "imagine" an alternative future for China and to muster the entrepreneurial skills and resources of the country to bring that about.

When Ringman's model is applied to a specific country, especially one as diverse and complex as India, several additional caveats need to be borne in mind. First, leaders may articulate visions more in response to past challenges than to future aspirations. Second, over time even the most carefully crafted institutions evolve in directions unforeseen by their creators. This is not necessarily a drawback as the change usually takes place in response to transformations in society and politics. Third, leaders may, and indeed very often do, attempt to postpone the resolution of a conflict instead of addressing its root causes. India's postindependence history is replete with such examples, but despite them, much has been accomplished: laws have been constantly reinterpreted, and new ones have been enacted; new institutions have been created to reconcile conflicting interests, and older ones that existed only on paper have been revived and put to use.[42] Change has therefore been incremental at the best of times, but its slowness has given India's myriad political constituencies time to adjust by striking new bargains with each other.

Indian leaders may have fallen short in envisioning change or articulating it clearly but this was at least partly because coalition governments could not come to power without striking a new bargain between likely parties to the coalition. Vision statements and election manifestos were therefore vague and more often than not quickly set aside. They give no clue to the direction in which policies will evolve. In post-2000 India, change is not driven from above but evolves out of an unceasing, reflexive dialogue between the central and state governments and between the state at all levels and civil society. It is the vector of all social and economic impulses in society. India's supposed weaknesses are therefore its strengths, for they give it the elasticity to absorb internal and external shocks and turn them into opportunities for change.[43] There is of course danger if the central and state governments' negotiations become paralyzed, which explains the stop-and-go pace of almost all policy changes in India. Change, however, accumulates and slowly builds national capabilities. An understanding of this process provides an insight into the reasons that India is becoming increasingly more capable of influencing the course of international events.[44] Cohen's poetic formulation—"India being itself"—captures this process without being able to describe how it works.

In this type of reflexive policymaking, manifestos and policy declarations are not the end point of decisionmaking they are its starting point. The government of the day lays out what it believes the people want it to do and waits for responses from the many levels of state and society. The final action often bears only a faint resemblance to the original policy statement.

For instance, the Congress Party has always stood for a strong center. For two decades it dominated not only the national Parliament but also each and every state legislature in the country. But it was the Congress Party that went against its own innate preference for centralization and created India's ethnolinguistic federation in 1956. Thirty-six years later in 1992, the same party created a third tier of democracy, the autonomous district councils, and empowered village councils (Panchayats), by making elections mandatory and devolving financial powers to them.[45]

Similarly, the Hindu nationalist Bharatiya Janata Party (BJP), India's other national party, was committed to economic self-reliance when it came to power in 1998, but it took only two years in office for the BJP to change its tune and become an ardent promoter of an open economy. The same party preached Hindu monolithism in theory but then pushed it onto a far back burner in order to form a coalition government at the center. The interactive process that has led to these dramatic U-turns by both the main parties is the very essence of Indian democracy as well as of all healthy democracies.

Ringman's second determinant—the capacity to create change-supporting and -sustaining institutions—encompasses entrepreneurial aptitude.[46] Focusing on a country's capacity for political innovation helps us assess the efficacy of new organizations, processes, legal frameworks, and social institutions that are created to guide the desired change. In India, the state has responded to the near-simultaneous end of dominant-party rule and the opening up of the command economy by creating a large number of new regulatory and coordinating institutions and reviving older institutions that had been enshrined in the Constitution but remained moribund. Thus, V. P. Singh's coalition government of 1989 revived the national Development Council as the main instrument for co-coordinating central and state political and economic policies. The central government coordinated economic policy by setting up regulatory commissions for public utilities and passing model acts on subjects ranging from power generation and distribution to land acquisition, value-added taxation, and right to information.[47]

What is true in the sphere of economic reforms is also true in defense and foreign policy. Post–Cold War coalition governments in India abandoned the principle of nonalignment that had guided them since 1947 and signed a defense framework agreement with the United States in 2005. Although a quest for autonomy in policy and for strategic restraint still remained watchwords of India's external posture, coalition governments gradually introduced new dimensions in India's defense doctrine that were more suitable to the post–Cold War world they faced. Indian military leaders sought the arms and weapons to extend India's influence well beyond its borders into what came to be defined as the "extended neighborhood."

New directions and new institutions inevitably change the distribution of power and benefits in society. Since this often engenders conflict, the capacity of a country to contain and resolve this conflict—Ringman's third determinant—is an important index of its power. India will face a whole set of new conflicts arising from growing inequality in rural areas, environmental depredation, declining water resources, and an unregulated grab for land. The violence triggered by the acquisition of land for Special Economic Zones (SEZs) in West Bengal and Maharashtra and generally from tribal populations in Central India underscores the nature of future conflicts. To these new confrontations will be added older conflicts of ethnic separatism and religious tensions that periodically challenge India's central and state governments. Facing these challenges, India's coalition governments have done in the political sphere what they have done in the economic sphere: they have responded in a slow and piecemeal fashion, which allows for a whole set of interested parties to adjust to the new dynamics produced by change.

This go-slow approach to political tensions was evident in the government's response to a demand for a new set of guidelines for acquiring land and setting up SEZs. It was also evident in relatively slow responses to demands for a separate state of Telangana, which was eventually carved out of the existing state of Andhra in 2011. The outbreak of violence over Telangana in 2011 was a failure of the United Progressive Alliance (UPA), led by the Congress Party, to resolve the conflict, but it was also the beginning of adjustment all around in preparation for the next round of negotiations for a new bargain.[48] The inclusion of a large number of political leaders in an October 2012 reshuffle of the UPA cabinet underlines the way in which the Indian political system seeks to accommodate dissent.[49] However, that ploy did not work and on July 30, 2013, the Congress Party Working Committee approved the motion to create the twenty-ninth state of Telangana.

If we apply Ringman's measures to the broader history of modern India, then the nationalist period, particularly from 1930 onward, could be considered a period of great innovation and entrepreneurship. It succeeded in producing a viable, alternative vision; mobilized required resources; and changed the rules of the game based on notions of nonviolence, civil disobedience, and the mass movement. Institutional developments and organizational innovation provided this vision. The evolution of the Indian National Congress Party (INC) and its pan-Indian grassroots organization was a testimony to the vision. The INC evolved mechanisms to resolve conflicts between the British colonial authorities and the nationalist movement and within the nationalist movement itself. It was predominantly a pluralist mechanism of conflict resolution; its one spectacular and tragic failure was the inability to contain the Muslim League (the political party representing Muslims in British India led by M. A. Jinnah), which successfully produced an alternative vision of a Muslim Pakistan carved out from pluralist India.

The early years of postindependence India, popularly known as the Nehruvian period (1947–1964), also saw enormous expansion in reflective and entrepreneurial capacity to resolve conflicts. It was a time of nation- as well as state-building and witnessed the creation of a spectrum of economic, political, and public welfare institutions. Indian leaders wrote and adopted a constitution, defining the rules of the game by which Parliament, the courts, and political parties were to operate. They created a planning commission to preside over the economic direction India would take. And, most importantly, they divided power between the central government and its federal units. In foreign policy, India settled for a position of nonalignment and forged an anti-imperial, anticolonial plank to unify the world's newly independent states in Asia, Africa, and the Middle East.

Prime Minister Jawaharlal Nehru has been criticized for neglecting national defense, for engaging in excessive moralizing, and for misinterpreting the intentions of China and Pakistan and the United States. But these mistakes in policy—and they are the subjects of fierce controversy—do not diminish his government's contribution to nation-building. Nehru created a distinctive, international persona for India that linked its civilizational past with its potential as a major international power. This vision was fully articulated on the eve of independence in 1947 in Nehru's first speech to the nation. He called upon his fellow citizens to embark on a new "tryst with destiny," in which, by its combined efforts, India would emerge as a great nation and a powerful voice on behalf of the world's oppressed. The two beliefs then articulated—India's civilizational greatness and its antic-ipated and deserved rise to international influence—have become the cornerstone of India's foreign policy aspirations and goalposts for every government in New Delhi.

Whereas Nehru had laid the institutional foundation for India's domestic and international direction, it was left to the subsequent Congress Party governments of Indira Gandhi and Rajiv Gandhi to nurture the dream and strengthen the institutions created in the first decade after independence. The Indira and Rajiv Gandhi govern-ments by and large failed in this regard, however. They held on to the rules of the game established under the Congress Party under Nehru even when party hegemony began to erode in the years after his death. The emerging centers of new dissent demanded decentraliza-tion of government and progressive democratization of social and political institutions, but neither Indira nor Rajiv Gandhi met these challenges with imagination or enlightened self-interest. In fact, they did the opposite. Each was deficient in evolving strategies to resolve social and ethnic conflicts and paid for this failure with their lives.

Insistence on maintaining Congress Party supremacy led Indira Gandhi to suspend elections (1975–1979) and tarnish the record of India's enduring democracy. It also convinced her to create a host of draconian laws and concentrate power in the hands of the police and government. Her insistence on imposing highly restrictive measures on foreign capital and domestic markets, all in the name of social jus-tice, led to what has been disparagingly referred to as the "license and permit raj," a regime that gave the bureaucracy inordinate con-trol over the economy and all but strangled growth. It also created opportunities for corruption throughout the chain of bureaucratic command. Despite these flaws, her conduct in the 1971 war with Pakistan and the liberation of Bangladesh were textbook examples of humanitarian intervention (and exit) that upheld international princi-ples and national interests.

Although Rajiv Gandhi tried to correct this situation and intro-duce greater probity within the Congress Party rank and file, he, too, failed before the power of the party machine. Both Indira Gandhi in her last few years and Rajiv Gandhi tried to liberalize the economy and introduce more competition; nevertheless, these modifications did not amount to a bold use of reflective or entrepreneurial power. In the realm of conflict resolution, both leaders failed to evolve mechanisms that could have prevented the ethnic violence that erupted in the state of Punjab, in the Northeast, and in Kashmir, although on balance, Rajiv Gandhi was more amenable to negotiations than Indira Gandhi.

By these yardsticks, the post-1990 coalition governments have fared at least as well and in some respects better than the preceding Congress Party–dominated governments.[50] Every coalition government reasserted the vision of a "great India" and changed the way the country would go about achieving this goal. Each did this in the face of intensifying social and economic challenges from the increasingly vocal and at times violent Dalits and "backward castes" parties and organizations; from extreme Hindu nationalists who espoused a radically different vision—monolithic and impatient of cultural diversity—of India from that developed by Mahatma Gandhi and Nehru; from those excluded from the gains of the market economy that replaced the former command economy; and from the fundamental shift of power away from the central state to region-based state governments, parties, and leaders.

These four challenges led to the collapse of several coalition governments and tested the resilience and strength of India's democracy. The Janata Dal coalition government of V. P. Singh collapsed under the twin strains of caste and religious violence. The BJP lost elections to the Congress Party–led coalition in 2004 for ignoring the poor and underprivileged. The Congress Party–led governments between 2004 and 2012 have been hard put to cope with the tribal insurgency led by Maoist ideologues commonly referred to as Naxalites in extremely poor parts of Central India that resulted from an increased commodification of land. Kashmir has remained an unsettled danger zone (although in 2007 India and Pakistan came close to an agreement to solve the dispute). And parts of the Northeast have periodically succumbed to violence and terrorist activities perpetrated by ethnic extremists.

What is more, the relationship between India's state and its society has fundamentally changed if the popularity and nationwide support for the anticorruption movement of 2010–2011 is any indication. Even though these challenges have been daunting and cause for much political instability and even policy paralysis, India's democracy has remained resilient and capable of functioning in the midst of turmoil and violence, and its economy has generated increasing surpluses to finance the ambitious military programs and foreign policy goals of great India.

To understand how and why India matters we need to measure the capabilities of India's coalition governments to balance between growth and equity and between domestic and international compulsions. These include flexibility in the management of caste, class, and ethnic revolutions; strategies to contain religious polarization; dismantling of restrictive economic legislation; and creation of new approaches to governing public and private investment. Capabilities can be measured also in the crafting of new defense and foreign policy, in the harnessing of new economic-cum-military assets to shape events in the neighborhood, in the forging of a new strategic and economic partnership with the United States and countries in Southeast Asia that boost India's standing in the world and give it greater leverage in international forums, and in the enhancing of strategic autonomy through the development of nuclear weapons. India's new outward orientation since 1991 stands in stark contrast to the inward preoccupations in the 1970s and 1980s.

India's rise challenges many theoretical propositions that have been the building blocks of political development theories[51]: that democracy cannot be rooted in a poor, underdeveloped, largely illiterate society; that primordial identities cannot be subsumed under larger identitics of a nation unless they are erased by force; that a multination-state is weak in matters of its own defense; that postcolonial leaders, trapped as they are in a nationalism derived and constructed under the influence of colonization, are incapable of independent reflection and lack the ability to build institutions and resolve conflict arising from change; and that conventional measures of power provide only a limited understanding of a country's potential for power. The list of the ways in which India challenges conventional notions of power and politics is endless.

This book seeks to explain the paradox of weak central governments in New Delhi and growing international stature abroad. It seeks to delineate through India's example an alternate way to understand national power and outline how culture, power, and the economy combine to permit a largely poor and deeply divided nation to rise to international importance. India matters because the odds remain in favor of its rise to the center of global politics and economy. But it also matters because India provides an alternative to the East Asian model of development in which political democracy takes second place to economic growth. India is a prime example of how a non-Western state can draw upon a deeply rooted cultural pluralism to combine democracy with rapid economic growth in what might prove a sustainable model of transformation into a modern state. It is also an example of the opposite, a paralysis in political will leading to economic setbacks that threaten the progress it has made. As a great experiment, India's achievements as well as failures matter; they provide important insights in how culture, power, and economy combine to shape a country's journey to modernity and wealth.

Organization of the Book

The next seven chapters expand on this theme. Ringman's three criteria for the acquisition of future state power—the capacity to reflect, the capacity to mobilize resources, and the capacity to resolve conflict arising from change—are interwoven in the narratives that follow. I have made no attempt to provide comprehensive accounts of India's past or present economic or international histories or policies. I have also refrained from moral judgment of events or policies, even if it is pertinent to ask if morally correct responses ought not to be a part of a nation's capabilities. I believe that India's coalition governments are opportunistic and in many instances behave reprehensibly. That judgment, however, does not alter my assessment of their capability to affect the post–Cold War transition, which by any yardstick has been dramatic but not always smooth. It compares well, though, with transitions in Indonesia, Yugoslavia, Russia, and the countries immediately surrounding India. What accounts for differences in India's experience and those of less fortunate parts of the post–Cold War world? I hope that this volume provides at least some insight.

Chapter 2 addresses India's history as a source of national identity. Torn asunder by a violent partition and poorly integrated, India was more an idea and an act of faith by its nationalist leaders than a coherent and territorially well-defined state. India's leaders reached into history to construct the idea of India, which they saw as a pluralistic, tolerant, and peaceful nation bound together by enduring bonds of shared culture and values. This self-image served to establish democratic institutions at home and a nonaligned stance abroad. By the end of the 1980s, India was struggling to cope with cataclysmic changes in its dominant-party democracy and the abrupt end of the Cold War rivalry between the United States and the Soviet Union. Chapter 3 outlines the emergence of coalition rule as a coping mechanism for change. It examines how the unstable coalition governments sought to balance the imperatives of survival with the demands of newly mobilized middle classes, Hindu nationalists, and ethnic separatists. Chapter 4 explores the economic transformation and gradual replacement of a command economy with one based on markets. Chapter 5 explains how foreign policy thinking underwent a dramatic change in response to the Soviet collapse and how coalition governments coped with the new challenges of a unipolar world that soon enough gave way to a polycentric international order. Throughout these changes, Indian leaders did not lose sight of their enduring goals of preserving the nation's strategic autonomy and establishing for India an enhanced standing in the world. Each required building up defense and cultivating an ability to project influence and power beyond India's borders, which was made possible by rapid economic growth. Chapter 6 discusses security imperatives and assesses the obstacles to power projection in the region. As a civilizational state, India possesses considerable soft power assets, particularly in the attractiveness of its arts, culture, and democracy and in the worldwide spread of the Indian diaspora. Chapter 7 explores the role of that diaspora. In conclusion, Chapter 8 explains why we need to think of India as a different kind of state, one that cannot be understood by applying the template of older established nation-states or the path that contemporary counterparts in Asia have pursued. India exists in contrast to each and illuminates a different path to international power and prosperity.

Notes

1. Hiton Root, "Do Strong Governments Produce Strong Economies?" *India Review* 5, no. 4 (Spring 2001): 565–566. See also Ann Sasa List-Jensen, "Economic Development and Authoritarianism: A Case Study of the Korean Developmental State," Development, Innovation, and International Political Economy, Research Working Paper No. 5 (East Aalborg, Denmark: Aalborg University, 2008), which argues that authoritarian states are more effective in achieving developmental goals.

2. David Scott, "The 21st Century as Whose Century?" *Journal of World-System Research* 23, no. 2 (2008): 109.

3. National Intelligence Council, "Global Trends 2025: A Transformed World" (published 2008), http://www.dni.gov/index.php/about/organization /national-intelligence-council-global-trends; Aaron Friedberg, *A Contest for Supremacy: China, America, and the Struggle for Mastery in Asia* (New

York: Norton, 2011); Thomas L. Friedman and Michael Mandelbaum, *That Used to Be Us: How America Fell Behind in the World It Invented and How We Can Come Back* (New York: Farrar, Straus and Giroux, 2011); Fareed Zakaria, *The Post-American World* (New York: Norton, 2009); Zbigniew Brzezinski, *Strategic Vision: America and the Crisis of Global Power* (New York: Basic Books, 2012).

4. Edward Kerschner and Naeema Huq, "Asian Affluence: The Emerging 21st-Century Middle Class," Morgan Stanley Global Investment Committee, June 2011, http://fa.smithbarney.com/public/projectfiles/3525 7b34-b160-45e4-980d-8bca327db92b.pdf; Homi Kharas, "The Emerging Middle Class in Developing Countries," OECD Working Paper No. 285 (Paris: Organisation for Economic Co-operation and Development, 2010), http://www.oecd.org/development/44798225.pdf.

5. Jane Golley and Rodney Tyers, "Contrasting Giants: Demographic Change and Economic Performance in China and India," CAMA Working Paper No. 10 (Canberra: Australian National University, Centre for Applied Macroeconomic Analysis, 2011), http://ideas.repec.org/p/uwa/wpaper/11 -04.html. According to the International Monetary Fund (IMF), "India's continuing demographic dividend can add about 2 percentage points to the annual rate of economic growth, if harnessed properly." Quoted in *Deccan Herald*, July 7, 2012, http://www.deccanherald.com/content /245837/demographic-dividend-can-boost-indian.html. See also Chris Barth, "Demographic Dividends," *Forbes Magazine,* June 25, 2012, http://www .forbes.com/forbes/2012/0625/investment-guide-12-india-china-demographic -dividends_2.html. Nandan Nilekani, *Imagining India: Ideas for the New Century* (New York: Penguin, 2008), stresses this point.

6. Jagdish Bhagwati, "Growth, Poverty and Reforms," in *India's Economy: A Journey in Time and Space*, ed. Raj Kapila and Uma Kapila (New Delhi: Academic Foundation, 2007), 81–89, says that economic reforms are the way to go if India is finally to fulfill its ambition to reduce massively its poverty and destitution. See also Jagdish Bhagwati and Arvind Panagariya, *India's Reforms: How They Produced Inclusive Growth* (Oxford: Oxford University Press, 2012), 82.

7. Evan A. Feigenbaum, "India's Rise, America's Interest," *Foreign Affairs* 89, no. 2 (March–April 2010), http://www.foreignaffairs.com/articles /65995/evan-a-feigenbaum/indias-rise-americas-interest.

8. Goldman Sachs regularly puts forward a well-researched assessment of global markets and regions in which it is heavily invested. For its assessment on India in 2012, see the video "A View from India with Tushar Poddar," http://www.goldmansachs.com/our-thinking/view-from/a-view-from -india/multimedia/video.html (accessed September 22, 2013).

9. For an optimistic view, see Sadiq Ahmed, *India's Long-Term Growth Experience: Lessons and Prospects* (New Delhi: Sage, 2007). For a cautiously optimistic view, see K. C. Chakravarty, "Prospects for Economic Growth and the Policy Imperatives for India," speech given at the plenary of

the National Conference on Leadership, Kolkata, India, December 10, 2010, http://www.bis.org/review/r101215e.pdf.

10. Nominal GDP list of countries for the year 2010, World Economic Outlook Database, International Monetary Fund, September 2011, http://www.imf.org/external/pubs/ft/weo/2011/02/weodata/index.aspx.

11. National Intelligence Council, "Global Trends 2010" (published 1997); NIC, "Global Trends 2015: A Dialogue About the Future with Non-government Experts" (published 2000); NIC, "Global Trends 2020: Mapping the Global Future" (published 2004); and NIC, "Global Trends 2025: A Transformed World," all available at http://www.dni.gov/index.php/about/organization/national-intelligence-council-global-trends (accessed October 4, 2013).

12. NIC, "Global Trends 2015," 30.

13. Ramachandra Guha et al., eds., "India: The Next Superpower?" (London: London School of Economics Ideas Section, March 7, 2012), http://www2.lse.ac.uk/IDEAS/publications/reports/SR010.aspx.

14. Rajeev Sibal, "The Untold Story of India's Economy," in ibid., 22.

15. Pankaj Mishra, "The Myth of the New India," *New York Times,* July 6, 2006, http://www.nytimes.com/2006/07/06/opinion/06mishra.html?pagewanted=all&_r=0.

16. Pankaj Mishra, "Tales of India's Economy Twistier Than Kama Sutra," Bloomberg View, May 27, 2012, http://www.bloomberg.com/news/2012-05-27/tales-of-india-s-economy-twistier-than-kama-sutra.html.

17. Mishra, "The Myth of the New India."

18. Similar views are expressed by Ramachandra Guha, "Will India Become a Superpower?" in *India: The Next Superpower?* 7–8.

19. For scholarly views critical of the Indian state and democracy, see Paul Brass, *The Production of Hindu-Muslim Violence in Contemporary India* (Seattle: University of Washington Press, 2003), which provides an extensive and authoritative commentary on Hindu-Muslim riots and causes of communal violence. Achin Vanaik, *Globalization and South Asia: Multidimensional Perspectives* (New Delhi: Manohar, 2004), covers the impact of globalization on the new neoliberal Indian state and its implications for redistributive justice. Atul Kohli, *Democracy and Discontent: India's Growing Crisis of Governability* (Cambridge: Cambridge University Press, 1990), analyzes the political economy of Indian democracy and concludes that India has a serious governability problem. Francine Frankel, *India's Political Economy, 1947–2004* (Oxford: Oxford University Press, 2005), similarly writes from a political economy perspective on India, but her more recent writings allow the possibility of India's rise. Baldev Raj Nayar, *India's Globalization: Evaluating the Economic Consequences* (Washington, DC: East-West Center, 2006), argues that India has the political will to secure and sustain economic growth. Other key scholars include Lloyd Rudolph and Susanne Rudolph, *In Pursuit of Lakshmi: The Political Economy of the Indian State* (Chicago: University of

Chicago Press, 1987); and Subrata Mitra, *The Puzzle of India's Governance: Culture, Context, and Comparative Theory* (New York: Routledge, 2006).

20. Rajesh Basrur, "Domestic Political Fragmentation and Constraints on Indian Security Policy," paper presented at the International Studies Association conference, New Orleans, Louisiana, February 17–20, 2010, http://citation.allacademic.com/meta/p_mla_apa_research_citation/4/1/6/2/8/pages416289/p416289-1.php.

21. "India's Growth Slowdown Calls for Reinvigorated Reforms," IMF Survey online, April 17, 2012, http://www.imf.org/external/pubs/ft/survey/so/2012/car041712a.htm.

22. James Lamont, "Be My Friend: World Leaders Compete to Build Ties with India," Beyond BRICS, December 6, 2010, http://blogs.ft.com/beyond-brics/2010/12/06/be-my-friend-world-leaders-flock-to-india/#axzz209KARkBI. See also "When the High and Mighty Came Calling," Rediff.com, December 24, 2010, http://www.rediff.com/news/slide-show/slide-show-1-chalo-india-say-world-leaders/20101224.htm.

23. In a November 2010 speech to the Indian Parliament, President Barack Obama said, "India is not simply emerging; India has already emerged. And it is my firm belief that the relationship between the United States and India—bound by our shared interests and values—will be one of the defining partnerships of the 21st century." See http://www.cfr.org/india/obamas-remarks-joint-session-indian-parliament-india-november-2010/p23329.

24. See Shankar Acharya, "India's Growth: Past and Future," paper presented at the Eighth Annual Global Development Conference of the Global Development Network, Beijing, China, January 14–16, 2007, Table 1, 2, http://depot.gdnet.org/cms/conference/papers/acharya_plenary1.pdf.

25. Kohli, *Democracy and Discontent,* 3.

26. Romila Thapar, the foremost historian of early India, argues that Ashoka Maurya laid down a code of conduct, which combined ideas of tolerance, equality, and nonviolence drawn from Buddhist teachings with Brahminical practices of statecraft based on Arthshastrato, to administer his diverse and extensive empire. Romila Thapar, "The Mauryan Empire in Early India," *Historical Research* 79, no. 205 (August 2006): 303. Similarly, Jalaludin Akbar, under whom the Mughal Empire reached its peak, preached religious tolerance and appointed Hindu officials as advisers and commanders of his army. He created a new syncretic religion—Din-I-Illahi—that sought to merge the best elements of the religions of his empire. His purpose was to create social harmony. See Makhanlal Roychoudhari Shastri, *The Din-I-Illahi* (Calcutta: University of Calcutta, 1941).

27. Romila Thapar and Makhanlal Shastri's writings suggest that religious confluence and syncretism were more a pattern than an aberration in Indian history. Thapar, "The Mauryan Empire"; Shastri, *The Din-I-Illahi.*

28. This is not to suggest a historical continuity from Ashoka Maurya to the modern nation-state of India but rather to argue that the idea of coexistence of socially diverse groups, communities, and regions is deeply

embedded in the historical memories of the Indian people. These memories have been reinforced by the nationalist narratives of India's rise and fall, but even those who argue that the idea of India is a modern artifact see the emergence of empire states based on accommodation of diversity as an undeniable fact. For a detailed development of the "historical state," an abstract idea that lays out the key features of how "empire states rose and unified their territorial possessions under a single authority," see Maya Chadda, *Ethnicity, Security, and Separatism in India* (New York: Columbia University Press, 1997), chap. 1.

29. Montek Singh Ahluwalia, "Economic Reforms in India Since 1991: Has Gradualism Worked?" *Journal of Economic Perspectives* 16, no. 3 (Summer 2002): 67–88.

30. According to Rajesh Basrur, coalition governments have been weak in protecting India's national interest. The delays in signing the nuclear deal and the near neglect of Sri Lanka and India's interests in the course of recent events there are cited as examples of how both these nonresponses cost India in terms of its regional interests. See Basrur, "Domestic Political Fragmentation."

31. The concept of power is one of the most elusive and contested concepts in political science. It has been defined generally as an ability to get someone to do what they might not otherwise do. This definition focuses on the outcome but other scholars define power as a relationship. Power is further defined as soft (attract by example) and hard power (use of military, economic, and diplomatic coercion). Political scientists also argue whether power should be seen as superior status, influence, or simply possession of superior resources. Three perspectives generally dominate interpretation of power as a concept: realist (typified by Niccolo Machiavelli), structural (Karl Marx), and constructionist (Michel Foucault). I refer to *power* as the capability to shape interstate relationships and not merely as an ability to coerce or serve by example.

32. Baldev Raj Nayar and T. V. Paul, *India in the World Order: Searching for Major-Power Status* (Cambridge: Cambridge University Press, 2004). For additional literature reflecting the realpolitik view, see Terasita Schaffer, *India and the United States in the 21st Century: Reinventing Partnership* (Washington, DC: Center for Strategic and International Studies, 2009); Rolie Lal, *Understanding China and India: Security Implications for the United States and the World* (Westport, CT: Greenwood Press, 2006); Alyssa Ayres and C. Raja Mohan, *Power Alignments in Asia: China, India, and the United States* (Thousand Oaks, CA: Sage, 2009); and C. Raja Mohan, *Crossing the Rubicon: The Shaping of India's New Foreign Policy* (New Delhi: Viking, 2003).

33. Nayar and Paul, *India in the World Order,* 206.

34. "Global commons" refers to international problems that span national boundaries and require a concerted global effort to tackle them. These include concerns over peacekeeping and peace-building in failing states and regions, over protection of sea-lanes, and over such problems as terrorism, trade in narcotics, and climate change.

35. Stephen P. Cohen, *India: Emerging Power* (Washington, DC: Brookings Institution Press, 2001). Others who also subscribe to this view are Subrata Maitra, "Nuclear, Engaged and Non-Aligned: Contradictions and Coherence in India's Foreign Policy," *India Quarterly* 65, no. 1 (2009): 15–35. Also see Sunil Khilnani, "Bridging Identities: India as Positive Power?" in *Through a Billion Voices: India's Role in a Multipolar World* (Berlin: Foresight, 2010), 13–17, http://www.foresightproject.net/downloads/Reader _FS_India_FINAL.pdf.

36. Cohen, *India,* 309, emphasis added.

37. Similar claims are made about China but also about the rapid growth of East Asian economies. In the case of India, ironically, civilization claims are often viewed by the media in a negative light because they conjure up caste, religious, and ethnic conflicts and passive acceptance of poverty and injustice.

38. Eric Ringman, "Empowerment Among Nations: A Sociological Perspective on Power in International Politics," in *Power in World Politics,* ed. Felix Berenskoetter and M. J. Williams (New York: Routledge, 2007), 189–203.

39. Ibid.

40. This is evident in the debates about the "new world order," the development of globe-spanning nongovernmental organizations such as Greenpeace and Médecins Sans Frontières (Doctors Without Borders), the emergence of global networks of terrorism and counterterrorism, the transformation of the UN's role from peacekeeping to peace enforcement (Lebanon, Somalia, Bosnia, East Timor), and the proliferation of international treaties on trade, AIDS, weapons, and the environment, mostly under the umbrella of the United Nations.

41. NIC, "Global Trends 2025," 81.

42. Arvind Subramanian, "The Evolution of Institutions in India and Its Relationship with Economic Growth," April 2007, http://www.iie.com /publications/papers/subramanian0407b.pdf. See also Govinda Rao and Nirvikar Singh, "The Political Economy of India's Fiscal Federal System and Its Reform," August 2006, http://www.escholarship.org/uc/item/3xf1752z ?display=all.

43. This is not true in every instance. For example, tardy response to communal riots not only costs lives but also exacerbates violence, as in the case of the Gujarat riots of 2002. Some might argue that the Gujarat state government deliberately delayed its response.

44. India's leadership role in the BRICS (Brazil, Russia, India, China, South Africa) nations, a promise of US support for membership in the Security Council, inclusion in several regional forums (East Asia Summit, G8+5 groups of nations, IBSA [India, Brazil, South Africa] Dialogue Forum), a growing contribution to UN peacekeeping efforts, and participation in joint naval exercises with the United States, Japan, and Australia are but a few examples of India's growing role in shaping international discourse on security, global finance, and trade.

45. Panchayat Raj Election Law, 73rd Amendment to the Constitution of India, enacted in April 1992, http://www.rajsec.rajasthan.gov.in/secraj /panchayat/PART1.1.htm.

46. In Ringman's view, "It is the entrepreneur who actualizes the potential that reflection has discovered." See Ringman, "Empowerment Among Nations," 10.

47. The postreform coalition governments created the Securities and Exchange Board of India, the Telecom Regulatory Authority of India, the Insurance and Development Authority, and the Central Electricity Regulatory Commission. The coalition governments strengthened the Election Commission and in 2010 passed the Right to Education Act in addition to a whole host of schemes to empower the poor and provide them with subsidies for food, jobs, and educational opportunities. The efficacy of these institutions and acts is fiercely debated, but they were created and with public pressure their performance could be improved.

48. "Telangana General Strike Continues," *Economic Times,* October 4, 2011, http://articles.economictimes.indiatimes.com/2011-10-04/news/3024 2523_1_telangana-issue-statehood-issue-congress-leaders; "AP Tops in Domestic Violence Cases," Associated Press, March 5, 2012, http://article .wn.com/view/2012/05/03/AP_tops_in_domestic_violence_cases/.

49. "Andhra Pradesh Takes the Cake in Cabinet Reshuffle," *Business Standard,* October 28, 2012, http://www.business-standard.com/generalnews /news/andhra-pradesh-takescake-in-cabinet-reshuffle/73359/.

50. This is described in detail in Chapter 4.

51. American sociologists and political scientists have favored three broad explanations of why democratization may succeed or fail in a country. Seymour Martin Lipset, Phillips Cutright, and Robert Dahl have argued that in order to succeed, a stable democracy requires certain economic and social background conditions, such as high per capita income, widespread literacy, and prevalent urban residency. These were absent when India embarked on the path to democracy. A long line of authors from Walter Bagehot to Ernest Barker have stressed the need for consensus as the basis of democracy in the form of a commonly held belief that creates a certain degree of common agreement among citizens about the fundamental values and procedures of governance. National consensus has remained elusive in the Indian democracy largely because of its segmented character and divisions based on religion, ethnicity, and caste. Daniel Lerner has proposed a capacity for empathy and a willingness to participate as necessary conditions, whereas Gabriel Almond and Sidney Verba talk about the ideal "civic culture" as a requirement for democracy. These preconditions were conspicuously absent in the Indian democracy. See Seymour Martin Lipset, "Some Social Requisites of Democracy: Economic Development and Political Legitimacy," *American Political Science Review* 100, no. 4 (2006): 675–676; Seymour Martin Lipset, "The Social Requisites of Democracy Revisited: 1993 Presidential Address," *American Sociological Review* 59, no. 1 (February 1994): 1–22; and Seymour Martin Lipset and Jason M. Larkin, *The Democratic Century* (Norman: Uni-

versity of Oklahoma Press, 2004). Robert Dahl, *Polyarchy: Participation and Opposition* (New Haven, CT: Yale University Press, 1971), 65, concurs with Lipset that modernization and development are conducive to democracy. Ross Burkhart and Michael Lewis-Beck, "Comparative Democracy: The Economic Development Thesis," *American Political Science Review* 88, no. 4 (1994): 903–910, explore the developmental prerequisites, which were also absent in democratizing India. For the argument that societies divided by ethnicity are not candidates for democracy, see Stein Rokkan, Derek W. Urwin, and the European Consortium for Political Research, *Economy, Territory, Identity: Politics of West European Peripheries* (London: Sage, 1983); and Gabriel Almond and Sydney Verba, *The Civic Culture: Political Attitudes and Democracy in Five Nations* (Newbury Park, CA: Sage, 1989). Dankwart Rustow maintains that national unity is a prerequisite for democracy; see his "Transitions to Democracy: Toward a Dynamic Model," *Comparative Politics* 2, no. 2 (April 1970): 337–363.

2

From Empire State to Multinational State

India's long and turbulent history is characterized by a succession of empires welding a host of autonomous ethnic and cultural groups into a single pan-Indian state. From the second century to the six-teenth, kingdoms and empires brought disparate regions of the sub-continent under a single suzerainty only to fragment into separate entities until another imperial state arose to create unity once more.[1] There were invasions and migrations from beyond the heartland—the Indo-Gangetic plains—of what is India today. There were conquests by foreign forces—Greek, Mongol, and Turkic—who then became assimilated, but there were also other invaders (e.g., Muhammad Gazhanavi) who came to loot and left when their mission was accomplished. Each event left marks, some deeply changing while others only superficially so, but all became part of a distinctive civi-lization that was India, or so it was recognized with the dawn of the modern era. By the eighteenth century, India was more or less under the rule of the British East India Company, bringing yet another imperial power, this time European, to the subcontinent. The East India Company came as a trading enterprise and stayed on to become the ruling power. Its possessions were transferred to the British Crown in 1857, thereby making India a prized colony in England's extended empire from the Middle East to the Far East.

Any meaningful survey of these centuries is beyond the scope of this chapter. In any event, it is not the argument here that "India's rise" in the twenty-first century can be traced in some identifiable way to events in ancient, medieval, or Mughal India.[2] Here the purpose is narrower: to understand, even if only imperfectly and selectively, the ways in which history has given India's leaders a vision of the future and the pathways to make that vision real.

This chapter looks at the perception of India's history among those who led it to freedom in 1947, determined what they wanted it to be, shaped institutions to achieve their goals, and adopted strategies to resolve the conflicts that inevitably arose from the changes they sought to bring about. It outlines four principal dilemmas of nation-building—unification, development, state formation, and foreign policy—and describes how the leaders' perception of history shaped their efforts to resolve them. This chapter is therefore less about historical accuracy than it is about the way history was interpreted and utilized to consolidate nationhood and create pathways to power.

The influence of the past on the present is a subject of immense controversy among India scholars.[3] Colonial and nationalist schools of historians, and more recently subaltern interpretations, have all proposed distinctly different perspectives. Although these debates deserve lengthy discussion, it is enough here to note that colonial (and Orientalist) narratives assume political fragmentation to be the natural tendency in the subcontinent. Nationalist histories, in contrast, regard India as a continuous whole characterized by an underlying unity of culture and civilization.[4] Historians of the subaltern school, furrowing a different path, see the nationalist version of history as an "elite" discourse, an attempt to legitimize elite power while ignoring the role of the underclass in the formation of the Indian state.

Just as the question of history's influence on the present is far from settled, there is no consensus on which history to look at in weighing influence. Nationalist narratives have nevertheless emerged as the dominant explanations of the evolution of the Indian nation and the main source of understanding by elites of their own past. The two strands of history—the nationalist and subaltern—whether they were constructed from above or below, are then impossible to separate.[5]

State Formation: India's Four Dilemmas

At the risk of oversimplification, I want to argue here that in modern times India has faced at least four grand dilemmas, the resolution of which has required drawing deeply on history as an experience and as a reading of that experience. The first dilemma is unification, that is, the task of welding diverse territorial fragments with distinctive historical arrangements of power and cultural autonomy into a single unified nation-state. The second dilemma is development, which encompasses shaping traditional communities of caste and kinship into citizens of India and modernizing a poor and underdeveloped economy to lay the basis for a future great power. The third dilemma is state formation, that is, transforming informal personalized power relations into a formal, legal-political arrangement by building a single center of legitimate and impartial authority to regulate conflict arising from competition for power and office. The fourth dilemma is foreign policy, meaning protecting and enhancing independent India's international interests while achieving territorial and political consolidation for the new state. Although conditions differed from one historic epoch to another, each successive empire state in the subcontinent had to resolve tensions between old and new patterns of power and order.

To get a fuller appreciation of what Indian leaders had to do to achieve this transformation, we need to understand how society connected with political authority in the empire states. In these preindependence, empire states, the central authority exercised only a modicum of control over the life of the communities and regions it ruled. It was marginal to the power relations within society and had little say in resolving disputes over land rights, maintaining law and order, or distributing wealth and status. Sudipta Kaviraj explains ancient India's power organization in this way: "Political arrangements in traditional India appear to have been stretched over three distinct levels. . . . The micro foundations of power lay in the structure of village communities over which regional kingdoms exercised a real and proximate political authority. At intervals these regional kingdoms were subordinated by majestic formations of large, temporarily powerful empires,"[6] which were fragile and short-lived. "Power at the level of the village community tended to be exercised through the . . . logic of the caste system. Its specific manner of allocating productive functions and rewards maintained a system of social repression without *making specific individuals the agents of these relationships of disdain and resentment.*"[7] Caste also established a differential system of status and authority; caste power did not coincide with divisions based on the control of wealth, office, or instruments of coercion.

India's caste order always determined how power was distributed, and even in modern India it has held sway over state-society relations. Under the caste arrangements of ancient India in the dharmic social order, the state was not the main source of justice or protection and therefore of authority. Those functions were performed by an impersonal, often uninstitutionalized religious order, which was itself an integral part of the caste universe. The state was simply implementing sacred social rules based on the duties and status assigned to castes. Although caste communities were geographically concentrated, their place in the universal caste categories remained fixed. A Brahmin might possess wealth and power in one region while a Brahmin in another region might be poor, but both still enjoyed the respect accorded to high caste status.

India's empire states could make wars, acquire territories, and collect taxes but could not make rules about caste order. Kaviraj explains that the state "was not an authority for appeal against widespread structural injustice, oppression, inequities, and irrationalities of social processes. It could not be expected to rectify them, because it had not created them."[8]

This relationship between state and society would have to undergo change if India were to modernize and become an advanced industrialized nation-state. In the course of its occupation, the British colonial authority changed India's caste arrangements in some important ways. It privileged certain castes and ethnic communities over others, labeled these groups at different times as backward, tribal, intelligent, or warlike. In the view of British administrators, modernity was good and all ideas and institutions they introduced, being modern, were good, whereas all other practices and institutions associated with traditional India were bad. In this scheme, Indian kingdoms, rituals, and caste were the domain of the traditional, and individual rights, private property, territorial sovereignty, and impersonal legislative authority were the domain of the modern. The British also legislated against reprehensible caste customs on moral grounds.[9] Abolition in 1829 of sati—a religious practice in some parts of India in which a recently widowed woman immolated herself on her husband's funeral pyre—was one such example.[10] But the British stayed away from denouncing the caste system itself and in fact extended special benefits to non-Brahmin castes to divide the nationalist opposition to their rule. The idea of protected castes and communities—following the British practice of extending special privileges to lower castes as they did for non-Brahmin castes in the Tamilnadu—has become entrenched since then. No government in New Delhi today can ignore the caste minorities without jeopardizing its political survival.[11]

India's nationalist leaders therefore inherited traditional power structures, although partially altered by a century of British colonial rule and an ideology of modernization originating in the West. Although subaltern historians have dismissed Indian nationalism as a "derivative" construct, on balance, however, they would be hard put to deny its capacity to envision a future and mobilize society-wide resources to resolve political conflicts. In fact, the era of nationalist struggle was a highly creative period in India's modern history,[12] as evidenced, for example, by the invention of satyagraha (commonly translated as "truth force")—nonviolent civil disobedience—as a mass strategy and its use to gain India's independence. Some historians may also differ over the "authenticity" of India's democracy and economic plans and condemn them as blind emulation of the West, but they would be wrong in dismissing what is a genuinely creative effort because of its family resemblance to Western concepts of development and modernization. Nor can such historians deny that Indian nationalism possesses a formidable capacity to effect change.

The Unification Dilemma

From some perspectives, the partition of British India in 1947 into the independent states India and Pakistan and the war that followed reflected a failure on the part of India's nationalist leaders: the Muslim League and the Indian National Congress attempted to create a loose federation but failed to make it work. And absent that failure, the ensuing communal violence that took more than 1 million lives could have been avoided.[13] British India could even have been divided into several states. Colonial India consisted of regions ruled directly by the viceroy and regions that were part of the British paramountcy but were under the nominal sovereignty of states ruled by

princes and maharajahs. Beginning in the 1920s, South India witnessed the rise of Dravidian nationalism, which drew a line between
what was believed to be a more egalitarian, Dravidian South and a
stratified, Brahminical, Aryan North. Under the aegis of the Muslim
League, Muslim elites were demanding an equal share of power for a
separate nation of Muslims, while Sikhs were arguing that they had
legitimate claims to a distinctive state in the subcontinent.[14] The
tribal regions in the Northeast, particularly the Nagas, were petition-
ing the departing British government to declare the Naga-inhabited
areas a separate region, and many Hindu and Muslim princely states,
reluctant to part with their power, were resisting the nationalist idea
of the civilizational commonality needed to create a single sovereign
state.[15]

Meanwhile, prominent nationalist leaders—Mohandas K.
Gandhi, Subhash Chandra Bose, Vallabhbhai Patel, and Jawaharlal
Nehru—held different visions for India. Gandhi saw India as a moral
force dedicated to empowering its poor and eschewing war; Bose
preferred a strong, unified, muscular India taking its rightful place in
the community of nations after independence. Patel, affectionately
known as Sardar Patel, disagreed with the effusively idealistic, liberal democratic, and secular India advocated by Jawaharlal Nehru.[16]
As a deputy prime minister (1947–1950) Patel did not hesitate to use
coercion to consolidate the princely states of Hyderabad and Juna-
gargh within the newly independent India. This suggests that he
favored order over self-rule and was less patient with democratic
niceties to secure unification. Historians characterize Patel as pragmatic; sympathetic to a more conservative, homegrown, realpolitik
worldview; and not averse to using force to achieve territorial unification. Socialists, led by Jay Prakash Narayan and later Ram Mohan
Lohia, were themselves riven by factionalism but considered Nehru
and Gandhi to have betrayed the cause of India's poor. Within this
widely differing spectrum of views were Hindu nationalists pushing
for the construction of an exclusively Hindu nation-state (*rashtra*),
Hindu supremacy, and a dominance of Hindu culture.[17] In 1948 one
of their followers had murdered Gandhi in the belief that he was
overly sympathetic to Muslims and Pakistan.

Even though Hindu nationalist organizations and parties did not
attract a mass following—that honor belonged largely to the Congress Party's moderate wing—they had considerable organizational
strength and a dedicated cadre. Socialist and other left-wing parties

had fairly wide public support as well, but factional conflicts prevented them from becoming a challenge to the Congress Party. When the Muslim League left to form the separate state of Pakistan, opposition to the Congress Party's supremacy all but disappeared. Having murdered Gandhi, the Rashtriya Swayam Sevak Sangh, a Hindu nationalist organization, had been banned. Gandhi's removal had eliminated the last opposition to the Nehruvian conception of India and its future. During the struggle for freedom, Nehru had willingly accepted Gandhi's leadership, but there were important differences between them on the economy, industrialization, foreign policy, and partition. Gandhi had argued in favor of a "village-based economy," stressed handloom and handicraft industries, and opposed the idea of a modern, industrialized India along the Western model. In his India, the rich would stand as trustees for the poor.[18] Gandhi did not envision class war but rather class cooperation. He also opposed the partition and rejected the idea of making India into a conventional strong state.

It was fortuitous for India that its founding leaders were able then to rescue their idea of a unified India from the ruins of the partition. To integrate what remained—a heterogeneous land torn by ethnic separatism and sectarian violence—required a powerfully attractive notion of a modern India, one that tugged at the past but caught the imagination of the people in the present and made them willing to sacrifice in its cause. Such a notion also required a strategy that would harness national resources to push India into modernization. This task now fell on Nehru, the sole surviving leader among the triumvirate—Gandhi, Patel, and Nehru—that had stood at the apex of the nationalist movement in 1947.

* * *

In contrast to Gandhi, Nehru envisaged a peaceful but strong and secular Indian nation with all the attributes of a modern state.[19] In a remarkable passage in his *Discovery of India,* Nehru writes that the first task was to recover the nation's history because to forget the past was to build without foundations and to cut off the roots essential for a healthy national growth. He derided the Communist Party of India for being totally out of touch with this past and called its members blind emulators of the West, who, he said, "talked glibly of modernization . . . and essence of western culture but were ignorant of their own." In his view, "National progress . . . lies neither in the repetition of the past nor its denial. New patterns must inevitably be adopted but they must be integrated with the old. Indian history is a striking record of changes introduced in this way . . . from the far distant days of Mohenjo-Daro to our own age."[20] Here was a continuity of cultural and historical forms offered as a characteristic of Indian civilization.

Nehru argued that his secular, democratic state would recreate within modern India its historical patterns of rule and unification, thereby giving it authenticity and deep social roots. Historians may disagree with Nehru's view, but his ideology became the official vision of the Indian state. In his view, the transformation would occur this way: an inclusive democracy would require an overarching ideology that would legitimize the establishment of a supranational state (one that transcended individual ethnic and religious parochialism). In Nehru's view, India's past empires had rested on the construction of just such a "universal" ideology. The Mughals had created the Indo-Islamic amalgam as the ideational umbrella for their empire. The Mauryas had forged a Hindu-Buddhist unity. And the British had established the notion of an impartial civil service, laws, and a government to legitimize rule. Nehru further argued that these past empires had rested on a layered administrative order and a central state that limited itself to the public domain. It did not interfere in the social order of caste and communities. We have already noted that dharmic strictures prevented India's historic state from altering the caste hierarchy and associated rules of work and status. Society preceded the state in traditional India.[21] Nehru's greatness therefore lay in the way in which he harnessed his understanding of India's history to create institutions of government.

Layering of the social and political order permitted diverse communities considerable cultural and social autonomy. This was largely true, in Nehru's view, of both the Mughal and the British Raj. The grant of regional cultural autonomy within an overarching ideology would make for an impartial state, which was the only way Nehru saw to ensure India's unity and development. The idea of a large degree of autonomy for the private sphere supported the liberal and secular elements in Nehru's vision. Because no single community could dominate, the modern state Nehru had in mind would be relatively free to promote the "common good." India's modern state would transcend individual and specific group interests while allowing them full play within the overarching order of unified rule. For Nehru, these historically defined strategies of unification would facilitate India's transition to modernity.

Nehru broke with the past in one important way: he eschewed the idea of flexible and vague boundaries in favor of the firm and defined borders bestowed by the last of the Indian empires, the British Raj. He believed that, even though the external boundaries of earlier empires had remained amorphous, the British had forged a territorial India that the nationalists could legitimately claim as their own.[22] Only a bounded modern state of India could take its rightful place in the community of nation-states. Given its cultural heritage, size, and population, India belonged among the world's first-ranking nations according to Nehru. Clearly, unification was a prerequisite for reaching that goal.

India's nationalist leaders deployed for this purpose a three-element strategy comprising *interlocking balance* and *relational control* within the frame of *Congress Party dominance*. Each element was meant to reinforce the other.[23] These same elements were also meant to resolve conflicts arising from change. It was a gradualist strategy that sought forward movement through accommodation, balance, and compromise; it foresaw no revolutionary change, no radical transformation, and no mass mobilization or massive use of violence to effect change. But this gradualism was hardly nonviolent; nor was it meant to serve primarily the "poor peasant" so central in the Gandhian design. Nehru had eschewed that design but had not abandoned the past, or at least his interpretation of the past. The imprint of history in the design of the three elements of unification cannot be overstated.

What kind of conflicts did the founding leaders think they would have to solve? For the most part, they believed that conflicts would arise from India's multiple cultural cleavages. They drew on colonial frames of reference to define tradition and modernity as opposites. Tradition included allegiance to linguistic, religious, and caste identities, whereas modernity belonged to free and rational individuals acting on self-interest. It was not class character but ethnic and religious identity that appeared to be the principal challenge in transforming India. In emphasizing caste and ethnicity, the nationalists believed they were seeing India as it was while they sought to modernize it out of backwardness. This could not be accomplished without legislative provisions that banned discrimination.[24]

The real purpose of the institutions they created was then to achieve national and territorial integration. Traditional divisions of ethnicity and caste were to be accommodated within an overarching frame, a democratic federation consisting of ethnolinguistic units that enjoyed a fair degree of autonomy. The new federation privileged larger, linguistic communities within a region and left local authorities to forge accommodations with their minorities. Electoral competition allowed majorities as well as mobilized minorities a chance to contest for office. State-led planned development, democratic institutions, and a nationalist-created body of laws gave India's leaders control over the transformative process.

In this design, stability depended on a smooth working of interlocking balances, the first element of the unification strategy, between and among culturally defined communities within and beyond India's borders.[25] For example, in Punjab the state government was formed by an electoral process based on mutual accommodation of Punjabi Hindus and Sikhs, the two dominant communities in that region. Peace and prosperity in Punjab would then depend on the longevity of this accommodation and a stable interlocking of ethnic futures. The next level of interlocking was between the state of Punjab and the central government. This was secured initially by the federal division of power and by the political parties that dominated the Punjab state and central government. Lastly, given that Punjab is on the border with Pakistan, the central state had to balance its domestic policies with security imperatives beyond Punjab. Although no significant number of Sikhs remained in Pakistan after the partition, a breakdown in Hindu-Sikh relations made India vulnerable to Pakistan. In the Indian Jammu and Kashmir (and also in the Northeast), the danger was even greater because Kashmiris were (and are) a divided people and sought independence from both India and Pakistan. Mutual cooperation among proximate ethnic communities was then critical to India's unity, particularly if these communities spilled across into neighboring countries and harbored separatist aspirations.

Even though ethnic accommodation frequently turned separatists into supporting blocs, it unfortunately had a cascading effect among such communities in other parts of India. For example, the extension of protection and quotas for the lower castes and tribes produced resentment among those excluded from these benefits.[26] The Constitution banned religious discrimination but granted Indian Muslims a separate personal law—freedom to apply Sharia in matters of inheritance, marriage, and divorce—which produced resentment among many Hindus who were inclined to support the Hindu majoritarian ideology. Modernity had thus produced new conflicts in its wake. Participatory democracy was not enough; it had to be supplemented with a grant of consociational rights, which provided special cultural and economic rights to subgroups within a nation. But frequently even those rights were not enough to prevent conflict from undermining stability.[27]

The preeminence of the Congress Party, the third unification element, enabled national leaders to turn conflict into an ordered contest for office and power, at least during the first two decades after independence. As an umbrella party, the Congress established a series of informal local and national alliances, which enabled the party to defuse and localize clashing interests. Until 1967, the Congress Party won unchallenged majorities in the national, local, and state elections. In its internal organization, the Congress Party reflected the Nehruvian element of interlocking balances. Its provincial units fit the pan-Indian party structure and interlocked with the party's high command.[28] Until 1967, competition for power and office took place within the Congress Party, not between the party and its rivals. There were, in fact, no rival parties to challenge its supremacy.

Nehru was the president and the unquestioned leader of the Congress Party, but the party depended on local ethnic and regional leaders to maintain its pan-Indian character. This mutual dependence permitted the party and Nehru to implement their nation-building program. Many have pointed out since then that these plans for poverty alleviation were seriously attenuated by the time they filtered down to the next layer of administrative government. And a vast number of village communities remained locked into traditional upper-caste-dominated structures that contravened constitutional promises in word and deed.[29]

The introduction of planned investment, laws, and regulations nevertheless created a new discourse of "development" along with that of competitive democracy and began slowly to transform India. The India that emerged after his passing was not the India Nehru had originally envisaged. It was nevertheless a grand experiment in rooting the ideals of the European Enlightenment in a non-Western setting. Its failure, and ironically even its success, cast doubts on the universality of these ideals. A failure to emulate obviously requires no explanation; we could argue, for instance, that India's democracy was flawed because of India's deeply unequal cultural ethos. But even the successes—stubborn adherence to electoral contests, constitutional government—raised questions because these could be achieved only after the standard template of Western liberal democracy had been compromised. We cannot know whether the emergence of a unified nation-state reflected India's civilizational strength or the power of the nationalist political classes. The unification strategy had achieved considerable success notwithstanding violent insurgencies in Punjab, Indian Kashmir, and the Northeast border regions. The violence pointed to the state's failure to secure interlocking balances, but there might have been many more Punjabs and Kashmirs had the strategy been absent altogether. An expanding economy was, of course, the other critical part of the interlocking balances.

The Development Dilemma

In 1947, the Indian economy was predominantly agricultural and agriculture accounted for more than 49.1 percent of gross national product (GNP). Large-scale industry and mining added up to about 6 percent of GNP, and the small-scale sector—primarily village industries such as weaving—contributed a further 9.5 percent. Trade and transport added another 18.5 percent, and services accounted for about 16 percent. More than 70 percent of the labor force made a living from land, less than 10 percent from manufacture, trade and transport employed 8 percent, and the rest were in service.[30] Indian agriculture was characterized by low productivity compared with that of other major Asian economies. Overall productivity was almost two times higher in China and in East Pakistan, three times higher in Malaysia, and five times higher in Japan.[31] India's low agricultural productivity was a result of lack of inputs, landlordism, high rates of indebtedness, and an absence of alternative opportunities for employment and income. Daniel Thorner and Alice Thorner write, "High rents, high rates of interest and low prices leave the mass of peasant producers with very little to invest in the development of the land and keep them at the mercy of the more powerful people in the village."[32] As Stuart Corbridge and John Harriss observe, the shift of employment and livelihood from agriculture to industry had not proceeded very far in India by the late 1940s or early 1950s.[33]

India's poor, stagnant, uneven economy was clearly an obstacle to unification and to the smooth working of the interlocking balances that were in turn important to the Congress Party's supremacy and control over the development agenda. Unless the national economic pie expanded, ethnic bargains could not be sustained. The question was how to do this without upsetting the class alliance the Congress Party had forged during the years of struggle for independence.

Party leaders chose a middle path. They rejected radical remedies and bent their energies to removing the most obvious and expendable obstacles to development. Partial land reform in the 1950s exemplified this choice. It was radical enough by the standards of Indian conditions at the time but not by much compared to development strategies in China, South Korea, and Taiwan. After all, independence had not been a result of peasant revolution in India; nationalist leaders represented the urban, Western-educated classes. Their choices reflected the interests of these classes. Their immediate priority was not to eradicate poverty as much as it was to unify postpartition India. Unification was then the first element in devising development programs.

The nationalist understanding of colonial and imperial history was the second element in shaping development strategy. The nationalists widely subscribed to the "drain" theory of British colonial rule, namely, that India had been drained of its wealth for imperial purposes.[34] They believed that British colonialists had deliberately destroyed indigenous manufacture and industry and pushed millions to depend on land, which had in turn impoverished rural India; that British taxation policies had siphoned off wealth and incomes; and that the modicum of modernization India had achieved under the British only facilitated more economic drain.[35] In the view of the nationalists, India needed structural transformation and a plan for self-reliant growth, but as the years unfolded, plans failed and the economy stagnated at an average of 3.5 percent in the decades from the 1950s to 1970s, what many disparagingly called the "Hindu rate of growth."

There were, of course, several separate visions for making the Indian economy strong and self-reliant. The Gandhian vision, for instance, argued that the Westernized pattern of industrialization would be highly dehumanizing and socially undesirable.[36] Nehru and Patel saw the Gandhian vision as impractical. They were convinced that India needed a strong and industrialized state that could defend its independence while meeting at the same time the needs of its poverty-stricken masses, but Patel favored private business and a limited economic role for the government. Nehru was, in contrast, committed to socialism. He believed that government control of the commanding heights of the economy would ensure that the masses were not exploited and development remained compatible with their needs. After Gandhi's assassination in 1948, the debate within the Congress Party was reduced to the scope and limits of planning and socialism; it was no longer whether to adopt socialist goals. The idea of the village-based economy vanished from the discourse.

Nehru could not, however, ignore the market-oriented advocacy within his party. The 1948 Industrial Policy Resolution marked a fundamental departure from the earlier policies of laissez-faire. According to this resolution, the government was to have a major role in initiating and regulating development in key sectors of the economy but agriculture and cottage industry, which employed the bulk of the population and constituted a large part of the economy at that time, were to remain in private hands. The 1948 resolution was then a compromise that reflected considerable deference to the right wing within the Congress Party. Following this resolution, the Nehru government passed the Industries (Development and Regulation) Act. This outlined the extent of state control of future industrial growth. Three actions followed immediately that set the stage for state-led growth: first the 1949 statement of policy on the future role of foreign capital, then the 1950 creation of the Planning Commission, and following that the 1951 publication of the first five-year plan. These actions established a legal-political framework and a blueprint for the economy. India embarked on a grand experiment of quasi-socialist development within the context of a liberal democracy. It eschewed the Russian and Chinese models and rejected the market-oriented, capitalist option; it avoided the path pursued by the East Asian economies. India embarked instead on a separate path based on its own experience and reading of history.

This strategy sought to reduce poverty by promoting equality—the two need not be achieved simultaneously, and indeed there were examples of newly independent economies that had expanded but with severe inequalities. These were, however, largely dependent on foreign capital for investment and tied to the imperatives of the Cold War. Anxious to guard against foreign interference, nationalist leaders sought to insulate the Indian economy.

Nehru therefore opted for a system of centralized planning and mixed economy in which a government-owned sector would dominate basic industry and the state would control, regulate, and protect the private sector from foreign competition. Foreign capital was permitted, but only under highly controlled and restricted circumstances. The scope of indigenous private capital was restricted to areas designated in the five-year development plans.

The conflation of poverty with inequality brought in an ever-expanding regime of bureaucratic controls and regulation that eventually produced a crisis of its own at the end of the 1970s, but a vast bureaucratic machinery provided national leaders with control over the commanding heights of the economy and a deep reach into national resources. The plans as well as the commitment to the public sector ran into serious trouble by the third five-year plan and were more or less abandoned by the 1980s. In fact, the first gesture toward probusiness liberalization occurred in the 1980s. Vast public-sector enterprises had become an albatross around the government's neck, and the economy was barely keeping up with a growth in population. Could India have developed more rapidly had the nationalists adopted a market-based strategy? Could it have emulated the East Asian economies and pursued a corporatist development path? Corbridge and Harriss note that before the "tiger" economies got started, their "historically dominant classes were all in disarray" because of military defeat (Japan) or the outcomes of armed revolutionary struggles (Taiwan, Malaya) "so that their ruling elites did not have to compromise with local power in the way that was characteristic of the Congress regime in India."[37] In India, the entrenched caste-based social order, particularly at the local level, had not changed with the transfer of power to the nationalist elites. It was to be expected that planned development and modernity would be slow to arrive or change rural India. Corbridge and Harriss further point out that "in the cases of Japan, Taiwan and South Korea, they [the elites] were shored up by US military power—under the umbrella of which successful redistributivist land reforms were carried through, completing the demise of the landed classes."[38]

These preconditions for rapid economic transformation were absent in India. In addition, in the tiger economies development took place under authoritarian dispensation. After seven decades of a nationalist movement for self-determination and political rights, this was not an option Indian leaders could follow. Nationalist leaders were committed to liberal democracy even though they disagreed about the scope and limits of equality, individual rights, and secularism that India should pursue.

* * *

The interventionist economic vision of the nationalists was matched by a reformist agenda in the social sphere.[39] There was no agreement, however, about how deeply to intervene in the existing caste and moral order or how to develop a "rational and scientific temper" among India's citizens. The cautious approach followed by colonial authorities was obviously no guide for leaders who were anxious to rid the country of encrusted traditions. Nationalist leaders had argued that India's "backwardness" and cultural divisions allowed the British to conquer India and that rejection of "casteism" was the first step in making it truly free. Even before the struggle for indepen-dence became a mass movement, several nineteenth- and early twentieth-century reform movements—the Arya Samaj of Dayananda Saraswati and the Brahmo Samaj led by Raja Rammohan Roy—had focused attention on the unjust role of caste and customs.

Nationalist-era leaders Gandhi and Bhimrao Ramji Ambedkar believed that independence was meaningless without social reforms. Each had rejected caste and untouchability and condemned the Brahminic order. Gandhi's reformist strategy, however, envisaged individual transformation as a basis for social transformation; Ambedkar, the leader of the Dalit movement in preindependent India and the principal architect of the Indian Constitution, wanted separate electorates (a precedent set by the British) to empower the lower castes. Nehru, in contrast, favored the more conventional path of legislating from the state to initiate reforms.[40] Ambedkar's demands proved too radical and divisive for the Congress Party. The Gandhian transformation depended on a "change of heart," which might take more time, if even possible, than the nationalists had. The Nehruvian solution had the virtue of requiring only a purposeful state. The last option emerged triumphant, making the state responsible for equal protection provisions and strong prominority legislation.

This preference for a purposeful state was in line with building a layered administrative and political order within the overarching ideology of unification. Accordingly, Indian Muslims were granted a separate personal law and the lower castes special quotas known as "reservations" in jobs and education. Both minorities were large enough in numbers to derail India's unification. Last but not least, economic plans gave the new state control over national resources. Riding on its national popularity, the Congress Party had built up a vast network of patronage, which endured even beyond the 1967 elections when the party lost many states to ethnicity-based opposition parties, although it could still form a government at the center until the late 1980s. The latter would not have been possible had the party not succeeded in retaining its exclusive, pan-Indian image and linking India's future with its civilizational past.

The State Formation Dilemma

Fortunately for India, although transforming informal personalized relations into a formal, legal-political arrangement was difficult, there was no leadership vacuum and the Congress Party had emerged as the natural and uncontested heir to the British after their departure. There was a single center of legitimate authority. This cannot be said of many countries that gained independence after World War II. Pakistan, the other half of British India, soon succumbed to military rule, and Nepal faced political turmoil. Although China's Communist Party eventually emerged triumphant, it had to overcome the trauma of a bloody civil war in which millions had perished. China's "stable" socialist government had emerged from a violent peasant revolution.

Why did India not descend into chaos and military coups or fragment into several smaller states and kingdoms following the partition and resulting communal holocaust? The partition dealt a severe body blow to the idea of a united and secular India, and more than 70 percent of its peasant population was destitute. As several historians have recorded, throughout the 1920s and 1930s violent peasant uprisings were quite common.[41] They could have radicalized the peasantry, but that did not happen largely because Congress Party leaders had built a broad alliance of urban middle classes, peasants, intelligentsia, and Indian business in support of their movement. The history of independence—the nature of the nationalist movement, the leadership's ideological preferences, the absence of a radicalized peasantry, and the strength of civil society institutions (party) over the military—set the stage for the triumph of a liberal democracy in India.

Even though India's liberal democracy bore a family resemblance to the early liberal democracies in the West, it in fact operated on a very different set of rules and practices: India recognized group rights and built institutions to privilege them.[42] In this, as in other respects, the national leadership had bought into the British view that

India was a society of compartmentalized communities. The nationalist leaders had, however, reversed the role of the state. It was no longer a passive entity imposing dharmic dispensation based on caste; the postindependence Indian state was an active and interventionist agency.

Could the Congress Party have imposed the authoritarian rule of a single-party dictatorship? The answer to this question would have to be in the negative, given the umbrella character of the party and the grand alliance of regional, ethnic, and religious communities that sustained it. In the early decades, opposition was contained within the party, and when it could not be so contained, new parties came into being to oppose the Congress Party at the province-state level.

Could the nationalists have chosen to establish a Hindu state? A short answer to this, too, is in the negative because of the existence of large religious minorities within India. Nevertheless, independent India's equidistant secularism was a world apart from secularism in the West. Prakash Chandra Upadhyaya argues that privileging primordial identities (as in Muslim personal law) was a ploy that permitted Indian leaders to avoid having to tackle class inequality. A society preoccupied with caste and ethnic conflicts is not likely to wage a class struggle.[43] He also argues that Gandhi, Patel, and Nehru were perfectly aware of the advantages of emphasizing religious over economic cleavages. "While it was Sardar Patel who implemented this brand of 'consensual' politics in practice, it was Gandhi," Upadhyaya writes, "who was its theorist and philosopher."[44] Gandhi had put forward an idea of trusteeship—the wealthy would take responsibility for the welfare of the rest who were less fortunate—as a way to prevent class wars and as an alternative to socialism.[45]

The Machiavellian designs Upadhyaya attributes to the nationalist leadership are, however, overdrawn. Surely, denying the existence of caste and ethnic division would not have erased them overnight. Nor could anyone have prevented their politicization in a competitive democracy. Could the weight of institutional and legal infrastructure have steered postindependence India to separate religion from politics more strictly? It is possible. But such a choice would not have been likely given the composition of the Congress movement and the party in the 1940s and 1950s. Nehru was staunchly secular and enjoyed huge popularity, but he could not have alone, without the support of the Congress Party's rank and file, imposed a strict separation of religion from politics. The rank and file reflected grassroots

divisions along language, caste, and religious lines. India's segmented democracy was then different from its namesake in the industrialized West; each segment had a different degree of commitment to
the Indian nation-state. Although political imperatives required a soft
separation of religion from politics, even that was a slippery slope
bound to deliver the country, as it in fact did, into the hands of Hindu
nationalists in the 1990s who subscribed to the idea of unifying India
on the basis of its Hindu majority.

We might then identify generally two competing approaches to
state formation in India. One might be referred to as "unity through
centralization" and the other as "unity through decentralization."
Congress Party leaders had opted for the first, but the center they
envisaged was a secular one representing no particular ethnic or caste
community.[46] The Hindu nationalists were the nonsecular variant of
unity through centralization. Unity through decentralization, in contrast, envisaged devolution of power from the center to the regions
and communities. The purpose was to turn localities into stakeholders in a unified India.[47]

We can now at least partly provide an answer to why coups and
revolutions did not then mark India's passage to modernization. It is
because of the ideological preferences of the nationalist leaders and
the umbrella character of the Congress Party organization. The broad
rules of the political contest were established early on. The pace of
change remained slow and economic growth modest. Each permitted
the political class to move forward incrementally. The success of
India's democratic state although imperfect, partial, and contested,
proves nevertheless that Indian leaders were capable of innovation
and institution-building to establish a democratic state that could
endure. Nowhere was this more evident than in independent India's
international stance.

The Foreign Policy Dilemma

Several India scholars argue that India has lacked a tradition of
strategic thought and produced no theory of the state.[48] The great
ancient texts had plenty to say about the emancipation of individuals
from the toils of material life but had little interest in the state or the
desirable scope of its power. Kautilya's *Arthshastra,* written in the
fourth century B.C.E., was an astonishing manual for administering
princely states. The *Dharmashastra,* dating a century earlier, made

references to *Matsyanyaya*, the rule of the fishes in which the "big eats the small," but the rest of Indian traditional literature was curiously uninterested in the powers of a state.[49] India's historians point out that there was no tradition of writing objective accounts or developing maps outlining the territorial scope of "India" in the region. Histories were usually hagiographies by court-appointed bards praising the deeds and achievements of a monarch or king. Maps were largely for administrative purposes or for the collection of revenues. They did not identify the boundaries of the empires or kingdoms.[50] Indeed, boundaries of kingdoms expanded and contracted depending on whether regional kingdoms accepted the paramount authority of the empire state.

The British established their Indian empire by breaking away from these traditions in at least one respect: they marked boundaries and drew detailed maps. The British kept records of economy, population growth and land revenue, ownership deeds of properties, and agreements with the princely states. They wrote histories of the regions and commentaries on policies. In short, a conscious effort at recording history began with the colonial administration. It is noteworthy that even in 1947 British India consisted of rings of control and authority that diminished with the movement from the center of power to the periphery—from areas ruled directly by the British to the tribal belt in the Northwest and Northeast where the British presence was weak. The nationalists inherited this uneven map of state presence from the British. Even after the princely states were integrated between 1947 and 1948, free India remained a polyglot of many nationalities, several of which lived on both sides of international borders.

As the Cold War penetrated into South Asia via Pakistan, India faced several urgent challenges: it had to manage these overlapping nationalities, consolidate territorial India, deter hostile states from derailing the nation-building agenda, and protect India's freedom in foreign policy. India adopted a strategy I have described elsewhere as "relational control."[51] This strategy was meant to give it a degree of control over developments in neighboring states, which shared borders, waters, and ethnic communities. The objective was to prevent a spillover of adverse developments from jeopardizing India's own efforts of national consolidation and state-building. Relational control was neither a quest for dominance nor was it meant to be passive if India's security and political unity were at stake. India sought to shape the power matrix within interstate relations and therefore opposed great powers from seeking military pacts and alliances (as the United States did with Pakistan in 1954 to 1955) among its neighboring states. The intervention in Pakistan's civil war in 1971 was a classic exercise in relational control, but the success of relational control depended on the strength of India's national unity. Forging interlocking balances based on ethnic accommodation was then a precondition for exercising relational control. The purpose of relational control, in turn, was to prevent regional developments from jeopardizing India's territorial and national unity. Although relational control was a defensive strategy, it was condemned by India's neighboring states as a quest for hegemony and dominance.

India's quest for relational control crystallized by the 1950s into an anticolonial, anti-imperialist, and staunchly independent foreign policy under the rubric of nonalignment. The purpose was to keep the United States and Soviet Union from changing the balance of power in South Asia. India's antipathy toward military blocs came as much from the nation's history of nonviolent struggle and the leadership's urgent need to secure the union as it did from a desire to be free of the Cold War power blocs. Nehru explained, "It is not our purpose to enter into other people's quarrels. If I may say so, I have more and more come to the conclusion that the less we interfere in international conflicts, the better, unless our own interest is involved. For this reason, it is not in consonance with our dignity just to interfere without any effect being produced. Either we should be strong enough to produce some effect or we should not interfere at all."[52] The sense of vulnerability he articulated could have predisposed India to align with one of the Cold War power blocs, and indeed several leaders in and out of the Congress Party argued in favor of alignment, but ultimately the choice of nonalignment prevailed.[53]

Even though vulnerability explains this choice, it does not explain India's high-profile diplomacy and lofty pronouncements on every issue, even those that did not directly concern India. What prompted Prime Minister Nehru to make India's views known when his pronouncements could only mean, in his own words, interference "without any effect being produced"?[54] In the 1950s and 1960s, India had little influence over its smaller neighbors, let alone the great powers. Several commentators have criticized Nehru for being naïve and for moralizing on issues that did not strictly involve India. Although a discussion about the merits of Nehru's policies is beyond the scope of this chapter and not particularly relevant here, what his pronouncements did show was his belief in India's civilizational greatness. Gandhi and Nehru believed that the West had a superiority in material sciences but of the spirit that moves and makes nations, and the arts and philosophy that constitute a great people, India had little to learn from others. It would be its own master, they declared. Nonalignment was more than a strategic posture; it was India's international identity.

Nehru's domestic and foreign policy visions were only partially successful. India did not succeed in preventing Pakistan from forging a military alliance with the United States. Its quest for relational control over Pakistan's policies thus failed. Nor could nonalignment resolve India-China border disputes or prevent China from forging strategic ties with Pakistan.[55] Despite these failures, the first generation of India's leaders established the foundations for a modern, secular, democratic India that was to endure, with only one interruption, for the next forty-two years after independence, a remarkable, post–World War II feat given that most newly independent countries succumbed to civil wars and military dictatorships.

Challenges After Nehru:
Setting the Stage for Post–Cold War India

Vastly weakened though it was, this vision—of interlocking balances, Congress Party dominance, and relational control—continued to guide India during the two decades following Nehru's death in 1964. Progeny and heirs of the first prime minister, Indira Gandhi and Rajiv Gandhi sought to protect the key principles of the Nehruvian blueprint, but that action was highly counterproductive. Insistence on maintaining the Congress Party's political hegemony led to increasing intolerance of dissent and splits within the party. To stem the erosion, Indira Gandhi split the Congress Party to form a new party, the Congress (I), which was made up mainly of her staunch loyalists. As prime minister, she frequently dismissed opposition state governments to clear the field for Congress (I) electoral victories.

These actions had damaging implications for the unification and development functions of the central state.[56] Nehru had argued that democracy and development would automatically replace India's primordial identities with a national identity, but Indira Gandhi's actions did the opposite. Opposition to the Congress (I) jelled along caste and ethnolinguistic lines. Ethnic nationalism in Punjab, Tamil Nadu, Kashmir, and Assam converged into mass movements that turned violent. Indira and to a lesser extent Rajiv Gandhi responded to this nationalism with force instead of accommodation. Coercion turned the demands for ethnic autonomy into demands for a separate state.[57] These conflicts lasted for decades, polarized society, and weakened India's control over its international borders.[58] Indira Gandhi's revenge killing by her Sikh bodyguards in November 1984 underscored the dangerous consequences of the path she had followed.

Preserving control over the state and party required control of the economy. During the eighteen years of Indira Gandhi's tenure as prime minister (from 1965 to 1977 and then from 1980 to 1984), India moved closer to the command-and-control model of the socialist economies. Bureaucracy expanded to regulate industry, banking, and trade. Her government created scores of new institutions to control private investment and markets. But by the mid-1970s, it was evident that state-led growth strategies had failed, poverty had not diminished, and India had become marginalized in international markets. Although the bureaucracy absorbed a good number of middle-class job seekers, it was hardly a venue for productive employment. The Green Revolution—with its introduction of high-yielding varieties of seeds, increased use of fertilizers, and focus on irrigation— had brought prosperity to some regions within India, but the gap between prosperous and poor widened as a result of its uneven progress. India was trapped for the first forty years of planned development at an average rate of growth of about 3.5 percent that failed to ameliorate underemployment, widespread undernourishment, and illiteracy.

Although post-Nehru leaders had by their actions aggravated the dilemmas of development and unification, some slow progress in laying an independent industrial base was visible. India had built a modicum of infrastructure and learned to administer a vast country divided by enormous diversity. It could produce all manner of industrial and manufactured goods by the 1970s, but these goods could not withstand competition in global markets. The positive part of the change was that economic planning created a reservoir of private and public managers skilled at running large-scale, technologically advanced enterprises. The civil service and bureaucracy also learned to regulate, anticipate, plan, and procure and distribute public goods to vast numbers of people living in rural India with rudimentary infrastructure and abysmal levels of literacy. Critics are right in condemning the red tape and delays, graft and corruption that the state-regulated economy produced, but India's maturing democracy began to devolve power downward and inspire increasing civil society activity by the 1970s.

An inward, self-reliant economy might have been compatible with the goals of nonalignment, but India's humiliating dependence on US food aid throughout the 1960s betrayed its failed quest for international stature.[59] Even the 1971 military intervention in Pakistan's civil war, hailed as a triumph of nonalignment, required signing a friendship treaty with the Soviet Union. The treaty was meant to counter any hostile Chinese military moves should a general war break out between India and Pakistan.[60]

These were hardly the actions of a strong and independent regional power. The 1971 intervention, which liberated Bangladesh from Pakistan, India's main adversary, did not bring enduring international status to India. Domestic weaknesses evident in perpetual ethnic challenges to New Delhi, not to mention a crisis-prone economy, dampened expectations abroad and made India turn inward in the early 1980s. A 1987 military intervention in Sri Lanka, designed ostensibly for peacekeeping between Tamil separatists and the government in Colombo, turned into a debacle.[61]

The Indira and Rajiv Gandhi era was a shift away from the Nehruvian schema of good neighborly relations, opposition to militarization, and adherence to the spirit of peaceful coexistence. The key element that had allowed for a smooth working of this blueprint had eroded. Nehru's Congress Party had withered away. It continued to win elections and form governments at the center (with the exception of the 1977–1979 Janata government), but its hold over individual states within the union had become tenuous. The entire 1970s and 1980s reflected a struggle for power within the party and between the Congress Party and its local rivals. Nevertheless, it remained the choice of the people until 1989. No viable alternative emerged, at least not for long and not at the center, to replace the Congress Party. But that was about to change.

Notes

1. See Marmann Kulke and Dietmar Rothermund, *A History of India*, 4th ed. (New York: Routledge, 2004); D. D. Kosambi, *The Culture and Civ-*

ilization of Ancient India in Historical Outline (New Delhi: Vikas Publications, 1994); Romila Thapar, *A History of India,* vol. 1 (London: Penguin, 1966); Irfan Habib, *The Agrarian System of Mughal India* (New York: Asia Publishing House, 1963); *An Atlas of the Mughal Empire* (Oxford: Oxford University Press, 1982); I. H. Qureshi, *The Administration of the Mughal Empire* (Delhi: Low Price Publications, 1979); and John F. Richard, *The Mughal Empire* (Cambridge: Cambridge University Press, 1993).

2. Although several historians have suggested that early Indian history shows a degree of familiarity with the notion of popular consent and have painstakingly researched the early republics of ancient India to prove their thesis, others have argued that the separatist conflicts in Kashmir, Punjab, or Assam echo the fissiparous trends embedded in India's history. The validity of these claims is best left to history scholars.

3. The list of eminent scholars engaged in this debate is long, but some key names and titles are Ranajit Guha, ed., *A Subaltern Reader, 1986–1995* (Minneapolis: University of Minnesota Press, 1997); Romila Thapar, *Cultural Pasts: Essays in Early Indian History* (New York: Oxford University Press, 2001); Irfan Habib, ed., *Akbar and His India* (New Delhi: Oxford University Press, 2010); Partha Chatterjee, *The Nation and Its Fragments: Colonial and Postcolonial Histories* (Princeton, NJ: Princeton University Press, 1993); Gyanendra Pandey, *Routine Violence: Nations, Fragments, Histories* (Stanford, CA: Stanford University Press, 2006); Sumit Sarkar, *Writing Social History* (New York: Oxford University Press, 1999); Peter Heehs, *Nationalism, Terrorism, Communalism: Essays in Modern Indian History* (New York: Oxford University Press, 1998); and Achin Vanaik, *The Furies of Indian Communalism: Religion, Modernity, and Secularization* (London: Verso Books, 1997). For comments and perspective on the debate, see Vinay Lal, "Subaltern Studies and Its Critics: Debates over Indian History," *History and Theory* 40, no. 1 (February 2001): 135–148.

4. Gyanendra Pandey, "Subaltern Studies as Postcolonial Criticism," *American Historical Review* 99, no. 5 (December 1994): 1475–1490, critiques colonial and nationalist history and comments on the flaws of postcoloniality.

5. Partha Chatterjee, an eminent critic of the nationalist and Nehruvian version of history and a proponent of the subaltern perspective, admits that each domain of history—subaltern and elite—"has not only acted in opposition to and as a limit upon the other but, through this process of struggle, has also shaped the emergent form of the other." See *The Nation and Its Fragments,* 12–13.

6. Sudipta Kaviraj, *The Dynamics of State Formation: India and Europe Compared* (Delhi: Sage, 1997), 228.

7. Ibid., emphasis in original.

8. Ibid., 230.

9. Kenneth Jones, *Socio-Religious Reform Movements in British India* (Cambridge: Cambridge University Press, 1990).

10. Lata Mani, "Contentious Traditions: The Debate on Sati in Colonial India," *Cultural Critique,* no. 7 (Autumn 1987): 119–156. (*Sati* is also spelled *suttee.*)

11. Ankit Vyas, "Relevance of Caste in Contemporary Politics—Part 2," *The Indian Economist,* January 16, 2013, http://theindianeconomist.com/relevance-of-caste-in-contemporary-politics-part-2/.

12. I have generally regarded the modern period to date from the establishment of East India Company rule in 1757 although admittedly this is arbitrary periodization and remains controversial among historians.

13. Mushirul Hasan, "Partition Narratives," *Social Scientist* 30, nos. 7–8 (July–August 2002): 24–53, describes the deep disagreement within the top leadership of the Congress Party and particularly the implications of M. K. Gandhi's isolation.

14. M. S. S. Pandian, "Notes on the Transformation of 'Dravidian' Ideology: Tamilnadu, c. 1900–1940," *Social Scientist* 22, nos. 5–6 (May–June 1994): 84–104.

15. For the Naga revolt, see Sanjib Baruah, "Confronting Constructionism: Ending India's Naga War," *Journal of Peace Research* 40, no. 3 (May 2003): 321–338. For integration of the princely states, see V. P. Menon, *The Story of the Integration of the Indian States* (New York: Macmillan, 1956).

16. For the Gandhi and Bose controversy, see Bhupinder Kumar Ahluwalia and Shashi Ahluwalia, *Netaji and Gandhi* (New Delhi: Indian Academic Publishers, 1982). For differences between Patel and Nehru, see P. N. Chopra and Prabha Chopra, *Inside Story of Sardar Patel: The Diary of Maniben Patel, 1936–50* (New Delhi: Vision Books, 2002). The diary of Maniben Patel, his daughter, serves to highlight the deep differences between him and Nehru on a host of issues: integration of Hyderabad; Kashmir; foreign policy, especially with regard to Tibet; Hindu-Muslim tensions; the refugee problem; the Nehru-Liaquat Pact; and, generally, issues of corruption, socialism, and centralized planning. Indeed, Patel's differences with Nehru were ideological and deep-rooted. In addition, Nehru resented his hold over the Congress Party machine. The Patel-Nehru differences over dealing with the leader of the Socialist Party, Rafi Ahmed Kidwai, and even Maulana Azad, the preeminent Muslim leader in the Congress Party, permeated the nationalist movement after 1935.

17. Chetan Bhatt, *Hindu Nationalism: Origins, Ideologies, and Modern Myths* (Oxford: Oxford University Press, 2001), 77–113.

18. Jagannath Swaroop Mathur, *Industrial Civilization and Gandhian Economics* (Allahabad, India: Pustakayan, 1971), explores the full range of Gandhian economic proposals.

19. For a succinct and highly readable account of Nehru's vision, see Sunil Khilnani, *The Idea of India* (New York: Farrar, Straus and Giroux, 1997); and Shashi Tharoor, *Nehru: The Invention of India* (New York: Arcade, 2003).

20. Jawaharlal Nehru, *Discovery of India,* centenary ed. (Delhi: Oxford University Press, 1989), 517.

21. Kaviraj, *The Dynamics of State Formation*. See also M. P. Singh and Rekha Saxena, *Indian Politics: Contemporary Issues and Concerns* (New Delhi: Prentice Hall, 2008), 48.

22. Subaltern historians see the Nehruvian vision as a highly romanticized version of history that had little to do with social reality. But in fairness, Nehru was not unaware of the gap between his vision and India's social reality. In speeches and statements, Nehru constantly worried about the disintegrative pulls of ethnicity, religion, and caste and exhorted his fellow citizens to reject their pull. He did not, of course, privilege them with independent accounts, as the subaltern historians tend to do.

23. For a detailed explanation, see Maya Chadda, *Ethnicity, Security, and Separatism in India* (New York: Columbia University Press, 1997), 1–26.

24. Rajni Kothari, "Tradition and Modernity Revisited," *Government and Opposition* 3, no. 3 (Summer 1968): 273–293, discusses the dichotomy of modernity and tradition embedded in the writings about Indian political development in the 1950s and 1960s.

25. For a detailed account of the smooth workings and failures of interlocking balances, see Chadda, *Ethnicity,* 49–102.

26. George Rosen, *Democracy and Economic Change in India* (Los Angeles: University of California Press, 1966), 195–211.

27. Hindu-Muslim tensions are a regular feature of Indian political life. These have been exacerbated since the rise of the Hindutva (Hindu nationalism) ideology and the Bharatiya Janata Party (BJP), which has espoused it. The BJP advocated replacement of separate Muslim personal law with a single civil code and the use of coercion to integrate minorities into the Hindu Rashtra (Hindu nation).

28. This was the Congress Party system Rajni Kothari wrote about in his early works on India's government and politics. See his *Politics of India* (Boston: Little, Brown, 1970).

29. Rosen, *Democracy and Economic Change,* 20.

30. Uma Kapila, ed., *India's Economic Development Since Independence* (New Delhi: Academic Foundation, 2008), 27.

31. Stuart Corbridge and John Harriss, *Reinventing India: Liberalization, Hindu Nationalism, and Popular Democracy* (Cambridge, UK: Polity Press, 2000), 10.

32. Daniel Thorner and Alice Thorner, *Land and Labour in India* (Bombay: Asia Publishing House, 1962), 3.

33. Corbridge and Harriss, *Reinventing India,* 11.

34. Ajit Kumar Dasgupta, *A History of Indian Economic Thought* (London: Routledge, 1993), 57–87.

35. R. C. Dutt, *The Economic History of India,* 2 vols. (London: Gollacz, [1901] 1950), was the first to articulate the thesis of drain in a systematic way. Similar arguments are to be found in Dadabhoy Naoroji, *Poverty and Un-British Rule in India* (New Delhi: Ministry of Information and Broadcasting, Government of India, 1962). Dutt represented the socialist

view; Naoroji was a successful businessman and industrialist who was later knighted by the British Crown. Both subscribed to the argument of drain.

36. Robert Hardgrave Jr. and Stanley Kochanek, *India: Government and Politics in a Developing Nation* (Boston: Thomson Press, 2008), 356.

37. Corbridge and Harriss, *Reinventing India,* 58.

38. Ibid.

39. Postcolonial research had shown that in many instances what we believed to be encrusted traditions were really mistaken interpretations of native conditions by colonial administrators or the result of policies they themselves had pursued.

40. For a succinct discussion of the differences among Nehru, Gandhi, and Ambedkar, see David Lelyveld, "Burning Up the Dharmashatras: Group Identity and Social Justice in the Thought of B. R. Ambedkar" (New York: Columbia University, April 14, 1990), http://www.columbia.edu/itc/mealac/pritchett/00ambedkar/timeline/graphics/txt_lelyveld_ambedkar.pdf.

41. Ranajit Guha, *Elementary Aspects of Peasant Insurgency in Colonial India* (Delhi: Oxford University Press, 1983), 2–3.

42. Special personal laws recognized the right of religious communities to practice their traditions and customs, including freedom to establish educational institutions for religious instructions of their young. In marriage, divorce, and inheritance the community could adhere to either civil law or its own religious laws.

43. Prakash Chandra Upadhyaya, "The Politics of Indian Secularism," *Modern Asian Studies* 26, no. 4 (October 1992): 832.

44. Ibid.

45. Gandhi to Agatha Harrison, April 30, 1936, cited in Kapil Kumar, "Peasants, Congress and the Struggle," in *Congress and Classes: Nationalism, Workers, and Peasants,* ed. Kapil Kumar (New Delhi: Manohar, 1988), 224.

46. In the early decades, Brahmin caste leaders dominated the top echelons of Indian government and civil service.

47. The unity through centralization approach was born out of the British colonial act of 1935, which permitted elections for provincial governments but the viceroy of India appointed by the British parliament could overrule the provincial legislatures. The creation of provincial legislatures was meant to appease the Congress Party and its demands for self-rule. But in many provinces Hindu nationalist ideology was popular and hence held considerable sway in shaping campaigns and their conduct. The unity through decentralization approach was advocated by ethnic nationalists: the Tamils, Sikhs, Nagas, and Indian Muslims. In the 1940s, they advocated a confederation of nationalities in a loose union.

48. Jaswant Singh, *Defending India* (London: Macmillan, 1999), 1–61; Stephen P. Cohen, *India: Emerging Power* (Washington, DC: Brookings Institution Press, 2001). Both Cohen and Singh stress this point.

49. Kamal Kishore Mishra, *Police Administration in Ancient India* (New Delhi: Mittal, 1987), 11.

50. Jaswant Singh writes, "This absence of a sense of geographical territory persisted from ancient India down the ages, to the medieval period and even later. . . . It is only during the British reign that territory, its survey, settlement, and mapping came . . . to India." See his *Defending India,* 17.

51. Chadda, *Ethnicity.*

52. Indian Constituent Assembly (Legislative), March 8, 1948, *Indian Information,* vol. 22, April 15, 1948, 412.

53. B. Shiva Rao and Hridayanath Kunzru, both leading members of the Constituent Assembly, pushed for India to join a military alliance, preferably on the Anglo-American side. See A. Appadorai, "India's Foreign Policy," *International Affairs* 25, no. 1 (January 1949): 42.

54. Ibid.

55. For a dispassionate analysis of Nehru's key decisions on questions of war and peace in the early years of India's foreign policy, see Srinath Raghavan, *War and Peace in Modern India* (New York: Palgrave Macmillan, 2010). Raghavan neither dismisses Nehru as an idealist, nor condemns him as an idealist unable to understand the international power play in the 1950s and early 1960s. On the contrary, based on a meticulously researched analysis of archival material, Raghavan in fact demonstrates that Nehru was a master realist who carefully weighed the pros and cons of every challenge India faced and sought to draw lessons from the past to carefully calibrate India's responses to new problems. According to Raghavan, Nehru's failings should be attributed to too much realism, not its opposite, as most assessments have tended to do.

56. Chadda, *Ethnicity,* 77–123.

57. Ibid.

58. Ethnic conflicts had another damaging effect: they tarnished India's international image as a secular country committed to preserving neutrality among India's multiple religions. In Punjab and Kashmir, ethnic nationalists belonged predominantly to the Muslim and Sikh religions, respectively. As violence in these provinces escalated, religious polarization dividing Hindus and Muslims and Hindus and Sikhs spread far and wide. It certainly poisoned communal relations in Punjab, Haryana, and Kashmir.

59. See Swaminathan Aiyar's commentary on the history of food aid in India, "Drought Not Big Calamity in India Anymore," *Times of India,* July 29, 2012, http://www.cato.org/publications/commentary/drought-not-big-calamity-india-anymore.

60. M. S. Rajan, "Indo-Soviet Friendship Treaty and India's Non-Alignment Policy," *Australian Journal of International Affairs* 26, no. 2 (August 1972): 204–215.

61. Chadda, *Ethnicity,* 164–170.

3

Managing
Political Change

History tells us that the leaders of modern India reconstructed
the state to make it an agent of economic and social transformation.
This reconstruction required a guiding vision and a set of institutions
that could cope with the multiple conflicts that such change would
inevitably produce. Where Prime Minister Jawaharlal Nehru's government built many key political institutions to secure independent
India's state and democracy, the succeeding governments of Indira
and Rajiv Gandhi did far less. Indeed, in their anxiety to ensure the
Congress Party's dominance, they undermined what the Nehru government had so painstakingly built.

By the 1980s, the pan-Indian Congress Party was a mere shadow
of its former self. Except when boosted by waves of sympathy, such
as those that followed the assassination of Indira Gandhi and Rajiv
Gandhi, its share of the vote had fallen steadily from a peak of 47.78
percent in 1957 to 34.52 percent in 1977. Divided by factional fights,
devoid of political vision, and organizationally weak, the party was
held together by personal loyalties and generous patronage. Its
resounding defeat in the 1989 elections in spite of the manifest personal popularity of its leader, Rajiv Gandhi, dealt a body blow to the
Congress Party and sent shock waves through the Indian political
system. The defeat, which was unexpected, could not have occurred
at a worse time for the country.

A balance-of-payment crisis in 1990, which coincided with the demise of the dominant-party system, was the most severe of the several that the country had faced since 1956.[1] The eruption of this crisis convinced the international community that India was politically incapable of making the changes necessary for its survival, thus radically lowering India's standing in the world. The very next year saw the collapse of the Soviet Union, and India lost not only a major source of defense supplies but also an important and protected export market for Indian goods. This had allowed India to maintain its overvalued exchange rate and thereby shielded its command economy. The Indo-Soviet friendship was almost as important for maintaining India's internal political stability as it was for sustaining India's balance-of-payments equilibrium. The Soviet Union had also shielded India from the hostility of China and from US resolutions on Kashmir in the Security Council that were critical of India.[2] The loss of the Soviet Union was therefore a serious blow to India. And it occurred at a time when China was dazzling the world with its double-digit growth while India remained mired in crisis.

While nuclearized China was making rapid strides, Pakistan was believed to be developing its own nuclear weapons, leaving India in the vulnerable position of being a nuclear-capable but not a nuclear-armed country.[3] The domestic situation was also in disarray. Insurgencies in Punjab and Kashmir threatened to unravel order in the northern border regions; at the same time waves of mass protests organized by the lower castes, advocates of Hindu nationalism, and disenfranchised landless rural poor imposed intolerable strain on the newly formed coalition governments at the center. As if all this were not enough, the end of Congress Party dominance touched off a frantic scramble among political parties of the left and the right to fill the space it had vacated. It seemed as if India's historic seesaw between centralization and decentralization, integration and disintegration, was about to be reenacted.

As noted in the first two chapters, political consolidation and formation of a stable center have been key challenges for India throughout its history. Empires rose and fell, creating their own waves of fragmentation that lasted until a new contender for imperial dominance arose and welded the disparate regions into a single entity. At no time, however, were these regions fully and completely within the direct control of the ruling authorities, whether they were the Mughal emperors or the British colonizers. The stability of India's central state depended largely on accommodating the local and regional aspirations of diverse communities. The end of the Congress Party's dominance confronted India with the age-old challenge of forming a stable state in the midst of multiple crises precipitated by external debt and a disintegrating center. Did India succeed in meeting these challenges? Ringman's yardstick for measuring potential for power indicates that if India made progress toward resolving these challenges, then it certainly moved that much closer to the goal of becoming an important actor on the regional and world stage. In the following I delineate the challenges as they arose and the success or failures of India's coalition governments to resolve them.

Many scholars pointed to weakening institutions and feared that India's coalition governments were too divided internally to meet the multitude of problems they faced.[4] These fears were understandable, given that for most analysts it was axiomatic that only a strong center, backed by a solid majority in Parliament, could make risky decisions or demand short-term sacrifices for long-term gain. A parliamentary majority provided government the necessary autonomy to make hard decisions.[5]

By this reasoning India's democratic system could have disintegrated under the pressure of events in 1989–1990. But this did not happen. On the contrary, even a cursory tally of India's achievements during the two decades that followed was impressive. India's commitment to democratic government and economic reform strengthened. Democracy deepened as even those who were historically among the most oppressed—the Dalits—began to exercise effective political power. No doubt inequality, too, increased under the spur of accelerated development, but even in regions that remained impervious to developmental efforts, poverty fell substantially.[6] There was an increasing diffusion of political and economic power from the center to the states and with it, ironically, an increase in interstate income disparities.[7] This "weakening," however, was offset by a broadening of a proreform consensus and a rapid growth in economically backward states such as Bihar, Uttar Pradesh, Rajasthan, Madhya Pradesh, and Orissa.[8]

The demise of single-party rule required that the newly elected parties forge a majority by working out a whole new set of arrangements to produce a stable coalition government. Reconciliation had to occur among numerous new constituencies that had arrived in the political arena but had little or no experience in forming governments at the center and taking on responsibilities for the whole of India. The formation of a succession of legitimate governments, however briefly in office, underlined India's adherence to constitutionality in the midst of vast domestic and international challenges and implied, in principle at least, a distinctive vision of the future. Unfortunately for the first ten years of coalition rule (1989–1999), such a formula eluded the competing parties. Nor did they figure out a formula for reconciling competing agendas within a potential coalition. The coalition led by the Bharatiya Janata Party (BJP), for instance, envisioned a muscular India that privileged the Hindu majority; the Congress Party–led coalition opted for a secular but strong India that would vigorously pursue a liberal international agenda; and the Janata Dal–led coalition envisaged a looser domestic federation in pursuit of a limited and selective foreign policy agenda. Although vague on all points, the competing coalitions did articulate distinctive visions of the India they wanted to build, thereby partly fulfilling Eric Ringman's first requirement for the acquisition of future state power: the ability to envision a well-articulated future for the country. The fact that between 1989 and 1999 coalition governments were formed but failed to live out their term in office, with the exception of the Congress Party–led government (1991–1996), shows that conflict got temporarily resolved but resurfaced quickly and repeatedly. These ten years of unstable coalitions could be viewed as a precipitous decline in the government's ability to solve conflicts or as a sustained effort by the government—with stops and starts—to articulate a set of rules for establishing stable majorities at the center. Both interpretations are valid. By 1999, competing parties had begun to forge more enduring mutual arrangements, which also reflected the preferences of their constituencies and their ability to settle interparty disputes. The latter also underscores the third element in Ringman's measure of power, the ability to resolve differences.

These developments cannot be attributed to any change in the character of India's political class, which remained both predatory and corrupt. On the contrary, the market economy created new avenues for the enrichment of the few at the expense of the many. There was much faltering and sliding back under the coalition governments, but the gains for the democratic system as a whole were undeniable. Within less than two decades after the end of the Cold War, international perceptions of India had begun to turn. Earlier predictions of doom were replaced by fulsome, often uncritical praise. In the first few years of the twenty-first century, international media, institutions, and agencies began to hail the emergence of a second Asian giant.

How are these very contradictory developments to be interpreted? If India's political institutions were as weak as critics have argued, how did the country manage the shift from single-party dominance to coalition rule so smoothly? How did it wind up the command economy and establish a market-directed economy in such a measured manner as to make the change relatively painless? How did it achieve the rapid acceleration of growth precisely at the time when the central government had lost its capacity to direct the course of development? The answer is that Indian leaders often backtracked but did not lose their way.[9] On the contrary, it was the sheer smoothness of the changes they presided over that led more and more observers abroad to bracket India and China together in discussions of power sharing in the twenty-first century and to expect India to play an active part in the formation of the post–Cold War international order.

The unexpected resilience of the Indian political system calls for a reexamination of the thesis, culled from the East Asian experience, that a strong central government is necessary to ensure economic growth, social progress, and political coherence.[10] The advocates of this thesis had argued that a strong state was necessary to act as a mediator among contending social forces. In order to play this role, the state had to be essentially independent of and above competing social groups. It would only then be able to effectively act on decisions it took. With some variations, Atul Kohli and Lloyd Rudolph and Susanne Rudolph had made this argument in explaining why India had been able to embark upon centralized economic planning and industrialization despite its enormous diversity and an increasingly powerful assertion of ethnic identity within a competitive party system.[11] The post-1989 experience therefore tends to reverse earlier theoretical assumptions. India presents the case of a strong society and a weakening state producing faster economic growth in a heterogeneous and contentious democracy.

Some scholars have modified the strong-state thesis to fit Indian conditions by suggesting that coalition governments at the center can exhibit the necessary strength provided they fulfill three conditions: (1) there is a single dominant party within each coalition, (2) the number of parties in each coalition is as small as possible, and (3) there is a degree of ideological coherence among its members. All three preconditions are also the measure of capabilities required in Ringman's yardsticks of power: a country capable of evolving a vision, mobilizing resources, and resolving conflicts. In India's case we need to modify the condition for ideological coherence as explained below.

The need for ideological coherence is obvious if a government is to be effective. Small coalitions are more stable because they permit each member of that coalition to maximize the benefits associated with incumbency. By the same token, larger coalitions mean fewer benefits for each party within it and therefore less incentive to stay within the coalition.[12]

India's experience does not fit entirely into this model. Admittedly, coalitions that have been formed with the Congress Party and the BJP at their core have been more stable than those formed without the support of either of these parties.[13] But these coalitions were not built around ideological coherence. Nor did they have optimally small numbers of members.

This chapter demonstrates that a different set of minimal conditions needs to be fulfilled to create stable coalition governments in an identity-based federal democracy such as India. It also highlights the remarkable capacity these coalitions can possess for innovating ways to produce a governing majority and policy consensus, however temporary these might turn out to be (see Box 3.1). As Table 3.1 shows, the twenty-three years since the advent of coalition rule can be divided broadly into two phases: the first from 1989 to 1999 and the second from 1999 to the present. Throughout these years, three main players and their allies contested elections: the much diminished Congress (I), the newly emergent BJP and its allies and affiliates, and the Janata Party and its various state-based fragments. The decade after 1989 was characterized by acute instability, frequent elections, and weak coalition rule. During this period, the Janata and its fragments attempted to assume the role of a core party but failed. The Congress (I), which had the characteristics of a core party, stayed out of government except during the coalition government formed by P. V. Narasimha Rao.

The second period witnessed the emergence of two broad coalitions led by the BJP and the Congress (I) separately, with each coalition completing its full term. By 1998, the BJP had expanded its electoral support and emerged as an alternative core party to the

Box 3.1 Key to Indian Government

National Government

India is the largest democracy in the world. The 2009 national elections involved an electorate of 714 million, which is larger than the electorate of the European Union and the United States combined. The size of the huge electorate requires that the elections be held in several phases (e.g., the 2009 general elections were held in five phases) over several weeks. Elections involve a step-by-step process that begins with the announcement of dates and phases of elections and ends with the declaration of results by the Election Commission. Once the results are final, a new government can be formed.

Constituted as a parliamentary democracy and a federal republic, India consists of twenty-eight states[a] and seven union territories. The central government and individual state governments each consist of executive, legislative, and judicial branches. A third tier of government at the village level is known as the Panchayati Raj system. The head of the state in India is the president of India, and the head of the government is the prime minister. The central Parliament is bicameral, consisting of two houses: the directly elected Lok Sabha ("House of the People"), the lower house, and the 245-member indirectly elected and appointed Rajya Sabha ("Council of States"), the upper house. A winning party or coalition of parties needs 273 seats (of the total 545 seats) to be able to form a government. Defection from the ruling coalition or loss of a no-confidence vote in Lok Sabha can lead to a collapse of the government. At that time, a new government can be formed from within Parliament. In the event no party gets the required 273-seat majority, Parliament is dissolved and new elections are held. The incumbent government carries out the role of caretaker government until elections return new winners—a party or a coalition of parties—to power. The prime minister, not unlike other members of Parliament, is elected from a single constituency and is subsequently selected to head the government by the winning party or a coalition of parties. The prime minister forms the cabinet, the council of ministers from within members of Lok Sabha and Rajya Sabha.

Note: a. If Andhra is divided into two states, there will be twenty-nine states and seven union territories—an issue not likely to be settled until after the 2014 elections.

(continues)

Box 3.1 Continued

State Governments

India's state governments are headed by a governor, who is appointed
by the president of India, and a chief minister elected from the Vidhan
Sabha, the lower house of the state legislature. Of the twenty-eight
states, six states have two legislative chambers while the rest have
only one. The upper house, if the state is bicameral, is called Vidhan
Parishad. The Vidhan Sabha is composed of members directly elected
from individual constituencies. The term of the Vidhan Sabha is five
years; one-third of the members of the Vidhan Parishad, in bicameral
states, are elected every two years for a six-year term. The governor
on the request of the chief minister may dissolve the Vidhan Sabha
even earlier than five years, or the term of the Vidhan Sabha may be
extended during an emergency, but not more than six months at a time.
The schedule of elections to Vidhan Sabha does not coincide with parliamentary election.

Congress (I). On its part, the Congress (I) had also learned from its
failures between 1989 and 1999 and devised effective strategies of
coalition formation. These developments account for the more stable
coalition rule in the second period.

Even though success or failure in forging preelectoral alliances
at least partly explains a coalition government's stability, it does
not tell the whole story. For that, we need to look at the context
within which coalitions have to function. For example, the V. P.
Singh and Chandra Shekhar governments faced the acute balance-
of-payment crisis along with caste agitations. The P. V. Narasimha
Rao government faced Hindu-Muslim riots triggered by destruction
of the Babri Mosque. The Vajpayee government had to cope with
rising tensions along Indo-Pakistani borders, which soon deterio-
rated into armed clashes in 1999 in the Kargil sector of the state of
Jammu and Kashmir.

Even during the stable period after 1999, the pressure of events
was relentless, mitigated only by compromises and skillful maneuvering on the part of the core party. For instance, Hindu-Muslim riots

Table 3.1 General Election Results at a Glance, 1989–2009

Election Year	Party/Coalition	Popular Vote (%)	Total Seats
1989	National Front		
	(coalition around Janata Dal)	40.66	143[a]
	Janata Dal	17.79	143
	Left Front[b]	8.23	43
	BJP	11.36	85
	INC	39.53	197
1991	INC-led coalition	35.66	244
	BJP	20.11	120
	National Front[c]		
	Janata Dal	15.10	61
	Janata Dal	11.84	59
	Left Front	8.65	49
1996	United Front	29.0	192
	National Front	14.33	79
	Janata Dal	8.08	46
	Left Front	9.10	52
	INC	28.80	140
	BJP	20.29	161
	BJP-affiliated parties	4.01	26
1998	National Democratic Alliance	37.20	254
	BJP	25.59	182
	INC	25.82	141
	Left Front	7.15	41
	BSP	4.67	5
	JD(U)	3.24	6
1999	NDA	37.06	270
	BJP	23.75	182
	INC	28.30	114
	Left Front	6.88	37
	BSP	4.16	14
2004	United Progressive Alliance	35.4	218
	INC	26.53	145
	Left Front	7.07	53
	NCP	1.80	8
	NDA	33.30	181
	BJP	22.16	138
	BSP	5.33	19

(continues)

Table 3.1 Continued

Election Year	Party/Coalition	Popular Vote (%)	Total Seats
2009	United Progressive Alliance	37.22	262
	INC	28.55	206
	NCP	2.04	9
	NDA	24.63	159
	BJP	18.80	116
	Left Front	6.76	20
	BSP	6.17	21
	Janata Dal	1.52	20

Source: Constructed from Election Commission reports (eci.nic.in/).

Notes: The votes of the winning party or coalition have been given first, followed by its major coalition partners. The table does not list all the contesting parties or their share of the popular vote. The total does not therefore add up to 100 percent. Only national parties of blocs have been included or those that became important to the formation of government in a given election. INC = Indian National Congress (Congress Party); BJP = Bharatiya Janata Party; BSP = Bahujan Samaj Party; JD(U) = Janata Dal United (in Bihar); NCP = National Congress Party (mostly in Maharashtra); Left Front = Communist Party of India (CPI), Communist Party of India (Marxist) (CPI-[M]), Forward Bloc, Republican Socialist party.

a. This refers to the preelection coalition of the Janata Dal. Its coalition partners did not win any seats. However, a large number of other smaller parties joined the coalition after the election. Their share of the votes is therefore reflected in the National Front's share of votes. Government was formed with support from the Left Front and the BJP.

b. Only CPI and CPI(M) votes have been included here.

c. These figures refer to the Janata Dal and the Samajwadi Janata Party.

in Gujarat in 2002 failed to undo the BJP-led National Democratic Alliance (NDA) government. Its successor, the United Progressive Alliance (UPA) government, also faced serious challenges from its own coalition partners. For instance, the UPA's main allies, the Left Front (LF) parties, threatened to withdraw support over the US-India civil nuclear deal. All post-1989 coalition governments struggled to survive in the face of these challenges; five collapsed well before their time, and only three managed to complete their tenure in office. The current UPA coalition is likely to complete its five years in office and these last four years have seen it paralyzed in face of economic slowdown and public protests, but if it stays in power until the elections of May 2014, it will be the fourth consecutive stable government in New Delhi since 1989.

The critics of coalition governments have seen only one side—the darker one—of a massive change of course in Indian democracy. They have dismissed coalition governments as a period of lost opportunities, but in so doing, they have overemphasized the disintegration and weakening of institutions that were built mainly to serve the purposes of a dominant-party democracy.[14] They have failed to see that dominant-party democracy itself was, of necessity, a transient phase in the building of a modern democratic system, and that it, necessarily, had to come to an end. The pertinent question was therefore not whether the years following 1989, which signaled the end of the Congress Party's dominance, would be turbulent, but how the turbulence would be managed.

The Era of Instability: Coalition Rule and State Capacity, 1989–1999

The First Coalition Government

The death throes of dominant-party democracy lasted a long time but effectively came to an end in 1989 when the Congress Party, which had secured more than 400 seats in Parliament and 50 percent of the popular vote in the 1984–1985 elections, found itself, astonishingly, with fewer than 200 seats in the 1989 general elections. Although the Congress (I) garnered the largest number of seats in the elections, they were not enough for the party to form a government alone. It chose not to form any government at all. That task fell to the leader of the National Front (NF) coalition, Prime Minister V. P. Singh. The NF won only 143 seats, a little more than half the number needed to form a stable government.[15] That this Janata Party–led coalition would have to seek support from both the communist left and the Hindu nationalist right to form a government was a foregone conclusion. This violated every rule of ideological coherence axiomatic to a stable coalition that the literature on coalition formation has so emphasized.[16] The NF collapse was not unexpected.

The NF government lasted barely eleven months, from December 1989 to November 1990. Its short tenure was marked by weak coordination among coalition partners and personality clashes among cabinet members. And as Table 3.1 shows, it was weakest in winning total popular support compared to most other viable parties. Prime Minister Singh could not agree with his partners in the coalition, and among themselves they could not agree on the distribution of ministerial positions. While these feuds within the ruling circles intensified, caste conflicts, triggered partly by the prime minister's announcement of the extension of reservations—quota-based affirmative action—for Scheduled Castes, Scheduled Tribes, and Other Backward Castes (OBCs), who together constitute close to 52 percent of India's population, pushed the coalition toward a collapse.[17] Although these castes do not vote as a single bloc, quotas in government jobs and seats in educational institutions are extremely popular among them and they constitute a highly important voting group in determining the outcome of elections in many Indian states. They have become even more important since the Congress Party system has been replaced by a fragmented party system and coalition rule.

Prime Minister Singh's announcement setting aside 27 percent of central government jobs for OBCs splintered the NF from within. His rivals in the coalition saw the announcement as a ploy to strengthen his individual faction and to concentrate power in his hands. The cabinet was thus bitterly divided. Popular agitations were launched, first by upper castes that stood to lose from the quotas and then by backward castes that wanted the government to stick by its promises. These conflicts plunged India into the worst caste wars in its modern history. Several Northern Indian cities and towns were scenes of violent demonstrations. Some seventy-five upper-caste youths died after setting themselves on fire in protest, and police firings meant to disperse demonstrators killed close to 200.[18]

Sensing the weakening of the NF, the BJP launched a nationwide campaign to demand that the Babri Mosque in Ayodhya city, located in Uttar Pradesh, be taken down so that a temple dedicated to the god Ram, a popular deity all over India, could be constructed in its place. The timing of the Ayodhya agitation—within a month of the quota announcement—was hardly accidental. The BJP meant to foil Janata efforts to consolidate the party's vote base. The launch of the Ayodhya agitation was meant to divide the Indian electorate along religious lines and displace the issue of caste discrimination with another political fault line in which "backward" castes and Dalits would be pitted against an imagined Hindu nation.

As the BJP's Ram temple campaign gathered speed and literally rolled toward the temple site in Ayodhya, Prime Minister Singh ordered the arrest of BJP president L. K. Advani. The BJP promptly withdrew its support of the NF government, which was then forced to face a confidence motion in Parliament. The Singh government lost the motion, thus making way for another coalition government, led by Prime Minister Chandra Shekhar, who, along with about sixty members, had previously defected from the NF to lead yet another party, Samajwadi Janata Dal.

The Singh government might have lasted longer had it not been confronted simultaneously with the twin challenges of Hindu nationalism and the backward class movement. The first tested its secular credentials and the second its promises to empower minorities, particularly the rural poor, lower and backward castes, and Muslims. Reconciling these opposed agendas was next to impossible, which Singh himself was the first to admit.[19] Judging by the yardsticks set out by Eric Ringman, the NF government had succeeded in articulating a distinctive vision for a more compassionate and just India but failed to resolve conflicts arising from this vision; nor had it mobilized sufficient political resources—the political support—to overcome opposition to its proposed changes.

The Second Coalition Government

The Chandra Shekhar government (November 1990–June 1991) was even weaker than the Singh government and was formed only because the Congress (I) chose to extend support in Parliament but refused to join the ruling coalition. This government assumed office in the midst of India's most severe foreign exchange crisis, which had been triggered by Iraq's invasion of Kuwait in 1990 and steeply rising oil prices. Unable to secure the Congress Party's support in pushing through necessary harsh economic reforms, Chandra Shekhar, too, resigned and catapulted India into another general election. His government collapsed within four months of its formation (after Chandra Shekhar's resignation in March, he carried on in a caretaker government until elections could be held in June 1991). But India's cup of woe was not yet quite full. While campaigning in

Chennai, Tamil Nadu, on May 20, 1991, Rajiv Gandhi was murdered by a suicide bomber belonging to the Liberation Tigers of Tamil Eelam (LTTE). This unleashed a sympathy wave in favor of the Congress Party, but because the assassination took place when three-fifths of the election was already over, this sympathy wave was insufficient to bring the Congress (I) to power with an absolute majority. In the months between 1989 and 1991, India faced a severe economic crisis, violent insurgencies in Punjab and Kashmir, and the death of a tested and tried national leader of the core party that had provided India with four decades of stable rule.

The Third Coalition Government

The Congress (I) returned to power in 1991, but it was a minority party in Parliament and had to depend for its survival on fractious regional parties. Unable to put forward an heir to the Nehru-Gandhi dynasty now that the heir apparent, Rajiv Gandhi, had passed from the scene, the Congress (I) turned to the octogenarian P. V. Narasimha Rao, a party loyalist, to lead the coalition.

The Rao government (July 1991–May 1996) managed to complete its term in office largely because no other party won enough seats to come forward as an alternative; the deep antipathy between the Janata cluster and the BJP—aggravated by the temple episode—ensured they would not join hands to unseat the Congress Party. Voters' reluctance to go repeatedly to the polls also favored the Congress Party. Its coalition, however, was under constant pressure to keep partners in line and maintain discipline within its own ranks. Challenges to the Rao government came from many directions: from within the ranks of the Congress Party leadership; from Hindu nationalists bent upon reclaiming the site of the mosque for a temple; from proreservationists pushing for an expansion of quotas; from urban and rural middle classes clamoring to widen job and education opportunities; from prosperous peasant proprietors who had forged a powerful lobby across several states; from insurgencies and violence in the border states of the Northeast, Punjab, and Jammu and Kashmir; and from changing international politics in the wake of the first international intervention in Iraq.

There was every possibility that the minority-led Congress (I) coalition would collapse under the strain of these events, but Prime Minister Rao capitalized on fears among opposition parties of a fresh election and neutralized challenges to his leadership from influential Congress Party rivals. He sacked recalcitrant chief ministers of the two large states in southern India, Andhra Pradesh and Karnataka. Rao gained some semblance of control by mid-1992, but it was precarious at best. The core party, the Congress Party, could not command a majority, while the BJP, which was not yet a core party, struggled to gather a following that would strengthen its claims to becoming one.

The BJP had increased its percentage of the popular vote from 11 to 20.11 percent in the 1991 general elections, but that still did not make it a core party, an anchor around which supporting parties could coalesce.[20] This vote share was roughly equal to the decline in votes for the Congress Party, although the percentages varied from one region to another.[21] The BJP had promised to serve as a loyal and responsible opposition, meaning it would not seek to bring down the government on issues relating to the Ram temple or religious-based demands. It had supported the Rao government on economic reforms, and in return Prime Minister Rao promised assistance to the BJP-led state governments of Madhya Pradesh, Rajasthan, Himachal Pradesh, and Uttar Pradesh.[22] But within a year, the BJP was again agitating to build the temple in Ayodhya. In 1992, its supporters succeeded in destroying the mosque in Ayodhya and virtually paralyzing the Rao government.

The ebb of support for the Congress Party had already begun in 1994 when it lost state elections in several important states.[23] The center could not hold without the party winning a sufficient number of states or securing support from sufficient regional allies to form a coalition. The Rao government survived because it was a core national party and its opposition was too divided and therefore unwilling to go to the polls during those five years. Janata and Left Front parties were locked in bitter internal fights, while the BJP lacked a nationwide presence to form a winning coalition. All three main players were therefore in a weak position, whether it was the Congress Party in the lead or the BJP and the Left Front in opposition.

Notwithstanding these obstacles, the Congress Party turned out to be decisive on the economic front. It eschewed the policies of piecemeal liberalization that its predecessors had followed from 1974 onward and reoriented the Indian economy, root and branch, toward the private sector and the world market. The result was an electrifying rise in the growth rate: from near 0 in 1991–1992 to 7.4 percent in 1995–1996. At the time, the proreform consensus was nonexistent. Very few among the electorate understood what the dismantling of the command economy would entail. The Rao government seized the moment of the balance-of-payment crisis to initiate fundamental reforms, but to carry them forward required building a proreform consensus among the national elites. The government could have given up on the reform argument once the economy stabilized, but instead it pushed for irreversible structural changes.

Not having been created by the sword, India's unity needed constant adjustment of relations among the diverse communities and classes. Narasimha Rao carried on the work of his predecessor Congress Party governments to accommodate ethnic nationalities within the Indian union by granting different degrees of autonomy and self-governance. In fact, the coalition era tilted the balance in favor of accommodation over force to integrate separatist, ethnic communities. Building on the work of these predecessors, Rao created the autonomous district of Bodoland in Assam, more or less ending a decade of violence there.[24] A similar hill district council was created in Leh, Ladakh.

Whereas his policies in the Northeast followed the lines of accommodation, his response to a separatist insurgency in Punjab was totally different and has remained mired in deep controversy. Rao's minority government took difficult political measures to end the insurgency in Punjab and the domestic component of an insurgency in the Kashmir valley. Human rights groups and Human Rights Watch charged that the government settled the Punjab insurgency at the cost of hundreds of unexplained disappearances, custody deaths, extrajudicial killings, and suspicious cremations of 6,000 bodies.[25] The coalition governments had not given up using force to keep India's territorial integrity intact, but the segmented nature of the ruling coalition allowed Rao to isolate the insurgency within Punjab while the rest of the state governments and ambitious regional parties that represented them continued to jockey for power at the center. By the early 1990s, Sikh separatists had lost popular support as well, and Rao gave the Punjab police a free rein while the state government turned a blind eye to police use of extreme measures.[26]

Rao carried forward Rajiv Gandhi's initiative in developing Panchayat Raj (local government through elected village councils) as a bottom tier of representative government. Panchayat elections had been initiated as far back as 1961, but the village councils that were elected through them had become moribund. Following a precedent set by the government of Karnataka in the 1980s, Rajiv Gandhi proposed an amendment to the Constitution devolving financial and administrative powers to the *Panchayats*.[27] But this bill did not make it through the Rajya Sabha, the upper house of Parliament, and languished even during the brief V. P. Singh interlude. It was left to Rao to implement the change, which has led to the election of close to 1 million officials, one-third of whom are women and one-fifth, Dalits.

The pressures for greater empowerment, and for a further devolution of power to smaller minorities and castes lower in the caste hierarchy, had been building within the political system throughout the 1970s and 1980s, nurtured by hot-button issues such as building the Ram temple in Ayodhya. On December 6, 1991, a 300,000-strong mob of Vishva Hindu Parishad (VHP) (Unite Hindus—Save Humanity!) and other BJP affiliates destroyed the Babri Mosque with pickaxes and hammers while the state police looked on helplessly. The demolition of the mosque sent a shock wave throughout India, causing communal riots in many cities and towns. The government faced charges of failing to prevent the destruction of the mosque. Stung by criticism, Rao dismissed four state governments in Northern India that had succumbed to Hindu nationalist propaganda. Arrests and the banning of Hindu communal organizations accompanied these dismissals, but the damage was already done. Religion and secularism had become polarizing issues rather than the unifying ones they had been in the decades of Prime Minister Nehru and Lal Bahadir Shastri.

The Rao government was able to weather the storm largely because coalition partners did not want to go to the polls. Many coalition partners depended on the support of Muslim minorities or other religious minorities, and they forcefully stopped the contagion of religious rioting from spreading into their states. Far from reducing the central government's capacity to deal with the demands of ethnic nationalities, the onset of coalition politics and minority rule actually increased it dramatically. India owes much of the political stability in the 2000s, and the resulting explosion of the country's economic growth, to the restoration of political flexibility that accompanied the advent of multiparty rule.

Despite the Rao coalition government's ability to stave off sectional divisions and bolster local government power, not to mention return stability to the economy, it was not successful in cementing a stable pro–Congress Party alliance among regional parties that would give it the required majority in future elections. The regional parties were themselves searching for a national platform and political allies that would provide them with consistency and predictability. The five years of Rao-led coalition restored a degree of stability to India but fell short of making the Congress Party a strong core party that could become a more permanent linchpin for future political coalitions. State-level political parties changed sides when the opportunity arose and without reference to ideology or policy. It would take the next three, short-lived governments for India's democracy to settle into a pattern of stable coalition rule led by two pan-Indian core parties. The Rao-led government had therefore articulated a new vision for the Indian economy and succeeded in implementing it by resolving differences over economic priorities and direction—in that the government had partly met the measures set out by Ringman but had not solved the conflict over power and office within the Rao coalition, or garnered sufficient popular support to win enough seats to form a government in the 1996 elections. Ringmans's remaining conditions of resource mobilization and conflict resolution had not been met.

The Congress Party won only 140 seats against the BJP's 161 in the 1996 elections. The United Front consisting of several regional parties in combination with the Left Front parties gained 131 seats. The nation was forced to confront the specter of a weak center amid powerful regional parties. What had seemed a passing aberration in 1989 was now a permanent reality.[28]

The Fourth Coalition Government

With 161 seats, the BJP was far from commanding a majority. On May 16, 1996, the president of India asked the BJP to form a government and prove its coalition majority in the Parliament by May 31. Its leader, Atal Bihari Vajpayee, decided to proceed in the hope that the Congress Party and the National Front–Left Front parties would remain divided and that the Congress (I) would not oppose the formation of the government. He also hoped to gain support from powerful regional parties, but in the intense maneuvering that followed the Vajpayee announcement, the Congress (I) switched positions and decided to support the NF-LF alliance, which had secured

131 seats to the Congress Party's 140 seats. Vajpayee managed to pull a coalition together that lasted all of thirteen days (May 16–June 1, 1996) in office. Facing defeat in a mandatory confidence vote, Vajpayee resigned. Because the Congress Party was uninterested in forming a government, the president had no choice but to invite the National Front–Left Front alliance to do so.

The Fifth and Sixth Coalition Governments

So great was the confusion following the fall of the BJP-led coalition that when the newly formed United Front (UF), the name that the National Front–Left Front government adopted, was invited to form a government, it did not even have a prime ministerial candidate. After considerable jockeying, its top leaders in Delhi settled on Deve Gowda, who until then was the chief minister of Karnataka. The UF coalition consisted of thirteen parties and lasted for eleven months (June 1996–April 1997) until the Congress Party, which had recovered enough to act again the spoiler, threatened to withdraw its support unless the UF came up with another leader. The UF complied and appointed a former minister from Indira Gandhi's cabinet and foreign minister in the Gowda government, Inder K. Gujral, as prime minister in April 1997. The Gujral government was sworn in on April 21, 1997, but in less than a year, the Congress Party became restive again, and with the UF having run out of leaders, the country found itself headed for another general election.

The immediate trigger that precipitated the fall of the Gujral government was the revelations of the Jain Commission, which had been charged with investigating the 1991 assassination of Rajiv Gandhi. The commission revealed ties between members of the Dravida Munnetra Kazhagam (DMK), a leading regional party in Tamil Nadu and UF coalition partner, and the LTTE, the Tamil militant organization and antagonist in Sri Lanka's civil war. The Congress (I) demanded that the DMK ministers be dropped from the UF cabinet. If the UF had complied, the DMK would have pulled out from the coalition, but the Congress (I) also threatened to withdraw support if the government failed to comply. The UF collapsed on November 28 and called for a general election. This was the third government collapse in less than two years. The Janata Party had tried hard since 1989—briefly in the NF and then in the UF coalitions—to coalesce into a third force with an alternate vision based on privileging minorities and lower castes as distinct from the upper castes and middle class who supported Congress and the BJP, but it failed to do so in the mid-1990s and has not succeeded thus far.

The Seventh and Eighth Coalition Governments

In the general elections held in March 1998, the BJP won 182 seats and clearly emerged as the largest party in Parliament. Its time had finally arrived. Csaba Nikolenyi observes that whereas in 1996 "the party did not have enough electoral allies that could have supported its efforts to form a government; this was not the case in 1998. The BJP-led bloc, the National Democratic Front (NDA) ended up only 18 seats short of a majority in the 12th general election, followed by the Congress led alliance and United Front."[29] In contrast, the Congress Party and the United Front, even when they combined seats, did not add up to a legislative majority.

The turbulence unleashed by the death of dominant-party democracy had not, however, run its course. In April 1999, the All India Anna Dravida Munnetra Kazhagam (AIADMK), a powerful southern coalition partner, demanded two ministerial positions—law and finance—in the Vajpayee cabinet in addition to the dismissal of the NDA defense minister, on the grounds that he had compromised national security by willfully meddling in the hierarchy of the Indian Navy. The AIADMK's motives had little to do with security. All that its chief, Jayalalitha Jayaram, was trying to do was pressure the NDA government, of which she was a coalition partner, into giving her party more ministries at the center and dropping the corruption charges that were even then being heard against her in the Tamil Nadu High Court.[30] Her move did set a fresh precedent because it was the first time a state party had directly raised the issue of national security, which thus far had been a preserve of the national parties. It was another telltale sign of the weakening of the center.

Although the BJP's Atal Bihari Vajpayee retained his position as prime minister, getting support from 286 members out of 545, the government collapsed having been in power for thirteen months from March 1998 when the AIADMK, with its 18 seats, withdrew its support, leading to new elections in 1999. This was the eighth change in government in the decade since the Congress had lost its dominance in 1989. As it turned out, however, the 1999 elections marked the end of the transition from a single-party to a truly multiparty government at the center.

The previous year had been momentous. The NDA had ordered nuclear tests within two months of its assumption of office, which had upset almost the entire international community, particularly the United States,[31] and brought sanctions on both India and Pakistan because the latter soon followed India and conducted its own nuclear weapons tests. Vajpayee traveled to Lahore in February 1999 to mend fences and underscore India's willingness to negotiate all outstanding issues that had prevented progress thus far, but upon his return, Indian troops discovered Pakistani guerrillas entrenched across the Line of Control (LoC) on the Indian side of the Kargil sector on the Kashmir border.[32] This violation of the LoC immediately triggered an armed clash, which lasted from May to July 1999. The outcome of the Kargil clash favored India and strengthened the BJP and Vajpayee.

The Period of Consolidation: 1999–2009

Construction of a Political Alternative: The BJP-Led NDA

Cheered on by victory against Pakistan, the NDA, now consisting of eight large and sixteen small parties, returned to power with an absolute majority in the March 1999 elections. On March 19, 1999, Atal Bihari Vajpayee became the prime minister of the NDA government, having secured support from some fourteen regional parties. It had won a total of 270 seats, of which 88 came from four Northern states and one Western state—Gujarat. BJP's allies spread over ten states won the remaining 182 seats. This was certainly not a small coalition of like-minded parties. The BJP had not published a manifesto, but in an attempt to appear moderate, it had carefully dampened the ardor of its party zealots and advertised itself as a consensus builder. Vajpayee was generous in sharing ministerial positions with allied parties. The wider sharing of the spoils of victory among coalition partners largely explains why the NDA survived its term in office, but other achievements contributed.

Despite the unwieldiness of the coalition, the NDA government proved to be surprisingly effective. In its five years in office, India weathered serious challenges at home and abroad. Each could have been devastating to the coalition government. A major earthquake hit Western India in January 2001 and killed close to 30,000 people. In September of that year, al-Qaeda attacked the World Trade Center and the Pentagon, thereby precipitating a US military invasion of Afghanistan that drove the Taliban out of Kabul and into southwest Afghanistan and northwest Pakistan. These developments reinforced Pakistan-based terrorist groups active in the Indian Kashmir. The Assembly House in Srinagar was attacked in September 2001, which was followed by an attack on the Indian Parliament on December 13, 2001. Lashkar-e-Toiba and Jaish-e-Mohammed, two radical Islamic organizations based in Pakistan, were said to be behind the attacks. These attacks led to heightened tensions, an end to all talks with Pakistan, and massive mobilization of the Indian armed forces along the Indo-Pakistan border in 2002.

The Vajpayee government used the 9/11 attacks to redirect the focus of India's external policy: India would no longer be nonaligned and will reserve the right to reexamine its traditional friendships and alliances. Vajpayee pointed to India's restraint in the 1999 Kargil clash to argue that the United States should stop equating India with Pakistan. His foreign minister, Jaswant Singh, entered into a sustained dialogue with the United States to set the stage for close strategic and defense cooperation. Vajpayee carried forward the normalization of relations with China that had begun in the Rao government and for the first time opened negotiations for military and political cooperation with Israel.

Following the Kargil war, relations with Pakistan remained tense, but the Vajpayee government revived the electoral process in Indian Kashmir and held the first free and fair elections in October 2002, which produced victory for the newly formed People's Democratic Party (PDP). The arrival of Mohammad Syed Mufti as the chief minister of Indian Kashmir turned out to be a game changer. With PDP on the scene, the National Conference, which had reigned unopposed in the previous five decades, could no longer take victory for granted in the Indian Kashmir. The rise of the PDP allowed Kashmiris an alternative to the National Conference, which had become synonymous in Kashmir with rule from New Delhi.

Despite its radically different vision of a more centralized, unitary, Hindu state, the BJP, when it assumed office, was forced to come to terms with the profound pluralism and diversity of the Indian state. Very early on after the BJP became a principal opposition party in Parliament, the BJP's leaders acknowledged that they would have to forego some of their cherished ideological demands to widen their popular support base.[33] The BJP dropped two of its three main party platforms—namely, a demand for a unified civil code in law and a demand for a repeal of Article 370 of the Constitution, which would have abrogated Jammu and Kashmir's autonomy and led to a forced integration of that state into the Indian Union. The BJP felt the full pressure of India's political pluralism after it came to power in 1998.

The first tangible consequence was the complete exclusion from the Vajpayee cabinet of hard-liners from the two organizations that were responsible for pulling down the Babri Mosque. One of these, the Vishva Hindu Parishad, made no secret of its anger and warned Vajpayee that it would not be taken for granted. Within weeks, the VHP began a campaign against Christian missionaries in tribal areas of Gujarat, Madhya Pradesh, and Orissa. Vajpayee did not make concessions, and after some days of initial hesitation, the central government issued a directive to the Gujarat government to take a firm line against Hindu extremists in its tribal areas.

Hindu-Muslim relations, however, remained the Achilles heel of the BJP throughout its six years (1998–2004) in office. The initial indecision with which the central government had reacted to the outbreak of anti-Christian violence was a forerunner of a far more damaging procrastination. Following the burning of a train carrying Hindu activists back from Ayodhya, BJP chief minister Narendra Modi ignored or even perhaps encouraged reprisal killings of Muslims throughout Gujarat by enraged Hindu nationalists of the Sangh Parivar.[34] Apart from issuing a few admonitions that Modi studiously ignored, the NDA was able to do little to stem the carnage or persuade Modi to hold off state assembly elections that were meant to gain from the wave of communal animosity sweeping through Gujarat.

Perhaps no other single event during the twenty-year interregnum that followed the end of Congress Party domination in 1989 did as much to harm India's reputation and shake people's faith in its capacity to resolve the manifold conflicts of its society as the communal violence in Gujarat in 2002. In the seven years (2002–2009) that followed, the Indian political system exacted a very high price from the BJP for its inability to resolve the conflict within itself and between Hindu and pluralistic views of India's future. In the 2004 elections, three of the NDA's partners ascribed their poor performance to the loss of the Muslim vote in their states (to the DMK in Tamil Nadu, the Telugu Desam Party [TDP] in Andhra Pradesh, and the Janata Dal, led by Ram Vilas Paswan, in Uttar Pradesh). Christophe Jaffrelot and Gilles Verniers writes,

> Parties like the TDP and the Bharatiya Janata Dal (BJD) were not comfortable with the Hindu nationalist discourse and practices of the Sangh Parivar. Former Andhra Pradesh Chief Minister, Chandrababu Naidu, might have come to the conclusion that the 2002 anti-Muslim pogrom in the BJP-governed state of Gujarat will dissuade Muslim voters to support its party and Navin Patnaik, current Chief Minister of Orissa, might have been indisposed by the anti-Christian activities of the Sangh Parivar in his very state. Not only did former allies abandon the BJP, but those which remained in the NDA were also not as successful as the Congress' allies.[35]

Had Vajpayee won the 2004 elections, the BJP victory might have resolved the conflicts within the party, but defeat perpetuated them. In the ensuing five years under L. K Advani, the BJP proved repeatedly that it could formulate neither a policy for a "Hindu" nation nor a broadly pluralistic platform for the party. BJP zealots had a field day—spreading rumors and mobilizing the people—in every state where the Hindu-Muslim issue raised its head even to the slightest degree. In the 2009 parliamentary elections, the main Oriya party, the Biju Janata Dal (BJD) in Orissa, broke its alliance with the BJP, causing a significant drop in the BJP's overall vote in that state.[36]

The NDA was able to weather the storm created by the Gujarat riots largely because of the federal division of power in India but also because of the BJP's handling of coalition politics. While the federal division of power provided the NDA with a fig leaf to hide its inaction, each state government took immediate steps to move against the slightest indication of attempts to incite Hindu-Muslim violence. More importantly, the coalition survived because of the reluctance of its allies to face elections so soon after 1999. The BJP's coalition partners were particularly apprehensive because the Congress (I) and its allies had shown unexpectedly greater strength in the state elections held in 2001. The 2002 assembly elections also confirmed the pro–Congress Party trend. The BJP's coalition partners in several states (Andhra, West Bengal, Uttar Pradesh, Bihar, and Assam) were locked in a competition with the Congress Party or its allies and had significant Muslim minorities to cater to within the state. They feared that the anti-Muslim image of the NDA would hurt them seriously in future polls.[37] The BJP's regional partners therefore distanced themselves from the events in Gujarat but did not withdraw support.

The BJP sought to soften its antiminority image by granting the demand for creation of three new states from Bihar and Uttar Pradesh. The Vajpayee government expended considerable energy on reviving the dialogue with the Naga rebels and building on the Rao government's policy, which had granted considerable cultural and administrative autonomy to the Bodo people in Assam by establishing the Bodo Territorial Council within that state. These internal territorial reorganizations reduced to a degree the incidence of separatist violence.

Reforms Under the NDA Government

The NDA made significant contributions by changing the framework for future economic reforms, the details of which are discussed at greater length in the next chapter. It used different tactics for different areas of reforms. In some areas, such as telecommunications, it moved forward to bring policies in line with changes that had already occurred. In other areas, the NDA "federalized" the reform—that is, allowed states to implement what would be difficult to legislate from the center, such as labor laws. In yet other areas, it proposed and then rolled back changes. Tax reform to standardize sales taxes across India was one such measure. In case of duties on the import prices of oil, the BJP government did not roll back any subsidies, but it lifted quantitative restrictions on more than 1,400 items and increased trade substantially.

By the end of the NDA's five years in office, there were strong signs that the economy had entered a boom period. Growth in gross domestic product for 2003–2004 was at a high of 8.2 percent, exports were growing at 20 percent annually, foreign exchange reserves accumulated to an unprecedented $110 billion, and food stocks were plentiful. In information technology India was gaining an international reputation, while portfolio investments were rising at an impressive rate. Baldev Raj Nayar reports, "Indian industry—after a wrenching restructuring since 1997 . . . had by 2002 established a stronger position from which to meet the challenge of global competition."[38] Economic success and India's recognition in world capitals had the salutary effect of routinizing reforms and suppressing the demand for Swadeshi (similar to "Buy American" campaigns) among BJP's Hindutva fundamentalists.[39]

Buoyed by the NDA's success, Vajpayee called for early elections, but his calculations went awry. The NDA ended up winning only 181 seats against the Congress Party–led UPA tally of 262. When the Left Front, which had secured 53 seats, decided to support the UPA, the Congress Party's return to power became a certainty. The UPA not only served its full five years in office from 2004 to 2009 but also came back with an even greater majority to form a UPA II in 2009. This was a clear indication that coalition rule had consolidated at India's center.

The Congress Party–Led UPA I and II: 2004–2014

In May 2004, a nine-party Congress Party–led United Progressive Alliance consisting of pre- and postelection alliances with seventeen parties formed a government. Four left parties and two additional regional parties from the outside supported it. Even though the Congress Party had formed a minority government under Narasimha Rao, it had not quite reconciled itself to the rules of the coalition politics emerging in India. With the 2004 elections and the formation of the UPA, it finally embraced the logic of coalition governments. For instance, in Tamil Nadu where the DMK and AIADMK were archrivals, alliance with the Congress Party or the BJP, respectively, offered each an option to participate at the national level. In addition to Tamil Nadu, the Congress Party gained by pitting rival local parties against each other in Uttar Pradesh and Bihar, two large Northern states.

Although successful alliance formation was part of the reason the Congress Party won the national elections, BJP's election slogan "India Shining" had little appeal in rural India and particularly for those at the bottom of the caste and income pyramid. The Congress Party made the needs of "Aam Adami," or the "common man," a central slogan and emphasized inclusiveness in the growth strategy it was proposing.[40]

Nevertheless, liberalization and market reforms remained the priority. The economy, in fact, boomed in the first term of the UPA tenure, growing at an unprecedented 9 percent in 2007. Investments and foreign collaborations poured into India. Manufacture expanded. The service industry, particularly the information technology sector, grew to account for close to 40 percent of India's total export earnings. Exports took off, and the government increased its spending on health, education, loan guarantees, and rural unemployment. Although the presence of a sizable Left Front in the coalition delayed or prevented deeper reforms in the financial sector, banking, and labor laws, the UPA pressed ahead with less controversial reforms. The four years of economic expansion had a visible effect on prosperity, especially on middle-class earnings, and even many parts of rural India saw easier credit, growing economic opportunities, and increased income. Recent findings have, however, forced an upward revision of the number of the poor in India.[41] So successful was the UPA I in projecting a positive image backed by a booming economy that it was reelected in 2009 for yet another term.

The UPA created nationwide welfare or poverty-reduction programs to which annual budgets allocated increasing amounts of funds. For instance, the Bharat Nirman (on rural infrastructure, launched in 2005) and Sarva Shiksha Abhiyan programs (free compulsory education, running from 2001) included financial commitments to education (primary and higher level), health, jobs, literacy, and other measures to increase social welfare for the poor. There were also debt-relief programs ($15 billion by 2010) and loan guarantees to farmers. UPA I passed a slew of legislation meant to empower civil society. It passed the Right to Information Act (which was to haunt it later) and Right to Education and Jobs Act (2010), and it proposed a new women's Reservation Bill that reserved one-third of Panchayat seats for Dalits and women.[42] It also passed the Forest Rights Act (2006), the Mahatma Gandhi National Rural Employment Guarantee Act (2005), and on September 12, 2013, an act subsidizing food grains for approximately two-thirds of India's 1.2 billion people. The last Right to Food Act was a response to a new estimate of poverty produced by a committee led by Suresh Tendulkar. The report recalculated poverty to be more than 32 percent, not the 27 percent the government had been publicizing previously.

Buoyed by an expanding economy and US backing, not the least of which was to be achieved through strategic and defense ties to make India a world power, India's international standing began to climb rapidly. This was evident in its inclusion in the G8 meetings and world forums for negotiating climate change. India came to be regarded by the United States as a serious partner in the protection of the world's economy and a potential bulwark against ambitious China. It was the UPA I that negotiated the civil nuclear deal with the United States in 2005, and although opposition from the Left Front parties that were part of the UPA I governing coalition stymied approval of the deal, UPA II managed to conclude it because by then the UPA no longer needed the left to stay in power. The UPA had foregrounded economics in its quest to make India an important player on the world stage. Growth had allowed it to purchase weapons systems that would give India the future capacity to project military power well beyond South Asia and into the extended neighborhood.

The resilience of the coalition government under the UPA was also evident in its ability to recover from the 2008 world recession. Although India's economy slowed to an annual growth rate of about 6 percent during 2008–2009, at the time it was still the fastest-growing economy in the world. The Manmohan Singh government coped with the recession by introducing a massive stimulus package to prevent the free fall experienced in the United States and Europe. In fact, by the first quarter of 2010 India had recovered much of the lost ground and was showing signs of resuming its earlier rates of 8.8 percent growth.[43]

The return of the UPA government in the 2009 elections suggested that performance had begun to shape public choices in government. In fact, the 2009 election results had freed the Congress (I) from having to depend on the left parties to follow its neoliberal agenda. Most commentators therefore expected that the UPA II would boldly move forward with the more difficult parts of economic reform, but, curiously enough, the UPA II appeared to be drifting.

Although economic growth had rewarded it with reelection, the deeper problems of inequality, corruption, government neglect, or, worse, complicity in the transfer of huge amounts of public funds and resources to private hands had finally boiled to the surface. The first signs of government complicity in kickbacks and corruption came to light over the transfer of land to industries, loggers, and real estate developers in restricted areas for which small landholders had not been paid fair compensation. As the prices of land skyrocketed largely because of the economic boom, farmers began to resist easy sales, and those given inadequate compensation clashed with the government to gain a more equitable deal from the market. Opponents of the UPA saw in the protests a golden opportunity to score points with the public. The UPA encountered a real contradiction for which it had no immediate answer: how to assuage urban India's hunger for land with rural India's right to a livelihood.

The Cycle of Fragmentation Resumes Course

Unable to resolve this contradiction, the UPA responded in a piece-meal and opportunistic manner and postponed the creation of a comprehensive land acquisition policy. The result was a series of violent confrontations, as in Eastern India, where South Korea's Posco started buying land after a tense five-year standoff with farmers for a $12 billion steel mill. Tata Motors had plans to build the world's cheapest car at Singur in West Bengal, but that ran aground in 2008 when farmers complained that they had been bullied and cheated out of their land. Indonesia's Salim Group abandoned plans to set up a chemical hub in Nandigram, also in West Bengal, after fourteen people were killed in clashes between farmers and police in 2007. Clashes over acquisition of land had become routine but several led to violent protests and deaths. In June 2011, in the villages of Bhatta and Parsaul, a little more than an hour's drive southeast of Delhi, farmers were originally told to make way for a new highway and industrial development. They soon discovered, however, that their land had been zoned for residential use instead of industrial use, making its value many times higher than the price they had been offered. They suspected that politicians and builders had colluded to corner all the profits while leaving them a small share of the total proceeds. In 2011, there were protests in 130 districts in the country. A report prepared by Washington, DC–based Rights and Resources Initiative (RRI) and the Society for Promotion of Wasteland Development predicted a sharp rise in similar conflicts against land-grabs all over India in the coming decade. The RRI estimates that by 2025, the government of India will need close to 11 million hectares of land for its infrastructure projects.[44]

To compound the public anger, in the first two years of UPA II a series of scandals and scams came to light that virtually paralyzed the Singh government. The first big scandal to hit the headlines was the 2-G spectrum scandal. In April 2011, the Central Bureau of Investigation, the government's chief investigating agency, charged several individuals including the minister of communications, A. Raja, of irregularities in granting licenses to private companies for spectrum rights. (A. Raja belonged to the DMK party in Tamil Nadu, an important UPA coalition partner.) It was alleged that he had short-circuited the bidding process and given telecommunication spectrum rights to big Indian companies at very low rates, leading to a loss of $27 billion to the public exchequer. These estimates are, however, contested. The Central Bureau of Investigation pegs the loss at $4.7 billion while the Telecom Regulatory Authority of India estimates it to be $460 billion.[45] If the comptroller general's audit report is to be taken as a true figure, the sum of money lost to companies could have bought the whole of the Indian public living below poverty line 77 pounds of grain every month for two consecutive years at the rate of Rs. 2 (3.1 cents) per 2.2 pounds. The Commonwealth Games scandal broke next, implicating the UPA minister for sports, who belonged to yet another important UPA coalition partner from the state of Maharashtra. He was indicted for corruption—inflating contracts and building substandard facilities for the games. The Adarsh Housing Society flats, which were at the center of the next scandal that made headlines in the summer of 2011, were constructed in greater Mumbai to provide shelter to the families of the martyrs following the Kargil clash. But instead, political, administrative, and defense "heads"—bureaucrats and public officials—grabbed the flats by fudging the forms and using political influence and bribes to secure possession. Names of present and former ministers of the Maharashtra state government, military generals, and bureaucrats surfaced in the scam.

The UPA's greater setback came in the UP state assembly elections in 2012. The Congress Party's share of the vote rose from 8.5 to only 11 percent, and its share of the seats hardly budged, despite months of hype by Rahul Gandhi, general secretary of the Congress Party and heir presumptive to the prime ministership. The wound was self-inflicted because the party ignored the ways in which the 1999 separation of Uttaranchal from Uttar Pradesh, with its substantial pro–Congress Party votes, would affect the party's prospects in subsequent state-level and national elections. The reorganization diminished the prospects for both the Congress Party and the BJP while promoting the fortunes of state-based parties. Rahul Gandhi's failure to bring Congress back in Uttar Pradesh further demoralized the UPA and began to make powerful constituents reassess their options for the 2014 national elections.

But the weakening of the Congress Party did not mean that the UPA coalition was a failed experiment. Two general elections (2004 and 2009) and two state assembly elections (2009 and 2012) in the truncated state of Uttar Pradesh brought into being what is looking increasingly like a stable bipolar party competition between the Samajwadi Party, led by Mulayam Singh Yadav and his son, and the Bahujan Samaj Party, led by Mayawati. Both coalitions represent backward classes, although the latter is identified with the Dalits. These changes in Uttar Pradesh's political landscape are highly significant because a two-party competition has generally stabilized state-level politics in India. This can only benefit the development of India's democracy.

Paradoxically, the Congress Party's humiliation and loss of a significant voter base in Uttar Pradesh have only served to underline the uniqueness of India's path to democracy. Its coalitions have been built around stronger central parties, but the continuing strength of these parties is not a prerequisite for the survival of the coalition. For instance, it is perfectly possible for the NDA to come back to power in 2014 with a smaller BJP. By the same token, in one or two elections hence the Congress Party may do the same. A gradual attrition of dominance within coalitions may pose no threat to the unity of the country or the effectiveness of governance.

Some Observations

The destruction of the old Congress Party–led system and the creation of new political institutions suited to multiparty rule are not yet complete. The institutional deterioration witnessed since 1989 is part of a larger process of political reconstruction that produced extraordinary results: a successful transition to a market economy, the second-highest growth rate in the world, a nuclearized India, and a far more responsive and flexible political system than anyone could have predicted. But this transformation has also unleashed unprecedented levels of corruption, massive protest movements, and violent responses by those who have lost their livelihoods to the cause of economic growth. At the heart of these contradictory developments are the problems of equity and social justice, the answers to which lie in improved governance and honest leaders. Both are difficult to achieve partly because of the diffusion of power away from the center to state-level parties and leaders and partly because of the rhythm of electoral contests. The latter is increasingly expensive. In the absence of public financing for elections, parties are left to build election war chests on their own. This has produced collusion among business, civil servants, and politicians and a resulting siphoning off of huge amounts of monies from public into private pockets. At the same time, the central government has come to depend increasingly on the state-level governments to implement the nation's policy agenda.

India nevertheless has moved steadily toward a hybrid political system that combines bipolar party contests in most state-level elections with multiparty national contests and weaker but more representative governments at the center. This has been possible only because most parties have not allowed their strategic purposes and shared goals to be overridden by ideological or identity-based loyalties. These had been spelled out in a succession of Common Minimum Programs drawn up by every new coalition upon coming to power. Although many of these goals have not been fulfilled, the premises upon which the programs have been drawn up are not generally challenged. All this has resulted from a shared vision of India's future (or a party's future) and the capacity to contain differences about how to achieve it within the limits of democratic contest.

India has thus met the first of Ringman's three measures of a nation's potential, namely, evolving a vision for a strong and powerful India. India's economic and political transformation could not have been achieved without the ability within the coalition to resolve differences and make winning electoral alliances, which also required a degree of agreement on policies and direction. This vision of India's future, together with the series of new model legislation and new institutions created after 1989 to turn a command economy into a market-friendly one, shows that India has met the three conditions of an ascending power proposed by Ringman, although the forward journey is far from smooth.

The Indian model is arguably sui generis and cannot be compared easily either with early industrial democracies, which were unitary nation-states, or with more recent East Asian success stories, which were based upon autocratic political models of government in their early stages. India needs to be understood on its own terms. The transition from dominant-party to coalition rule is still a work in progress, and the jury is still out on whether India will attain its great-power ambitions. There is no doubt, however, that it has been successful in transforming its economy, politics, and foreign policy while expanding and possibly deepening its democracy.

Notes

1. Kartik Rai, "The Indian Economy in Adversity and Debt," *Social Scientist* 20, nos. 1–2 (January–February 1992): 8–28.

2. The Soviet Union repeatedly vetoed anti-India Security Council resolutions on Kashmir. For a comparison between Soviet and Western economic ties with India, see Peter Duncan, *The Soviet Union and India* (London: Routledge, 1989), 71–76. See also Ramesh Thakur, "The Impact of Soviet Collapse on Military Relations with India," *Europe-Asia Studies* 45, no. 5 (1993): 831–850.

3. Pakistan's premier nuclear scientist, Abdul Qadir Khan, revealed in a March 1987 interview to Kuldip Nayar, an Indian journalist, that Pakistan had manufactured a nuclear bomb. Although Khan later retracted his statement, India believed that Operation Brass Tacks (executed during 1986 to 1987), a large-scale exercise along the Pakistan-India border, had unnerved Pakistan and that its leaders were thus warning India that they would use nuclear weapons should India cross a red line. Quoting Khan, Kuldip Nayar remarks, "What the CIA has been saying about our possessing the bomb is correct and so is the speculation of some foreign newspapers. . . . They told us that Pakistan could never produce the bomb and they doubted my capabilities, but they now know we have done it. . . . Nobody can undo Pakistan or take us for granted. We are there to stay and let it be clear that we shall use the 10 bombs if our existence is threatened." See also Shamaz Khan, "Nuclear Doctrine of Pakistan: Dilemmas of Small Nuclear Force in the Second Atomic Age," Red Storm Rising, December 19, 2010, http://shamaz khan.wordpress.com/2010/12/19/nuclear-doctrine-of-pakistan-dilemmas-of -small-nuclear-force-in-the-second-atomic-age/.

4. Dipankar Sinha, "V. P. Singh, Chandra Shekhar, and 'Nowhere Politics' in India," *Asian Survey* 31, no. 7 (July 1991): 598–612.

5. There is considerable scholarship on the subject of strong and weak states. For one recent work on South Asia, see T. V. Paul, ed., *South Asia's Weak States* (Stanford, CA: Stanford University Press, 2010). Guillermo O'Donnell and A. O. Hirschman have written on the bureaucratic authoritarian states in Latin America and their ability to preserve law and order and bring about economic transformation. Indeed, these scholars argue that only a strong state can rapidly grow the economy because it enjoys a greater degree of autonomy from society and has the institutional capacity to maintain order while initiating development. See Guillermo O'Donnell, "Reflections on Patterns of Change in the Bureaucratic-Authoritarian State," *Latin American Research Review* 13, no. 1 (1978): 37; and A. O. Hirschman, *A Bias for Hope: Essays on Development in Latin America* (New Haven, CT: Yale University Press, 1971). A similar argument is advanced by T. B. Gold and Alice Amsden for East Asian states. See T. B. Gold, *State and Society in the Taiwan Miracle* (Armonk, NY: M. E. Sharpe, 1986); and Alice Amsden,

"State and Taiwan's Economic Development," in *Bringing the State Back In,* ed. Peter Evans, Dietrich Rueschemeyer, and Theda Skocpol (New York: Cambridge University Press, 1985), 78–106.

Scholars of India agree that the state plays a prominent role in economic development, but they differ on the level of autonomy the Indian state enjoys. Atul Kohli denies the Indian state any autonomy, whereas Pranab Bardhan argues that it is able to formulate policies independent of social interest groups. All agree, however, that a strong state—able to formulate policies, penetrate society, and deal impartially with social diversity—is necessary to perform its proper functions. See Atul Kohli, ed., *State and Development in the Third World* (Princeton, NJ: Princeton University Press, 1986); Atul Kohli, *The State and Poverty in India* (Cambridge: Cambridge University Press, 1987); and Pranab Bardhan, *Political Economy of Development in India* (Oxford: Blackwell, 1984).

6. Jaya Mehta, "Poverty in India," http://www.saunalahti.fi/otammile /povindia.html (accessed February 13, 2013), writes that government statistics seriously underestimate the extent of poverty. She recalculates the poverty line based on calorie intake and comes up with a figure of 54 percent of the rural population living below the poverty line. Estimates of poverty remain highly debated, and the latest one by Suresh Tendulkar puts the figure at close to 32 percent. In any event, one-third of the Indian population definitely lives below the poverty line. Even though this number may reflect the truer statistical measure, the state of Bihar, frequently considered the poster state for poverty and corruption, was posting 11 percent growth in 2010. See "Press Notes on Poverty Estimates," Government of India, Planning Commission (New Delhi: Government Printing Press, January 2011), 2, http://planningcommission.nic.in/reports/genrep/Press_pov_27Jan11.pdf. Also see Santosh Sinha, "At 11.03 Per Cent, Bihar Growth Rate Only a Step Behind Gujarat," *Indian Express,* January 10, 2010, http://www.indian express.com/news/at-11.03-per-cent-bihar-growth-rate-only-a/563018/.

7. Mehta, "Poverty in India."

8. T. Ninan has an interesting argument about why there might be growing support for reforms in India. He suggests that if per capita incomes rise faster than inequality, the average individual will support market reforms; that, Ninan says, has been the case for a larger number of people in India between 2000 and 2010. See his "Why Poverty and Inequality Are Rising in India," *Business Standard,* September 21, 2009, http://business .rediff.com/column/2009/sep/21/guest-why-poverty-inequality-are-rising-in -india.htm.

9. Dhruva Jaishankar, "A Wider View of India's Foreign Policy Reveals Clear Strategy," *New York Times* (global edition), June 14, 2013, http://india.blogs.nytimes.com/2013/06/14/a-wider-view-of-indias-foreign -policy-reveals-clear-strategy/?_r=0.

10. Jose Edgardo Campos and Hilton Root, *The Key to the Asian Miracle: Making Shared Growth Credible* (Washington, DC: Brookings Institution Press, 1996); Peter Evans, "The State as Problem and Solution: Preda-

tion, Embedded Autonomy, and Cultural Change," in *The Politics of Economic Adjustment: International Constraints, Distributive Conflicts, and the State*, ed. Stephan Haggard and Robert Kaufman (Princeton, NJ: Princeton University Press, 1992), 139–181.

11. Kohli, *State and Development*; Kohli, *State and Poverty*; J. S. Migdal, *Strong Societies and Weak States* (Princeton, NJ: Princeton University Press, 1988); Lloyd Rudolph and Susanne Rudolph, *In Pursuit of Lakshmi: The Political Economy of the Indian State* (Chicago: University of Chicago Press, 1987).

12. Sanjay Ruparelia and Csaba Nikolenyi have written several analytical articles on this subject. See Sanjay Ruparelia, "Managing the United Progressive Alliance: The Challenges Ahead," *Economic and Political Weekly* 40, no. 24 (June 11–17, 2005): 2407–2410; and Csaba Nikolenyi, "When the Central Player Fails: Constraints on Cabinet Formation in Contemporary India," *Canadian Journal of Political Science* 37, no. 2 (June 2004): 395–418. K. K. Kailash, "Middle Game in Coalition Politics," *Economic and Political Weekly* 42, no. 4 (January 27–February 2, 2007): 307–317, shows how coalition governments learn from their own internal conflicts as well as from success and failures of past coalitions and develop mechanisms to ward off collapse.

13. The Janata Party–led coalitions were short-lived because the Janata Party was not and could not become a core party.

14. Swaminathan Aiyar, "Falling Governance, Rising Growth," *Economic Times,* August 2, 2006, http://articles.economictimes.indiatimes.com /2006-08-02/news/27441147_1_governance-ncaer-economic-growth. Arvind Subramanian, "The Evolution of Institutions in India and Its Relationship with Economic Growth," April 2007, http://www.iie.com/publications /papers/subramanian0407b.pdf, provides a different argument. He suggests that India's institutions have been more robust than critics think.

15. The elections were held in two phases on November 22 and November 26, 1989, for 543 seats (2 are appointed bringing the number to 545) in the Lok Sabha, the lower house of Parliament. The National Front managed to secure a simple majority in the Lok Sabha and formed a government with the outside support of the Left Front and the BJP. The Janata Dal, the National Front's largest constituent, won 143 seats, with the CPI(M) and the CPI (the Communist Party of India [Marxist] and the Communist Party of India) securing 43 in all. Independents and other smaller parties managed to win 59 seats.

16. Morris Fiorina, "Coalition Governments, Divided Governments, and Electoral Theory," *Governance* 4, no. 3 (July 1991): 236–249; Josep Colomer, "Measuring Parliamentary Deviation," *European Journal of Political Research* 30, no. 1 (July 1996): 87–101; Gerald Pech, "Coalition Governments Versus Minority Governments: Bargaining Power, Cohesion, and Budgeting Outcomes," *Public Choice* 121, nos. 1–2 (October 2004): 1–24.

17. There was a gradual erosion of the Nehruvian secular-nationalist imagination along with the emergence of caste in public discourse. The

watershed in this respect was the famous Mandal Commission instituted in 1978 during the Janata Party government, under the stewardship of B. P. Mandal, a socialist leader from a "backward caste." He was given the task of looking into the question of the "backwardness" of certain castes and suggesting remedies for discrimination as a result of prejudices against lower caste status. For about a decade after that—through the governments of Indira Gandhi (1980–1984) and Rajiv Gandhi (1985–1989)—these recommendations remained unattended. They were implemented under extremely contentious circumstances in 1990 when V. P. Singh held the position of prime minister.

18. Prem Shankar Jha, *In the Eye of the Cyclone: The Crisis in Indian Democracy* (New Delhi: Penguin, 1993), 11.

19. See ibid., 132–222.

20. James Heitzman and Robert L. Worden, eds., *India: A Country Study* (Washington, DC: GPO, 1995), http://countrystudies.us/india/113.htm. The BJP's seats in the Lok Sabha increased from 85 to 120, and its vote share grew from 11.4 to 20.11 percent.

21. Walter Anderson, "Election 1989 in India: The Dawn of Coalition Politics?" *Asian Survey* 30, no. 6 (June 1990): 527–540.

22. Yogendra Malik and V. B. Singh, *Hindu Nationalists in India: The Rise of Bharatiya Janata Party* (New Delhi: Vistaar, 1994), 91.

23. Walter Anderson, "India in 1995: Year of Long Campaign," *Asian Survey* 36, no. 2 (February 1996): 167.

24. For instance, whereas Indira Gandhi had reorganized Assam and the entire Northeast into seven ethnically determined, small federal states in 1971, Rajiv Gandhi two decades later created the Autonomous District Council (ADC) of Gorkhaland as a third tier of Indian democracy. A number of states with tribal populations, particularly in the Northeast, have provisions for ADC. The ADC elected its own council members, was devolved funds from the state budget, enjoyed limited powers of taxation, and, most important of all, was given control of land, law and order, and education.

25. "Protecting the Killers," *Human Rights Watch,* October 17, 2007, http://www.hrw.org/en/node/10644/section/4.

26. See Virginia Van Dyke, "The Khalistan Movement in Punjab, India, and the Post-Militancy Era: Structural Change and New Political Compulsions," *Asian Survey* 49, no. 6 (November–December 2009): 990–997.

27. Accepting recommendations of the L. M. Singhvi Committee, the central government, headed by Rajiv Gandhi, introduced the 64th Amendment Bill, which was passed by the Lok Sabha on August 16, 1989. This was a comprehensive bill covering all vital aspects of the Panchayat Raj Institutions. Unfortunately, this bill could not be enacted, as the Rajya Sabha did not approve it.

28. As several commentators noted, it was the "regional factors more than national issues" that had shaped voter sentiments. See Sumit Ganguly, "India in 1996: A Year of Upheaval," *Asian Survey* 37, no. 2, part II (February 1997): 129.

29. Nikolenyi, "When the Central Player Fails," 408.

30. Vaasanthi, "Amma-Mia," *India Today,* April 12, 1999, http://www.india-today.com/itoday/12041999/jaya.html.

31. For official statements and comments from world governments, see "World Reaction to the Indian Nuclear Tests," Archived Material, Resources on India and Pakistan, James Martin Center for Non-Proliferation Studies, Middlebury College, Vermont, http://cns.miis.edu/archive/country_india/reaction.htm.

32. The Line of Control was the cease-fire line drawn after the first war between India and Pakistan in 1948. This was turned into the Line of Control in 1972 by mutual agreement.

33. Davesh Kapur and Bhanu Pratap Mehta, "India in 1998: The Travails of Political Fragmentation," *Asian Survey* 39, no. 1 (January–February 1999): 164.

34. "'We Have No Orders to Save You': State Participation and Complicity in Communal Violence in Gujarat," quoted in *Human Rights Watch* 14, no. 3(C) (April 2002), http://www.hrw.org/reports/2002/india/.

35. Christophe Jaffrelot and Gilles Verniers, "India's 2009 Elections: The Resilience of Regionalism and Ethnicity," *South Asia Multi-Disciplinary Academic Journal* 3 (December 2009), http://samaj.revues.org/index 2787.html.

36. Ibid.

37. Subrata Mitra, "The NDA's Minority Politics," in *Coalition Politics and Hindu Nationalism,* ed. Katherine Adeney and Lawrence Saez (Oxford: Routledge, 2005), 92.

38. Baldev Raj Nayar, "India in 2004: Regime Change in a Divided Democracy," *Asian Survey* 45, no. 1 (February 2005): 71–82.

39. For analysis of the problems the BJP-led NDA faced, see Kapur and Mehta, "India in 1998."

40. The UPA promised to deliver on the national Common Minimum Program, which meant a higher allocation of funds for welfare and poverty alleviation programs. See "UPA Government to Adhere to Six Basic Principles of Governance," *The Hindu,* May 28, 2004, http://www.hindu.com/2004/05/28/stories/2004052807371200.htm.

41. R. Ramakumar, "The Unsettled Debate on Indian Poverty," *The Hindu,* January 2, 2010, http://beta.thehindu.com/opinion/lead/article 74196.ece.

42. On May 6, 2008, UPA II introduced the Women's Bill, meant to reserve one-third of the total seats in the Lok Sabha and state legislative assemblies, including the National Capitol Territory of Delhi, for women for a period of fifteen years. The Rajya Sabha passed the bill on March 9, 2009. A bill has also been introduced in the Lok Sabha providing 50 percent reservation to women in urban local bodies. The UPA set up the National Mission for Empowerment of Women in March 2010 to secure the intersectoral convergence of all prowomen or women-centric programs, cutting across ministries and departments, states, and Panchayat Raj Institutions. See

"Women's Bill Part of Venture to Ensure Equality: UPA Report," *DNA,* June 1, 2010, http://www.dnaindia.com/india/report_women-s-bill-part-of-venture -to-ensure-equality-upa-report_1390739.

43. "Economy Growth by Around 9% in 2010–11: India INC," *Times of India,* September 1, 2010, http://articles.economictimes.indiatimes.com /2010-09-01/news/27601537_1_gdp-growth-estate-and-business-services -farm-sector-performance.

44. "Land Acquisition in India Leads to Widespread Conflict," press release by Rights and Resources Initiative, Washington, DC, December 2012, http://www.rightsandresources.org/pages.php?id=69.

45. Report of the Comptroller and Auditor General of India, "Performance Audit Report on the Issue of Licenses and Allocation of 2G Spectrum by the Department of Telecommunications Ministry of Communications and Information Technology," Union Government of India, No. 19, March 2010–2011, New Delhi, http://cag.gov.in/html/reports/civil/2010 -11_19PA/Telecommunication%20Report.pdf. The audit covers the period 2003–2010.

4

Economic Growth
and India's Rise

India owed its rising importance in the global economy to a
sustained 7 percent rate of growth for twenty years from 1992 to
2011—and a near 9 percent rate of growth from 2003 to the end of
2010. (See Table 4.1.) In the following two years, these rates came
down sharply because of the adoption of a policy of high interest
rates by the government of India, implemented by the Reserve Bank
of India, allegedly to control inflationary expectations arising from
an increase in money supply and its budget deficit resulting from
financing a fiscal stimulus in 2008 and 2009. The high interest rate
policy did not bring down inflation, largely because the inflation was
not caused by excess demand in the domestic economy but by the
global supply shortages, rising oil prices, and a 40 percent devalua-
tion of the rupee, which higher interest rates could not affect. However, the rise in interest rates slowed industrial growth from 8.2 percent in 2010–2011 to 2.9 percent in 2011–2012 and just about 1
percent in the following sixteen months.[1] In fiscal year 2012–2013,
India's growth declined from January to March 2013 to a mere 4.8
percent. Most economists both within India and abroad believed that
a sharp lowering of interest rates would lead industry to bounce back
within as little as a year. Whether that happens or the economy continues to spiral downward depends largely on the urgency with which
the new government tackles yawning fiscal deficit and sluggish
growth.

99

Table 4.1 Rate of Growth for India's Economy, 1951–2013

	1951–1956	1956–1966	1966–1975	1975–1981	1981–1991	1991–1992	1992–1997	1997–2002	2002–2007	2007–2011	2011–2012	2012–2013[a]
GDP	3.7	3.3	3.3	4.3	5.5	1.4	6.8	6.0	8.9	8.2	6.2	5.0
Capital formation	8.9	14.0	14.0	16.6	20.2	22.1	22.4	22.5	31	31.6	35.7	n.a.
ICOR	2.4	4.2	4.2	3.9	3.6	[b]	3.3	3.8	3.4	3.8	n.a.	n.a.

Sources: Government of India Economic Survey 2007–2008, Statistical Tables 1.4 and 1.5; Economic Survey 2011–2012, Statistical Table 1.6. Union Budget and Economic Surveys are published and posted by the Government of India's Ministry of Finance each year, assessing the past year's economic performance.

Notes: n.a.: data are not available. Capital formation is expressed as a proportion of the GDP. ICOR: Incremental Capital to Output Ratio.
  a. Estimated.
  b. Transitional year; the ICOR for that year is an anomaly.

These cautious hopes of restored growth were based on India's surprising resilience in the recent past. In 2008, when global markets succumbed to a deep recession bordering on depression, India's economy also plunged. But within a year of the 2008 recession, India had recovered most of the ground it had lost and posted an 8.4 percent growth in 2009–2010 and 2010–2011. As Table 4.1 indicates, the growth rate of the GDP, which had fallen to 1.4 percent in 1991–1992, peaked at nearly 9 percent in the five years before the global economic crisis of 2008, giving India an average growth rate of 7.2 percent till 2007–2008, second only to China's.[2] India's growth was accompanied by an impressive accumulation of foreign exchange reserves, and the country established a preeminent position in the Internet-enabled global services market, comparable in many respects to China's dominance of the market for manufactured consumer goods.[3] In absolute terms, however, India's per capita gross domestic product (GDP) is far behind China's GDP, largely because the latter began its explosive development in 1980, thirteen years before India entered its high growth phase. The impetus for India's growth between 2003 and 2010 came from the sweeping economic reforms enacted by the Narasimha Rao government to meet the requirements of its creditors and the International Monetary Fund (IMF). These reforms broke the hold of the command economy and, belatedly, made it possible for India to integrate itself with the global economy.

According to the Government of India's Economic Survey of 2011, the country had moved from tenth in 2000 to fifth in 2011–2012 in the Index of Government Economic Power for 112 countries.[4] This ranking was based on a country's ability to raise resources, its credit-worthiness and credibility in international financial markets, and its importance in multilateral forums.[5] This rapid rise electrified the industrialized world. Manufacturers and service providers woke up to the fact that consumer demand was growing at more than 7 percent a year in a country that contained one-sixth of the world's population. What is more, India's large reservoir of young people virtually ensured that the country would be able to sustain this, or a similar, rate of growth for several decades to come.[6] Along with China, it was hoped that India could become the market that would revive flagging demand and profits in the industrialized countries in the twenty-first century.

How had a succession of short-lived minority governments based upon unstable alliances been able to steward such a profound transformation? To answer this question, we need in this chapter to explore the course of the economic change according to the three broad measures proposed by Eric Ringman. First, have reforms been inspired by a continuing vision of India as a strong and self-reliant but compassionate nation? Second, did India's leaders succeed in adapting existing institutions and creating new ones that would make this transformation possible? Third, were these leaders successful in resolving most, if not all, of the social and economic conflicts that the changes in policy had unleashed? The answer to all three questions is a qualified yes.

The Era of State-Led Growth

The Indian state first demonstrated its capacity to reassess its policies and change course sharply in 1975 when, taking advantage of the Green Revolution in agriculture, Prime Minister Indira Gandhi embarked upon a long period of cautious and phased liberalization that has come to be known as Reform by Stealth. This involved liberalizing industrial production, imports and exports, and rules governing industrial production as well as the financial sector in stages but without altering the fundamental inward-looking structure of the economy. This approach was maintained through high tariff walls and an overvalued exchange rate.

These reforms pushed up the rate of growth to 5.1 percent in the first half of the 1980s and to 5.9 percent in the second half of that decade, but the growth occurred within a closed economy that was becoming steadily less able to compete in international markets. This trend could not go on forever because the accelerating growth increased India's need for imports while the inward-looking economy continued to discourage exports. This contradiction came to a head when Iraq invaded Kuwait. The way in which the state handled the resulting foreign exchange crisis is perhaps the best demonstration that there is not a necessary connection between a nation's strength, as measured by conventional yardsticks, and its capacity to take hard decisions in pursuit of a shared national vision.

When Iraq invaded Kuwait, India had been living on external borrowings for the best part of five years. This had pushed up its external debt from a modest $14 billion in 1985 to $76 billion in 1990. Once bankers became gun shy about lending to India, the government started to rely increasingly on short-term borrowing and to cover repayments of past loans through fresh borrowing. Iraq's invasion of Kuwait choked off remittances from the Gulf just when oil prices spiked from $18 to $31 a barrel. India suddenly found itself with foreign exchange reserves that would cover barely ten days of imports. To continue receiving short-term loans in order to avoid a ruinous default, India had to ship all the gold reserves of the Reserve Bank of India (RBI) to London to provide surety against its loans.

The crisis struck during the weakest coalition India had ever lived under. Prime Minister V. P. Singh headed a party with 144 members in a Parliament of 542 (see Table 4.2). For the previous ten months, he had ruled with the support of two other parties, the left and the Bharatiya Janata Party (BJP), but within a month of Iraq's invasion of Kuwait, the BJP had all but withdrawn support from him. Singh knew that his government had only weeks of life left, but instead of leaving the problem to his successor, he initiated a string of exceedingly harsh austerity measures, including the transfer of the RBI's gold to London. His successor, Chandra Shekhar, headed an even weaker coalition of fifty-five members of Parliament supported from the outside by the Congress Party. But his government, too, did not shirk the challenge of taking hard decisions. When the Congress Party balked at endorsing another spate of austerity measures included in the budget, Chandra Shekhar resigned but left behind a blueprint that became a working draft for the reforms that followed under Prime Minister Narasimha Rao in July 1991. Even the Congress Party did not enjoy an absolute majority in Parliament when it enacted the reforms. Thus, the change of direction upon which India's future rapid growth was founded was the product of three competing political formations in Parliament, all weak but united by a shared vision of India.

India's Change of Course: Crisis and Reforms

In 1991, the Rao government did what Congress Party governments since the 1970s had shirked doing: instead of continuing Congress Party reforms and making still more piecemeal changes, his government opted for comprehensive changes in policy that put India firmly on the road to integration with the world market.[7] Economists have debated whether Rao did this under duress from the World Bank and

Table 4.2 Prime Ministers of India, 1947–2014

Name	Tenure	Elections	Political Party/Alliance
Jawaharlal Nehru	August 15, 1947–May 27, 1964	1952 (1st), 1957 (2nd), 1962 (3rd)	INC
Gulzarilal Nanda	May 27, 1964–June 9, 1964	3rd	INC
Lal Bahadur Shastri	June 9, 1964–January 11, 1966	3rd	INC
Gulzarilal Nanda	January 11, 1966–January 24, 1966	3rd	INC
Indira Gandhi	January 24, 1966–March 24, 1977	1967 (4th), 1971 (5th)	INC
Mararji Desai	March 24, 1977–July 28, 1979	1977 (6th)	Janata Party
Charan Singh	July 28, 1979–January 14, 1980	6th	Janata Party with INC
Indira Gandhi	January 14, 1980–October 31, 1984	1980 (7th)	INC
Rajiv Gandhi	October 31, 1984–December 2, 1989	1984 (8th)	INC
V. P. Singh	December 2, 1989–November 10, 1990	1989 (9th)	Janata Dal–led coalition with NF
Chandra Shekhar	November 10, 1990–June 21, 1991	9th	Samajvadi Janata Party with INC
P. V. Narasimha Rao	June 21, 1991–May 16, 1996	9th	INC-led alliance
Atal Bihari Vajpayee	May 16, 1996–June 1, 1996	1996 (11th)	BJP-led alliance
H. D. Deve Gowda	June 1, 1996–April 21, 1997	11th	Janata Dal United Front (UF)
I. K. Gujral	April 21, 1997–March 19, 1998	11th	Janata Dal United Front
Atal Bijari Vajpayee	March 19, 1998–May 22, 2004	1998 (12th), 1999 (13th)	BJP-led National Democratic Alliance (NDA)
Manmohan Singh	May 22, 2004–(incumbent)	2004 (14th), 2009 (15th)	INC-led United Progressive Alliance (UPA)

Note: These prime ministers were not elected for the indicated years. When the government loses the confidence of the Parliament and the prime minister resigns, a new government is elected from within the Parliament. In the event no compromise is reached, a new national election is held. India will hold its sixteenth national elections in 2014. INC = Indian National Congress; BJP = Bharatiya Janata Party; UPA = United Progressive Alliance; NDA = National Democratic Alliance; NF = National Front; UF United Front. Since the ninth elections, all governments have been formed by coalition of several parties.

foreign creditors or in response to internal pressures for liberalization. The answer is that he was responding to both. Between 1985 and 1990, India's external debt had risen from $14 to $71 billion, and an unhealthily large proportion was short-term debt. Since 1987, it had increasingly been borrowing in the short-term money market to repay maturing, long-term debt and finance its current import surpluses. Even before Iraq invaded Kuwait in 1990, bankers had raised an alarm and told India that they would be unable to continue lending if it did not change its policies in a manner that restored their confidence in its ability to repay its debt.

Internal pressures also played a part. V. P. Singh, when he was Rajiv Gandhi's finance minister in 1987, first proposed rationalizing and lowering domestic taxes and import duties at a time when the foreign exchange crisis was nowhere on the horizon. Pressure for liberalization was coming from the private sector, particularly from a younger generation of owners who had accumulated large amounts of capital during the higher growth years of the 1980s and were eyeing the world market not as a threat but as an opportunity. The Congress Party's fear of other entrenched interests, such as trade unions, rich farmers, state-owned enterprises, and older, more traditional entrepreneurs in the private sector, had prevented it from implementing these reforms. The same inhibitions prevented Rajiv Gandhi from implementing a far more comprehensive set of reforms suggested early in 1989 by Gandhi's economic adviser, Montek Ahluwalia (who later became one of the chief architects of the economic liberalization). Gandhi purportedly accepted the reforms but deferred them until after the elections, which were scheduled for December 1989. As a result, when India signed a standby agreement with the World Bank and IMF in 1991, all but a handful of the preconditions were already a part of the government's avowed but as yet unimplemented policies.[8]

The Narasimha Rao government's minority status, however, prevented it from adopting any but a step-by-step process of reform. The 1990 foreign exchange crisis that triggered the reforms had come at a time when India's manufacturing growth rate (from April to August) had touched 12.8 percent. In such a buoyant economy, few people immediately comprehended the need for any, let alone drastic, changes in policy. The reforms therefore had to be from the top down. Lacking a solid majority in Parliament, Rao had to generate a consensus behind the reforms, even as he and his finance minister, Manmohan Singh, gradually implemented them. As a result, India devalued the rupee and removed all controls on the buying and selling of foreign exchange in three stages spread between 1991 and 1994, opened the economy to foreign direct investment (FDI) on progressively more liberal terms, removed most remaining restrictions on imports, and lowered and rationalized customs duties incrementally.

The central government made similar changes to domestic indirect taxation. In both foreign and domestic areas, there had been a wide range of tax rates, ranging from 5 to 330 percent. In addition, both were riddled with ad valorem and specific tax rates, which made them a nightmare to administer while also making it impossible for manufacturers to determine how much of their cost of production was made up of government taxes. Because other countries exempted their exports from domestic taxes, India found itself at a severe disadvantage in the world market. Most importantly, Narasimha Rao also pushed for a virtually complete abolition of all domestic controls on private investment in international trade that had held back industrial growth during the previous four decades.

These reforms took the shackles off the production, sale, and export of all goods and services and led to a huge burst in private investment, which quadrupled between the years 1992 and 1996.[9] But Rao was unable, because of his government's minority status, to tackle the far more difficult task of reforming the market in factors of production, namely, land, labor, and capital. Stiff opposition from the left parties and public-sector trade unions prevented him from amending labor laws to allow employers to lay off surplus workers. At the same time, strict controls on the use of land for industry, governed by the 1976 Urban Land Ceiling Act and other acts, made it difficult for owners to move industries out of urban areas and to sell valuable urban land to finance expansion and modernization in new locations.[10] Last, in a bid to open up sensitive sectors such as banking and insurance to foreign investment, he tried to privatize state enterprises but met with little success.

Rao's enthusiasm for reforms was always tempered by his awareness of the fragility of his government.[11] It was no surprise, therefore, that he lost his appetite for pushing ahead with what Manmohan Singh had called the second, more difficult phase of reforms. In December 1994, the Congress Party lost the state assembly elections in Andhra Pradesh and Karnataka, two southern states that had until then been staunch bastions of Congress Party power. In the soul-searching that followed, Rao and the party concluded that curbing rising prices, which had marked the previous four years, had to take precedence over all other objectives. Structural reforms were therefore pushed onto the back burner.

Reforms Under Unstable Coalition Governments

The United Front (UF), which came to power in 1996, was even weaker than the Congress Party at its weakest. Not only did it depend upon the Congress Party's support from the outside to survive, it also required the support of the left. Both the Congress and the Left Front parties harbored the ambition to become the kingmaker if not the pivot of the next national government. They had little inclination to see the UF succeed. The Congress and the Left Front parties' non-cooperation ensured that the UF could not move vigorously forward with economic reforms. Yet by then the consensus within India for reform had strengthened to the point where no one, even in this motley coalition, sought to reverse it. On the contrary, the UF's new finance minister, P. Chidambaram, initiated cuts in the central government's bloated budget by reducing the bureaucracy and raising the price of gasoline, diesel, and other subsidized oil products. He was, however, brought up short on both issues not only by the left but also by the Congress Party, which refused to be a participant in unpopular measures.[12] Electoral calculations outlined in the last chapter explain why the Congress Party considered it prudent to distance itself from the painful reforms the UF thought necessary. The finance minister took his cue from the Congress Party and let lie unchanged other prickly issues such as labor policy and privatization. The only reforms that he could proceed with were a further lowering and rationalization of customs duties and domestic indirect taxes.

Throughout this period, the rhetoric of reform remained unaffected. This bestowed unanticipated side benefits: for instance, when Ministry of Industry bureaucrats, sitting on the board of Maruti Udyog, the nation's premier automobile plant, got into a head-on collision with the Suzuki Motor Company (which owned half the shares of Maruti Udyog) and came within inches of forcing it out of the collaboration, Prime Minister Inder Gujral was able to step in quietly and make key personnel changes in the ministry without being accused of selling out to the multinationals. Paradoxically, in view of what was to follow, the one moment when the reform process came under real threat was in 1998 at the very beginning of the National Democratic Alliance's (NDA) term in office. Whereas members of the UF cabinet had all been part of either the Rao or the V. P. Singh governments and had therefore been exposed to the relentless pressures that had opened up India's autarchic economy, the BJP had never tasted power at the center. It came to New Delhi with an economic ideology that had been framed on the basis of its abstract nationalist ideals, the ideology of *Swadeshi*.[13]

Mahatma Gandhi had coined this term in the 1920s to give his nonviolent revolt against British rule an economic dimension. Throughout the years of the freedom struggle, Congress Party agitators had exhorted the Indian people to boycott British-made goods and to buy Indian instead. At the violent fringe, the movement burned British textiles and other manufactures in the bazaars of Delhi and other large cities. With the achievement of independence, the movement's time had passed. Nevertheless, the BJP resuscitated it in the early years of economic liberalization to oppose foreign investment and the too-hasty opening up of the economy to trade. "We want computer chips, not potato chips," was one of many emotive slogans that its rhymesters coined at that time.[14] When the BJP came to power, it had to deliver on its commitments. It did not, however, manage to go very far. Its finance minister, Yashwant Sinha, who had held the finance portfolio in the short-lived Chandra Shekhar government (November 1990–March 1991), resisted the demands of the Swadeshi movement zealots but was unable to do more. The result was a lackluster budget that drew only derision from the media and the establishment in Delhi and Mumbai.

It is difficult to surmise how the BJP would have gotten out of the hole in which Swadeshi had landed it had it not been for its decision to test nuclear weapons, which took the matter out of the ideologues' hands. The international community reacted to the May 11–13, 1998, nuclear tests by imposing economic sanctions on India. Foreign direct investment dried up (partly on account of the sanctions and partly on account of political uncertainties) precisely when the previous five years of reforms had opened the way for large-scale foreign investment in infrastructure and manufacturing projects.[15] India was running a trade deficit that was made good by inflows of remittances and savings of Indians living abroad, but the sanctions revived the fear that these inflows would dry up and push India into another foreign exchange crisis. The government reacted by raising interest rates for nonresident Indian deposits and by floating two bond issues abroad, Resurgent India bonds and India Millennium , to make good the anticipated shortfall of foreign exchange. Quite suddenly, keeping on the right side of international economic opinion became a matter of supreme importance. Swadeshi became expendable.

The two bond issues were heavily oversubscribed. This not only reinforced the clout of reformers within the party but also brought its leaders into direct contact with the large Indian diaspora. The BJP was well aware that it had already won admiration and support from the latter for having the courage to defy the world and go nuclear to defend the country's security interests. It was therefore predisposed to listen to the voices of the Indian diaspora, especially from the United States, on issues of economic policy. This developing relationship was institutionalized by the government hosting an annual reunion in New Delhi of Indians living abroad and by appointing a special representative with the rank of ambassador to act as a liaison between Indians in the United States and the NDA government.[16]

Economic Reforms Under Stable Coalitions

The NDA's commitment to economic reforms strengthened after October 1999 during its second term in office. It continued to lower and rationalize domestic, indirect taxation and tariffs and to open up the economy further by inviting foreign investment in the automobile and power sectors. It fully honored India's commitments under the World Trade Organization and eliminated all quantitative restrictions on traded goods by 2001. Its most important contribution to the economy, however, was to lower interest rates. After the onset of an industrial recession in November 1996, the demand for manufactured products showed signs of reviving in 1997–1998, but the fear of a "flight of dollars" from India, generated by the economic sanctions imposed on the country following its 1998 nuclear tests, forced the Reserve Bank of India to raise interest rates. In the meantime, inflation had subsided to historically low levels of 3 and 4 percent. The RBI raised real rates of interest and the cost of borrowing to unprecedented levels. Not surprisingly, fresh investment came to a near halt.

By 2000, however, India had withstood the impact of the sanctions. Its foreign exchange reserves were rising, and it had a surplus in its external account. The government therefore aggressively lowered interest rates to half their earlier levels over the course of the next two years. To stimulate private investment even more, Prime Minister Atal Bihari Vajpayee also announced the construction of a golden quadrilateral of four-lane highways connecting Delhi, Mumbai, Chennai, and Kolkata.[17] Although the implementation of this project soon got bogged down in disputes over the acquisition of land, these measures became the genesis of the sustained growth that began in 2003 and was interrupted only by the global recession of 2008.

The NDA also made a significant contribution to the creation of legal and regulatory mechanisms for an increasingly privatized infrastructure sector. The most important of these was the Stock Exchange Board of India and the Telecom Regulatory Authority of India. The NDA's most ambitious effort yet was the passage of the Electricity Act in 2001. The act had been incubating since 1996 but could not get passed because most power generation and all of its distribution were in the hands of the state governments, which were adamantly opposed to giving up their monopoly, especially in the area of distribution.[18] The central government's failure to break this monopoly was the main reason that India had not succeeded (and still has not), despite strenuous efforts, in attracting a single transnational company into the power sector. The lone exception, Enron, had run afoul of the government of Maharashtra, the state in which it was located, and was preparing to take India to international arbitration when the parent company collapsed in the United States.[19]

The Electricity Act laid down the ground rules for private participation in both power generation and distribution. It also articulated the principles on which state governments would allow private distribution and the "wheeling" charges that they would levy to let private distributors use the state power grid. These were only the highlights of a comprehensive bill that also established guidelines for the resolution of a host of other issues, such as the acquisition of land and the safeguarding of the environment. The absence of ruling on land had discouraged private investors from entering the field.[20]

Another vitally important reform was the repeal of the Urban Land Ceiling and Regulation Act (ULCRA). Passed by Indira Gandhi's government in 1976, it had been intended to prevent rampant speculation in the dwindling amount of vacant land that remained in the large cities, but all it had succeeded in doing was to replace—in China fashion—private speculation with speculation by minions of the state. By 1991, it had become the accepted practice for ministers and senior officials in the state housing ministries to extract large considerations for exempting specific pieces of land from the purview of ULCRA. But even this privatized market worked only for residential housing and office buildings. When it came to the sale of mill-owned land, no government functionary was prepared to stand up to the wrath of the unions and the adverse publicity they were capable of generating. As a result, although as far back as the early 1990s Manmohan Singh had been among the first to recognize the need to do away with the act, neither the Rao government nor its successors had been able to crack the opposition of the state governments. The NDA managed to do this by offering funds to the state governments provided they were willing to undertake seven key reforms that included repeal of ULCRA; reform of rent control laws; rationalization of stamp duty; reform of property taxes; and computerized processes of registration. The NDA allocated about $110 million to promote these reforms.

Among the NDA's other reforms were opening up the insurance sector to international capital, despite severe opposition from state-sector employees and trade unions, and opening up Internet service provision to the private sector. This spate of reforms raised the ire of the radicals in the Sangh Parivar (the BJP's more militant affiliates) and sent them into the streets to mount protests against Vajpayee's betrayal of Swadeshi.[21] But by then they had been reduced to an irrelevant cluster on the Hindu right and even failed to hold media attention for long.[22]

The NDA's most courageous effort at reform, however, was one that remained incomplete during its tenure and had to be bequeathed to its successor, the United Progressive Alliance (UPA) government of Dr. Manmohan Singh. This was to bring the consolidated fiscal deficit of the central and state governments down from 6 to 8 percent of GDP, at which it had remained obstinately stuck since the early 1990s, to the internationally accepted norm of 3 percent. To do this, the NDA passed the Fiscal Responsibility and Budgetary Management Act (FRBMA) in August 2003 and invited the state governments to enact complementary legislation that would give their budgets some teeth. The act required the center to reduce its fiscal deficit by 0.5 percent of the GDP per year beginning in 2004–2005.

With great political skill, the NDA combined the stick with the carrot to bring the state governments around. On the one hand, it helped them refinance their huge accumulated debts at the drastically lower interest rates that its monetary reforms had made possible after 2000. On the other, it offered a variety of inducements to make them replace sales tax, their main source of tax revenues, with a value-added tax.[23] State governments were initially hesitant to do this because they feared the leap from the known to the unknown, but the central government offered a variety of transitional revenue packages that would insure them against risk. In fact, few of these were invoked because the value-added tax proved a bonanza to the state governments, increasing their revenues by 50 to 100 percent, depending upon their level of development. Finally, to reduce the central deficit, the NDA drew up a five-year blueprint for eliminating administered pricing from the petroleum and fertilizer sectors—the two areas that accounted for most of its subsidies. The NDA was, however, unable to implement its own act because it lost the elections to the UPA in May 2004.

Overall, the fiscal deficit of the center as a proportion of GDP came down from 6.2 percent in 2001–2002 to 3.8 in 2006–2007.[24] The reduction in revenue and fiscal deficit as proportions of GDP by 0.6 percentage points and 0.5 percentage points, respectively, in 2006–2007 was higher than the levels prescribed under the FRBMA rules.[25] The fiscal situation of the states showed even greater improvement. As a proportion of GDP, the fiscal deficit of the states declined by 1.9 percentage points, post-FRBMA, from 4.5 percent in 2003–2004 to 2.6 percent in 2006–2007.[26]

To sum up the transition, India made a right-angle turn in its economic policies at a time when single-party dominance had irretrievably collapsed. The change was effected over a twelve-month period by three minority governments interspersed by two parliamentary elections. What is more, three succeeding minority governments forced to rule with the help of regional parties continued the process of reforms in a graduated manner that gained the approval of international financial institutions. What made this possible was the shared underlying vision of India's future that bound the entire polity despite it numerous differences on specific issues. This vision assumed concrete forms through passage of model legislation on key issues that fell within the purview of the states and the development of consultative center-state institutions to forge the necessary consensus.

Reforms and Recession Under the UPA

The UPA was led by the Congress Party, which, somewhat unexpectedly, emerged as the largest single party after the 2004 elections. But because it had won only 145 seats, it was compelled to form a coalition, and this time it could not take refuge, as it had in 1989 and 1996, in supporting a coalition of minor parties from the outside. By 2004, the Congress Party had grown tired of living in the political wilderness. It had reluctantly come to the conclusion that it would need to steal certain slogans from and cede certain states to parties that it hoped to turn into long-term allies, even if this meant allowing its own organization in these states to wither. In 2004, however, the party's job was made much easier by the left, which had won a record sixty-two seats but had no ambitions to become a part of the government.

Although the left maintained its separate identity, it was prepared to take the initiative in bringing a number of smaller parties into the coalition. As a result, with the support of the Dravida Munnetra Kazhagam in Tamil Nadu, which had won thirty-nine seats, the Congress Party was able to cobble together a majority without having to make too many concessions to regional parties elsewhere. Its reluctance to do so is evidenced in its rejection of support from the Uttar Pradesh–based Samajwadi Party, a powerful regional party representing backward classes, which had won thirty-six seats in Parliament.

In the years that followed, this reluctance on the part of the Congress Party was to cost it dearly in terms of effectiveness, for it became wholly dependent on the Left Front for its survival. What this meant became apparent within a week of the formation of the new government, when it issued its National Common Minimum Programme (NCMP). The NCMP was full of huge disbursements for social spending on health, education, and rural development, along with an employment guarantee program, but the NCMP gave no hint on how to raise the money.[27] To no one's surprise, the stock markets crashed and trading had to be suspended for several days to let the panic subside. It was only when the new finance minister, P. Chidambaram, presented his first budget that investors felt reassured that the UPA government would not roll back reforms but would continue on the path to India's integration with the global economy.

The UPA lived up to the first but not to the second expectation. An overview of its first five years shows that it shunned all but one of the difficult reforms needed to complete the transition to a market economy. Labor law reform ground to a halt. The NDA had left two important reform bills on the table in Parliament. One of these was a contract labor bill that would have legalized the hiring of workers to meet seasonal demand. This was essential for many export industries, particularly garments. The second was an amendment to the Industrial Disputes Act of 1947 that would have made laying off workers easier, at least for small and medium-sized companies. Neither bill passed in Parliament. The UPA also shelved the very idea of privatizing state-owned enterprises, even those that were incurring losses. At the same time, it found itself unable to break free of the regime of government-administered pricing in the petroleum and fertilizer industries.[28] The UPA was unable to muster support even for price increases that would simply offset the rise in oil prices that had begun in 2004 when China abruptly turned from being a petroleum exporter to an importer. Instead, the alliance preferred that the oil companies pile up losses. This repoliticization of oil-product pricing drove private entrepreneurs that had ventured into oil distribution out of business.

The rise in the losses of state-owned oil companies came on top of a threefold increase in central outlays on rural development, education, and health and a huge outlay on the National Rural Employment Guarantee Scheme. When the UPA also hastily accepted the recommendations of the government-appointed Pay Commission to increase the salaries of 18 million civil servants and waive Rs. 600 billion ($15 billion) in farm loans, these actions came close to breaking the bank.[29] The only reason that the fiscal deficit did not soar out of control was the country's 9 percent growth rate. This pushed up current revenues by 15 percent a year and enabled India to stay abreast of its rising expenditure until 2007–2008.

When the global recession hit the Indian economy in 2008, the chickens came home to roost. In 2008–2009, the growth of the GDP dipped sharply to 6.7 percent. The Pay Commission's awards of salary arrears to government servants contributed at least 1 percent of the purported GDP growth, but that increase resulted from a UN accounting convention that treated the back pay as a real increase in the GDP. The rise in the real GDP, and therefore the taxable base, of the Indian economy was therefore smaller than it might appear. The fiscal-deficit-to-GDP ratio would therefore have risen in any case, but it was further expanded by the government's decision to make a virtue out of necessity and pile on a series of other subsidies to the farm and economically weaker sectors under the common (and politically acceptable) rubric of a fiscal stimulus. In all, the fiscal deficit ballooned once more in 2008–2009 and 2009–2010, and the targets of the FRBMA were quietly shelved. In hindsight it is apparent that for its first two years in office, the UPA was able to resist populist pressures from the left and from social activists in the Congress Party National Advisory Council (established to advise the prime minister of India), but as the UPA lost one state assembly election after another, the pressure from within the party mounted and encouraged a fresh round of populist spending.

The constraints imposed by the left did not stop the government from trying to enact new market reforms. But because only left-supported reforms stood any chance of being enacted, the coherence and purpose that had characterized Singh's reforms between 1991 and 1996 disappeared. Among the measures enacted by the UPA during this period was the establishment of Special Economic Zones (SEZs). This was a belated attempt to emulate the Chinese and integrate at least a certain number of small enclaves within the country into the global economy by providing them with quality infrastructure and a cosmopolitan lifestyle. The move turned out to be hasty and based upon an incomplete understanding of what had actually happened in China. In 2005, Hu Jintao closed down 4,755 of approximately 7,000 SEZs.[30] Although announced by the central government, the creation of the SEZs was left to the state governments, which provided local officials the same opportunity to make money that Chinese local cadres had sensed in the late 1980s when Beijing allowed provinces to open up to Special Economic and Development Zones. In the ten months that followed the Indian central government's decision, the states opened an SEZ every two days. In no time at all, farmers had been evicted from more than 1 million acres of land, most of which was under cultivation. The forcible purchase of land from farmers did not attract immediate attention because the left was doing precisely this in West Bengal. By the end of the year, however, several civil society organizations and smaller parties across the country had taken up the cry against the SEZs.[31] Belatedly, in December 2006, the government announced a revision of the guidelines. Three months later, additional guidelines specified that the state should take no part in land acquisition and that deals would have to be struck solely between buyers and sellers, but UPA I and even UPA II failed to come up with a comprehensive land acquisition policy that would reflect the alliance's professed concern for the common man.[32]

Another controversial reform was the decision to allow foreign retailers into the Indian market. Every previous government had resisted this, but the UPA succumbed to pressures from the George W. Bush administration. However, it took the precaution of allowing only foreign, single-brand retailing. This kept out giants such as TESCO and Wal-Mart.[33] Undeterred, both these corporations concluded wholesaling arrangements with prominent Indian companies, which had set up mass retailing outlets. Most businesses in India concluded that this was only a halfway house to full entry by the multinationals. Unlike most of the reforms that had been enacted until then, this opening of the Indian market aroused serious misgivings across all strata of society because of its capacity to destroy tens of thousands of small retail establishments.

The only measure that was unambiguously welcomed by the entire business community was the Indo-US nuclear deal. While public attention remained focused throughout the two years of its negotiation on the deal's political and military implications, these aspects were far outstripped in importance by the economic opportunities the deal afforded the country. Not only did India get a chance to update its obsolete nuclear power technology and to import the uranium it needed, the deal also lifted decades-old US-imposed sanctions on the sale of dual-use technology to India, sanctions that had begun to suffocate the country's scientific and technological progress.[34] The deal very nearly failed because of the adamant opposition of the left. Although the two governments initialed it in July 2005, and signed it in July 2007, New Delhi was unable to take the follow-up steps to bring it into operation because the left threatened to withdraw support every inch of the way. The deal finally went through only because the prime minister made it clear that he would resign if his own party and the UPA's other allies denied support.[35]

In 2009, to the surprise of most political analysts, the Congress Party increased its share of both the vote and seats in Parliament. The reasons were the five years of uninterrupted high growth, which had created millions of new jobs, albeit mostly in the informal sector, and a determined bid to make the benefits of growth reach the poor through programs such as the National Rural Employment Guarantee Scheme. The UPA therefore returned to power as a more homogeneous coalition free from the constraints placed upon it by the left during the previous term in office.

Despite these advantages, the UPA's second term in office was in sharp contrast to the first. For whereas the first saw dramatic initiatives on issues ranging from the Indo-US nuclear deal and the National Rural Employment Guarantee Act, the second was characterized by an absence of concrete policy outcomes. The UPA did propose a whole slew of rights legislation to realize its campaign promises of inclusive growth, such as the Right to Information Act (2005), the Food Security Act (2013), the Right to Education Act (2009), the Land Acquisition Rehabilitation and Resettlement Bill (2013), and the Jan Lok Pal Act (yet to be passed), though many of these languished in Parliament or existed largely on paper. Within the first two years of its second term in office, the UPA government was paralyzed by a spate of corruption scandals involving high officials and cabinet ministers. Prime Minister Singh's government faced repeated demands from the opposition to resign. Industrial production plummeted to just a little more than 4 percent from a high of 10 percent the previous year. The economy as a whole slowed to 6.1 percent between January and April 2012 while inflation was at an all-time high.

This dramatic slowing of the growth rate immediately triggered speculation about India's economic future. Many within and outside India argued that perhaps India's growth story had come to an end. Ajay Vaishnav wrote in the *Times of India* that the "Indian economy being the world's talking point is by now yesterday's story."[36] India's "chances of getting into an economic slump are high considering policy paralysis, political uncertainty, coalition compulsions, an anti-reforms mindset and corrupt governance. For starters, the country's much-touted growth story has fizzled out." In a new book, Ruchir Sharma, Morgan Stanley's head of emerging markets, observed that the possibility of India growing at a brisk and sustained pace in the future was only 50:50.[37] But the *Times of India* was more optimistic: "The economic history of the country shows that it is very much capable of reform. The liberalisation policies of 1991, brought on by the balance-of-payments crisis, are a case in point. Similarly, the reforms initiated during the second phase of the NDA regime allowed for high growth during the first tenure of the UPA dispensation."[38] Even Sharma admitted that there were several factors in India's favor: India's low per capita income, which allowed for greater headroom for growth; a rapidly expanding middle class; and a large youth

population.[39] These advantages, in his and other commentators'
views, were likely to provide the necessary impetus for growth if
Indian leaders carried out a second generation of economic reforms
and liberalization that would free up the labor market and concentrate on building the country's physical and legal infrastructure to
sustain a 9 percent rate of growth. The *Times of India* agreed: an editorial pointed out that to leverage the available resources, all that
India needed was "market-oriented reforms that incentivise competition, bring in FDI [Foreign Direct Investment], observe fiscal prudence and invest in critical infrastructure. Aspirations have exploded
across the country—thanks in no small part also to the information
revolution—and the genie cannot be put back in the bottle any
longer."[40] Tyler Cowen, writing in the *New York Times,* agreed that,
even though failures to engage in deeper liberalization had slowed
the economy, India's growth potential remained intact.[41]

A closer look at the interplay of political forces during this
period shows that the paralysis was caused by political developments
that were likely transient in nature and will be resolved through the
electoral process. The same cannot be said of the deeper malaise: a
dysfunctional state that fails both because it procrastinates over decisions and because the decisions it does choose to make widen the gap
between the rich and the poor and hence the danger of social conflict.
The immediate cause for the UPA paralysis after 2010 was a struggle within the Congress Party between its radical wing, centered on
Sonia Gandhi and the party organization, and the parliamentary party
and cabinet, headed by the prime minister, for control over policy.

Prior to 2004, from the first days of India's independence, the
parliamentary wing had always dominated within the Congress Party
and framed its agenda. The circumstances in which Sonia Gandhi,
chair of the Congress Party National Advisory Council, led the party
to victory but stayed out of the government sowed the seeds of a
dyarchy within the UPA government. But during its first term, the
struggle between the radicals in the party organization and the mod-
erates in the government took place within the coalition because the
left could plead the radicals' cause within Parliament and the UPA
coordination committee. With the absence of the left from the second
UPA government in 2009, the struggle between the party in Parliament and its organizational wing reverted to within the Congress
Party and therefore went out of public view. This conflict not only
limited the initiatives the UPA was able to take, but also the few that

the parliamentary wing took were marked by an unseemly haste and lack of preparation. The attempt to open up the retail trade sector to FDI was a case in point, for it aroused a storm of protest, was rejected outright by a majority of state governments (in whose purview retail trade falls), and therefore had to be withdrawn for "reconsideration."

The paralysis, however, was by no means complete. Behind the storms in the media created by the FDI and other controversies, the UPA government had forged ahead with a spate of new legislation designed, as mentioned earlier, to achieve "inclusive" development. The tilt toward radicalism within the party was translated into a whole range of fresh legislation that attempted not only to confer concrete benefits upon the poor but also to enact rights that the poor could adjudicate in the courts. In all, as of 2013 seven such bills were pending before Parliament of which three were meant to confer economic rights. The most important of these was the Land Resettlement and Rehabilitation Bill, which sought to make those who lose their land to development permanent beneficiaries in its future use; the Right to Food bill, which will guarantee nearly free food to 160 million families in the country; and the Right to Education bill, which provides compulsory but free education for all children. The extent to which these rights will be enforceable in a judicial system that already has a backlog of more than 300 million cases remains to be seen, but if the Right to Information Act is any guide, the poor are likely to share in the benefits of growth more than skeptics believe possible.

The Direction of the Economy

If skepticism about the future of the Indian economy persists despite the successes since 1989, it is because of an all-pervading belief that their base remains fragile and large structural problems remain unaddressed. In fact, several commentators argue that the first-generation economic reforms were relatively painless but that they unleashed growing inequality, a rampant and predatory business class aided and abetted by a shrinking state both unable and unwilling to protect the poor, and growing vulnerability to the vagaries of global markets. This commentary on the course of India's economic reforms confuses two separate streams of criticism: one about the kinds of policies, their sequencing, and their pace and the second about the morality of neoliberal reform. Although the latter criticism frequently draws a causal link between impoverishment and growth, for the most part the focus in this set of criticisms remains on the exploitative and predatory nature of state policies.[42]

Commentary belonging to the first set of criticism goes as follows: Since 1989 India has been able to enact only the easiest parts of the reforms. These include reform of its external trade and exchange rate regime and the freeing of product markets from oppressive government intervention. But India has failed, despite repeated efforts, to free a large part of the factors of production, it has signally failed to privatize state-owned enterprises, it has turned away deliberately from privatizing the banking and insurance sectors, and, most important of all, it has failed to free up the market in labor and land. These failures are caused largely by the decision to reform in a gradual and piecemeal fashion, which has in turn permitted opponents to consolidate opposition and robbed reforms of coherence and momentum. Under coalition rule India has turned from a "license and permit raj" into a "subsidy raj." Motivated by politics as they often are, these subsidies fail the test of economic rationality and reduce India's competitive advantage in global markets. Failure to build adequate and modern infrastructure in power, water, roads, ports, and communication and the red tape associated with start-up business or FDI are additional reasons that sustained and robust economic growth has been held back.

The second set of criticism is as follows: the neoliberal growth strategy adopted by successive government is slave to FDI and consequently both undemocratic and antipeople. Had the public been consulted, the shift from poverty reduction to capital accumulation would not have taken place and the consequent tragedies of large-scale suicides by indebted farmers and clashes over establishment of SEZs could have been avoided or mitigated. The reforms have created only an illusion of growth because nearly 40 percent of India still continues to live on $2 a day. The persistence of large numbers of poor, along with spiraling inequality, has led to violence and class wars and thereby checked growth. These interconnections among poverty, discrimination, and violence are already apparent in the resurgence of Maoism across Central India from Maharashtra to West Bengal. India still ranked only 136 in the United Nations' 2013 Human Development Index (HDI), which underlines the failure to provide even a modicum of social security to its vast unorganized working class. By even a conservative reckoning, the number of workers in agriculture and in nonagricultural occupations exceeds 440 million. In the latter sector, employment rose throughout the first two years of the second UPA government partly owing to the National Rural Employment Guarantee Act, but study after study shows that workers enjoy no social security. This, too, is a product of the shift toward industrialization, growth, and international trade.

The criticism that coalition governments have taken the easiest way out and allowed the opposition to consolidate is, at best, partly correct. Capital markets have many components, and most of these have been freed from government controls. The buying and selling of land is subject to laws besides those of the market. Private companies have entered markets hitherto restricted to state-owned enterprises whose market share in most cases is at less than half. This "green field" privatization has been remarkably successful in areas as diverse as steel, telecommunications, airlines, port facilities, banking and insurance, and oil exploration and refining. In these industries, the presence of the public sector has acted as a brake on private profit making, while the entry of the private sector has forced state-owned enterprises and banks to transform themselves. Indeed, a strong case can be made for the claim that by creating a competitive mixed economy, India has managed to combine advantages of the public and private sectors.

By the same token, even though the formal laws governing the labor market remain unchanged, flexibility has been introduced informally. The Rao government initiated a voluntary retirement scheme (VRS) under which owners and trade unions could negotiate terms by which employees were free to leave a company. The private sector immediately took advantage of this scheme and offered terms of separation, which were often so generous that the employee suffered little or no reduction in monthly emoluments. Not long after, the public sector followed suit. The result was not always what the government had intended, for it was often the best managers and workers who left first. But slimming down enterprises improved profits and efficiency. The nationalized banks, for example, computerized their transactions and reduced staff levels by about one-third. Of course, the VRS was not an entirely satisfactory substitute for labor law reform. It did not, for instance, provide a means to lay off workers when a company wanted to close down altogether. Taking advantage of the scheme was, moreover, most difficult for companies that were financially weak and therefore most in need of personnel reduction. All in all, however, the VRS worked reasonably well because most of the shakeout of surplus workers took place when the economy was growing rapidly. In the fast-growing states of the West, the South, and the North, those seeking new jobs could find them.

Lastly, the entire financial market was deregulated in stages. To begin with, the Rao government removed restrictions on the sale and purchase of government bonds, making their prices and yields subject to market forces. Successive governments progressively lifted controls on interest rates and abolished sectoral lending targets. The Reserve Bank of India eventually took control of the entire banking sector through the use of conventional monetary instruments such as a cash reserve ratio and interbank interest rates.

Criticism that transitional governments implemented reforms without prior public consultation confuses the real world with an idealized construct of the critic's own making. At the time when India embarked on reforms, "shock therapy" was the accepted mode of transformation. Politics had little to do with this. Russia, Poland, Hungary, and, for that matter, the entire Eastern bloc resorted to it. Shock therapy relied for its success on stealth and speed of execution. Judged by this yardstick, Manmohan Singh's reforms were a model of inclusive decisionmaking. After the first emergency measures to restore India's capacity to borrow abroad, he adopted a strategy of appointing an expert committee to lay out a blueprint for the reforms he intended to pursue. He would then release the committee's report to the public and leave it there for every industrialist, economist, and commentator to voice his or her views. All that was missing was the American system of holding a formal public hearing, but this hardly made the decisions arbitrary.

In the ensuing fifteen years, as coalition governments became the norm, proposed reforms were discussed more and more fully in the cabinet prior to being placed before Parliament and the public. As a result, every party came gradually to "own" the reform process, including the Left Front governments in West Bengal and Kerala. Indeed, the course of Jan Lok Pal Bill and the Land Acquisition Rehabilitation and Resettlement Bill (LARRB) shows the tortuous but determined commitment to consult the ever-widening circle of stakeholders in the proposed legislation.

Critics of the performance of the state during the post-1989 period have also been guilty of selective perception and overgeneralization. The absolute measure of poverty is only one indicator of social well-being. Social mobility is another. It is true that the poor still constitute a substantial portion of the population and are concentrated in the North and the eastern parts that have recorded low growth rates despite the acceleration in India's overall growth since the mid-1990s. Nevertheless, we need to look at poverty in tandem with social and economic mobility to build a better picture of peoples' subjective assessment of their own condition. The balance between discontent and satisfaction rests more on the availability of upward mobility than critics would have us believe. Under the command economy, upward mobility was insignificant. A combination of democracy and upward mobility can be destabilizing as well, but behavior during the coalition era suggests that the post–Congress Party polity is far more sensitive to popular discontent than it was during the days of the Congress Party's dominance. This responsiveness acts as a corrective and a safety valve that prevent Indian democracy from collapse.

The National Council of Applied Economic Research estimated that in the decade between 1988–1989 and 1998–1999, the number of urban Indian households in the lower classes (making below Rs. 35,000) declined from 83.4 million in 1989–1999 to 52.1 million in 1998–1999.[43] Those belonging to the lower middle classes (Rs. 35,000–70,000) increased from 78 to 93 million (rounding off numbers), while those in the middle class (Rs. 70,000–105,000) increased from 40 to 62 million in the same ten years. Those in the next income category, the upper middle class (Rs. 105,000–140,000), increased in numbers from 14 to 33 million, while those in the higher middle classes witnessed the sharpest increase, from 8 to 34 million.[44] Rural areas show a different variance. Here, the upper- and higher-middle-class categories jumped sharply, while there was a slower decline in those belonging to the lower-income classes. But the rural middle classes rose substantially from 40 to 70 million households in ten years. Overall, these numbers support the conclusion that since the 1980s there has been a remarkable expansion in the middle class, broadly defined, and considerable mobility between classes, especially within the top three categories comprising the middle, upper-middle, and higher-middle classes.[45]

What is more, in a vast and diverse country like India, there are bound to be wide-ranging differences not only in income and welfare but also in the performance of the state. These differences have been exacerbated by India's federal structure. India's low ranking on the Human Development Index is not conclusive evidence of lack of progress because other strong indicators, such as a decline in infant mortality and an increase in life expectancy, point the other way. Even if we accept the HDI as a useful indicator of relative changes over time, however, what it really demonstrates is that the conscious attempts by successive central governments to improve rural health, education, and development have not borne fruit because of the "filtering" effect of inefficient and corrupt state governments.

This is not new. The center was no more able to oversee the performance of the states in the days of Congress Party dominance than it is today. Consequently, what the post-1989 governments must be judged by is their effort to increase outlays for planned expenditure. On this score, at least in the two spells of Congress Party–led coalition governments, there has been no dearth of effort. The outlays under Manmohan Singh tripled between 2003–2004 and 2007–2008.[46] His administration also made determined efforts to ensure that money reached its intended beneficiaries. It enlisted nongovernmental organizations to regularly monitor and report on the implementation of the National Rural Employment Guarantee Scheme and created eight national missions in health and education to demand an accounting of how state governments spent the money.[47]

In addition, in 2009 the UPA government initiated the Unique Identification Authority of India (UIDAI), headed by former Infosys CEO and prominent businessman Nandan Nilekani. The purpose was to issue identity cards to all citizens to prevent fraud in elections and embezzlement that had affected the reach of the government's poverty-alleviation programs. The unique ID card is meant to verify and ensure that state assistance goes to the correct individual and is not diverted by bureaucrats and middlemen through fraudulent use or process manipulation. By April 2012, the UIDAI had issued close to 200 million IDs. The success of these measures is doubtful, but in the view of several commentators they will improve the accountability and administration of government assistance to the poor and disadvantaged compared to the situation before 1989.

Critics have also confused poverty with social and economic exclusion. Every quinquennial survey by the National Sample Survey of India, howsoever its results may have been parsed, shows a continuing and in some periods steep decline in the proportion of the population living below the poverty line.[48] But these figures have not captured the exclusion of specific categories of the poor from the very process of development. And although this was happening even during the days of the command economy, there is growing evidence that it may have accelerated with the acceleration of growth after 1992. It is economic exclusion, not poverty, that is responsible for the Maoist resurgence, as it turns people into victims of economic growth, a subject to which we turn below.

An overall assessment of the period since 1989 shows that just as the advent of coalition rule made it necessary to adopt a consultative form of democracy, market-oriented reforms imposed a need to build a consensus on matters of economic policy. The constant process of dialogue and exchange among different levels of government and between government and business widened the participation of economic actors and of state-level politicians and increased their understanding of the compulsions emanating from the economy. Given the strength of the entrepreneurial class, regional political formations including political parties, and the trade unions, it was unlikely that any government would have opted for shock therapy. What the Rao government's minority status did was to remove the temptation to go down that road. Gradual reforms and their immediate success created a powerful consensus in favor of the transition to an open economy, a consensus that never seriously wavered. Ideologies had, in any case, played only a minor part in Indian politics. The BJP's hasty abandonment of the Swadeshi agenda and the contrast between the Left Front's policies in New Delhi and those in West Bengal showed that ideology played only a peripheral role in the actual framing of policy. In effect, economic reform gained a measure of immunity from the vagaries of Indian politics, although its pace remained hostage to the rhythm of coalition rule.

What political instability did was determine the pace of change. In these years of transition, coalitions with greater political coherence pushed ahead with reforms a good deal faster than those without it. The first Congress Party government under Rao had no option but to act in response to the crisis. It therefore had to make sweeping changes at a time when there was no domestic consensus behind it. Subsequent governments lacked internal coherence but were able to ride upon the consensus his reforms had generated. The UF government, by contrast, was both the weakest and the least coherent. The first Vajpayee administration was far weaker and less coherent than the second. As a result, a great acceleration of reform occurred under the NDA but was concentrated entirely in its second term in office. The contrast between the first and second Congress Party–led governments is particularly instructive. The UPA's dependence on the left between 2004 and 2009 deprived its economic policies of the coherence and synchronicity that had characterized the policies of the Rao government. Having returned with a majority, UPA II expected to push reforms and welfare, but sadly it has been paralyzed because of revelations of massive corruption and waves of popular protest and the virtual dyarchy in its ruling strategy. It is difficult to tell whether it will be able to overcome this paralysis and move forward with an inclusive economic growth. Popular democracy, particularly dispersion of power to regions and regional parties, has reduced the central government's room for maneuver and made cross-party consensus increasingly more difficult.

If the reform process is to be judged by its success in integrating India into the global economy, however, it has so far been less than wholly successful.[49] After more than twenty years of economic liberalization, the indisputable fact remains that, while India is a part of the global marketplace, it is still not a part of the global manufacturing system. India has built up a commanding position, not unlike China's in manufacturing, in the service sector, where it is home to roughly one-third to two-fifths of outsourced service provisions. The value of transactions and the employment generated in this sector, however, do not bear comparison with China's manufactures.

The paramount reason for this failure is India's inability to raise its energy, transport, and communication infrastructure to the level where it can compare in reliability and speed with what East Asia, and more recently China, has to offer.[50] To do this, the country could have followed the Chinese approach of building large SEZs equipped with world-class infrastructure. Alternatively, it could have opened up the energy, transport, and communications sectors to the private sector and adopted a uniform investor-friendly regulatory framework in the first few years of liberalization. India's federal structure, and the end of dominant-party rule in 1989, ensured that the country did neither. The first option, creating SEZs, requires drastic changes in land-use laws. These laws fall within the purview of the state governments, which were adamantly opposed to giving up a principal source of private and party funding for their leaders. The second alternative, privatization and regulatory consistency, also required, at the very least, that the state governments be under the same party or coalition during the transformation period. Such a situation had ceased to exist as early as 1967. Since then, the required consensus for concerted action has been absent. The experience of the NDA and UPA governments has shown that the state governments can be persuaded, but it has necessarily been a tedious process.

The second major area of failure has been the government's inability to eliminate its perennial fiscal deficit. The causes of this are almost too numerous to list, but a constant leitmotif has been the competition among political parties to woo voters by promising them an unending flow of giveaways. Over the years, these have included not only food subsidies, which are common to most governments in the world, but also subsidies on fertilizers, kerosene, diesel and cooking gas, electricity, water, and housing. What is worse, political competition has also ensured that these giveaways are periodically revised upward. The central government has financed deficits year after year by borrowing from the public.[51] After remaining at tolerable levels between 2003 and 2011, the fiscal and balance-of-payment deficit in India began to rise with the slowdown in the global economy (it was estimated to be close to 4.9 percent in October 2013), as did fears that the economic crisis of 1991 was about to be repeated. International rating agencies, such as Moody's, had warned that India could face a lowered rating should the fiscal situation remain unchanged. What is more, the deficits have ensured that the cost of investment remains high, which has discouraged private investment. Thus, even more than two decades after the beginning of economic reform, the share of manufacturing in the GDP has remained virtually static at 16 to 18 percent.

The pervasiveness of subsidies is also a reason that foreign investment has been wary of India. For instance, the low electricity prices promised by each government to farmers and poorer consumers have pushed every state electricity board into a loss. The mere existence of any form of administered pricing acts as a strong disincentive to foreign investment because it makes investors vulnerable to political forces that they cannot predict and over which they have little or no control. The Enron power project in Maharashtra foundered and was headed to international arbitration when Enron collapsed because the power purchase agreement had been signed by a Congress Party government in Maharashtra in 1993, which was replaced by a BJP government in 1995. When officials of the Maharashtra State Electricity Board pointed out major flaws in the agreement, the BJP did not feel bound to honor an agreement entered into by its predecessor. Enron's long battle in Maharashtra has made foreign investors extremely wary of investing in the infrastructure of utilities in India.[52]

In addition to the problem of government subsidies, a lack of labor law reform has stymied foreign investment. Being unable to close down a plant because workers cannot be laid off introduces a measure of uncertainty and raises costs, affecting the calculus of gain and loss that precedes the decision to invest in India. China has no such restraints in its SEZs.

In sum, while India has moved a long way toward full integration with the global market, the process is still incomplete. Vestiges of inward-looking policies still survive in the factor markets, notably the labor market, and these vestiges have so far sufficed to keep India from becoming a part of the global production chain. Yet India's stage-by-stage change has been relatively painless. In fact, every step on the road to the market economy has been rewarded by an acceleration of growth and a rise in employment, which have built a powerful, near-unanimous consensus to complete the opening of the economy. This consensus has allowed the political system to remain stable through wrenching economic changes.

Not all segments of society have benefited equally, and some of the poorest and least organized have been left out, but all transitions to capitalism have experienced such conditions. India's gradual transition has limited economic exclusion and given the political system time to identify the threat that exclusion can pose. The most striking proof is the manner in which the Trinamul Congress (TMC) in West Bengal decided to champion the cause of those who were being forced off their land by the Left Front government to provide land for a small car plant. This was the first mainstream political party to enter what had so far been the preserve of the Maoists. The TMC's success in the 2009 elections and its subsequent entry into the ruling UPA coalition brought the issue of the traditional land rights of forest dwellers and tribal peoples out of the violent fringe and into the mainstream of Indian politics. Indeed in 2011, the TMC ousted the Left Front parties that had dominated West Bengal politics since 1967 and won a majority to form a state-level government on its own. The party's career path provides a striking demonstration of the ways in which the need for consensus- and alliance-building inherent in multiparty rule has widened political participation and increased the country's capacity to reconcile the political conflicts that market-led growth invariably creates. Nevertheless, economic growth continually tests the reconciliation capacity of coalition rule. It has ignited too many fires, and as was evident in the government's failure to preempt Maoist violence with policy changes, gradualism can be a decided disadvantage.

Looking Back

Two significant observations emerge from the above examination of the development of economic policy. First, India's economic trajectory, and for that matter its political trajectory as well, can no longer be determined by a blueprint created by its central leaders as used to be done in the early decades of Congress Party dominance and a centralized planned economy. More than six decades of democracy have allowed power to diffuse from the center to numerous political and economic groups in the states and districts. Policy increasingly emerges from a constant and complex process of negotiation between center and state and among caste, class, and ethnic groups. But if growth can be taken as a proximate yardstick of effectiveness, this system has harnessed the potential of the people to a far greater extent than the top-down system existing in the days of single-party dominance and the command economy. And arguably much of this diffusion has occurred since the demise of Congress Party dominance, the dismantling of the command economy, and the resulting rise of coalition rule.

Second, it is no longer possible to predict the course of India's future development—the policies it will adopt and the turns its economy will take—with the degree of certainty that scholars were accustomed to. But if the progress made since 1989 is any indication, then this unpredictability should not be confused with weakness or a lack of vision and direction. On the contrary, coalition governments have been challenged by crises in the economy and the polity to an extent that the Congress Party governments of the past never experienced. And they have shown a resourcefulness, an ingenuity, and, above all, a determination to arrive at decisions by building consensus in shaping legislative and administrative responses that few could have anticipated. The course of Land Acquisition Resettlement and Rehabilitation Bill is a case in point. In its original form, the LARRB was, in fact, two separate bills, one dealing with acquisition and the other with rehabilitation of those impacted by the sale of land. Since then, the bill has undergone several drastic changes, each in response to objections by key stakeholders. It is still far from perfect, but there is little doubt that the LARRB (which passed in September 2013) will lay the foundation of rapid economic growth impelled by modern infrastructure and manufacturing capabilities. In the next five years, (2013–2017) the government of India is poised to spend over $1 trillion on infrastructure raised from both private and public sources. Such a huge infusion of money is likely to restore the lost momentum to the economy. Whether it is able to balance and manage the goals of reducing the deficit, protecting the poor by curbing inflation, and opening the economy to global markets remains to be seen. But that is the test facing India in the future.

Notes

1. *Union Budget and Economic Survey, 2012–2013* (New Delhi: Ministry of Finance, 2013), 2, http://indiabudget.nic.in/es2012-13/echap-01.pd.

2. *Union Budget and Economic Survey, 1993–1994* (New Delhi: Ministry of Finance, Government of India, 1994), 1, http://indiabudget.nic.in /es1993-94/1%20General%20Review.pdf. "The growth of GDP at factor cost (at constant 1999–2000 prices) at 6.7 per cent in 2008–09 nevertheless represents a deceleration from high growth of 9.0 per cent and 9.7 per cent in 2007–08 and 2006–07, respectively." See *Union Budget and Economic Survey, 2008–2009* (New Delhi: Ministry of Finance, Government of India, 2009), 2, http://indiabudget.nic.in/es2008-09/chapt2009/chap12.pdf.

3. In September 2011, the foreign exchange reserves stood at $311 billion, against $199 billion five years earlier. See *Union Budget and Economic Survey, 2011–2012* (New Delhi: Ministry of Finance, Government of India, 2012), Table 6.4.

4. "India Fifth in Global Economic Power: Survey," *Economic Times,* February 26, 2011, http://articles.economictimes.indiatimes.com/2011-02 -26/news/28636057_1_economic-power-global-slowdown-economic-survey.

5. "Global Economic Power List: India Enters Top 5," *Indian Express,* February 26, 2011, http://www.indianexpress.com/news/global-economic -power-list-india-enters-top/755105/.

6. According to Nandan Nilekani, an eminent entrepreneur who has designed and implemented a nationwide identification system, "No country

is better poised to take advantage of the demographic dividend than India. In 2020, the average age in India will be only 29 years, compared with 37 in China and the United States, 45 in Western Europe, and 48 in Japan. Moreover, 70 percent of Indians will be of working age in 2025, up from 61 percent now. Also by 2025, the proportion of children younger than 15 will fall to 23 percent of India's total population, from 34 percent today, while the share of people older than 65 will remain around just 5 percent. China's demographics are not as rosy as India's, because the government's policies to limit population growth will have created an abnormally large cohort of people over age 60 by 2040. Other emerging nations, such as Pakistan, Indonesia, and certain countries in Latin America and Africa, will produce much larger workforces in the coming years. But their demographic dividends may be inhibited by political and social instability that impedes efforts to put this young population to productive use; a country with massive numbers of unemployed young people and no constructive economic outlet for their dynamism is headed for trouble." See his "India's Demographic Moment," *Strategy + Business,* Autumn 2009, http://www.strategy-business.com/article/09305?pg=all.

7. "Why Did India Reform?" *Business Standard,* Rediff.com, February 24, 2004, http://www.rediff.com/money/2004/feb/24guest1.htm. Marshal Bouton, a scholar and commentator on South Asian affairs, did not think the initial reforms were that big a deal, but he noted that subsequent stabilization efforts turned India in a different direction. According to a report from the University of Chicago Task Force on Economic Reforms in India, "The experience of enacting smaller reforms in the 1980s gave Rao's team the confidence to react swiftly with broader reforms like market determined exchange rates, liberalization of interest rates, reductions in tariffs, and a dismantling of the License Raj." See Sandeep Ahuja et al., "Economic Reforms in India" (Chicago: Harris School of Public Policy, University of Chicago, January 2006), http://harrisschool.uchicago.edu/News/press-releases/IPP%20Economic%20Reform%20in%20India.pdf.

8. The promarket team included Manmohan Singh, Montek Singh Ahluwalia, and Abid Hussein. Each of them had been in and out of government in very high advisory positions throughout the 1980s and again in the 1990s.

9. *Union Budget and Economic Survey, 1995–1996* (New Delhi: Ministry of Finance, Government of India, 1996).

10. The Urban Land Ceiling Act was repealed in 2007.

11. Gurcharan Das, *India Unbound* (New York: Anchor Books, 2002), 218–219.

12. Anil Padmanabhan, "Fuel Prices Decontrol: History Repeating Itself?" Livemint.com (*Wall Street Journal*), February 7, 2010, http://www.livemint.com/2010/02/07230959/Fuel-price-decontrol-history.html.

13. Baldev Raj Nayar, "The Limits of Economic Nationalism in India: Economic Reforms Under the BJP-Led Government, 1998–1999," *Asian Survey* 40, no. 5 (September–October 2000): 792–815, explains it as a policy of economic nationalism.

14. "BJP vs History," *Asian Wall Street Journal,* March 20, 2001, http://www.saliltripathi.com/articles/Mar2001AsianWallStreetJournal Europe.html.

15. India's share in net portfolio investment flows to the developing countries declined to 5.1 percent in 1997, after having increased to 8.7 percent in 1996. See *Foreign Investment in India,* http://www.indiaonestop.com /economy-fdi.htm (accessed February 19, 2013).

16. The annual gathering is called Videshi Pravasi Divas and usually takes place in January. The BJP appointed Bhishma Agnihotri as a nonofficial ambassador to liaison with the Indian diaspora in the United States.

17. Dinesh Chandra, "Golden Quadrilateral Highway Project Completion Advanced by 2003," *Financial Express,* January 9, 2000, http://www .expressindia.com/news/fe/daily/20000109/fec09041.html.

18. For a discussion of this, see Jagdish Sagar, "Power Sector Reforms in Delhi: The Experience So Far," http://info.worldbank.org/etools/docs /library/86464/ses2.1_powersectordelhi.pdf. Sagar is a former chair of the Delhi Electricity Board.

19. Toney Ellison, "Enron's Eight-Year Power Struggle in India," *Asia Times* online, January 18, 2001, http://www.atimes.com/reports/ca13ai01 .html.

20. Government of India, Electricity Act 2003, March 2006, http://www .powermin.nic.in/acts_notification/electricity_act2003/preliminary.htm.

21. R. Upadhyay writes in "Globalisation Versus Swadeshi" that Rashtriya Swayamsevak Sangh (RSS) affiliate Swadeshi Jagran Manch called for protests and warned the public that Vajpayee was straying from the agenda of the Sangh Parivar. It warned the Vajpayee government that "India may face a crisis like that of South East Asia and appealed to general public and all other mass organizations to participate in Swadeshi Movement and become soldiers of second freedom struggle." *Swadeshi Patrika,* a monthly magazine published by Swadeshi Jagran Manch, is full of articles severely criticizing the NDA's economic policies. See "Globalisation Versus Swadeshi: A Tricky Problem for Vajpayee," South Asia Analysis Group, Paper No. 134, July 8, 2000, http://www.southasiaanalysis.org/paper134.

22. "Sangh Parivar Assails Centre," *Times of India,* August 4, 2002, http://articles.timesofindia.indiatimes.com/2002-08-04/patna/27322167 _1_sangh-parivar-sjm-bms.

23. "Tax Measures," *Union Budget and Economic Survey, 2001–2002* (New Delhi: Ministry of Finance, Government of India, 2003) http://india budget.nic.in/es2001-02/chapt2002/chap27.pdf.

24. *Union Budget and Economic Survey, 2007–2008* (New Delhi: Ministry of Finance, Government of India, 2008), Table 3.12; *Union Budget and Economic Survey, 2006–2007* (New Delhi: Ministry of Finance, Government of India, 2007), Table 2.11.

25. Ibid.

26. Ibid.

27. *National Common Minimum Programme of the Government of India,* May 2004, http://pmindia.nic.in/cmp.pdf.

28. It decontrolled gas and fuel prices in June 2010 but has run into a storm of criticism because of increases in gas prices.

29. Ashok Sharma, "Farm Loan Waiver: Timely Relief but Doubts Remain," *Financial Express,* March 10, 2008, http://www.financialexpress.com/news/farm-loan-waiver-timely-relief-but-doubts-remain/282223/.

30. Prem Shankar Jha, *Crouching Dragon, Hidden Tiger: Can China and India Dominate the West?* (Berkeley, CA: Soft Skull Press, 2010), 78.

31. The acquisition of land for SEZs provoked violent protests in many parts of India. The protests by farmers in Nandigram, West Bengal, whose cause was espoused by Mamta Banerjee and her Trinamul Congress Party, a mainstream political party, led to the killing of several protesters by the West Bengal police. Ironically, the police action was ordered by the ruling Left Front government in West Bengal, which had signed an agreement with industries and business houses to create the SEZs. See "Six Killed over SEZ Land Acquisition in W. Bengal, 8th January 2007," *The Hitavada,* January 8, 2007, 1, 5; and "Nandigrammed," *Outlook,* February 19, 2007, 20. For details on the SEZ, see Jona Aravind Dohrmann, "Special Economic Zones in India—An Introduction," *ASIEN* 106 (January 2008): S60–80, http://www.asienkunde.de/articles/a106_asien_aktuell_dohrmann.pdf. See also Amitendu Palit, "Growth of Special Economic Zones (SEZs) in India: Issues and Perspectives," *Journal of Infrastructure Development* 1, no. 2 (December 2009): 133–152.

32. A draft land acquisition bill had been presented to the Lok Sabha in 2007 but saw no further movement for the next four years largely because of the controversy surrounding it. Many politicians—ministers and political leaders—were making huge sums of money from the current system. They had no interest in changing that state of affairs, but the Anna Hazare stir forced them to table a bill on land acquisition. The UPA II tabled a revised bill that removed several defects of the 2007 draft and, more importantly, provided a share of the benefits from the future produce of the land to those who had lost land and were without livelihoods as a result of its sale.

33. "Wal-Mart to Enter Indian Market," BBC News, November 27, 2006, http://news.bbc.co.uk/2/hi/6186930.stm; "TESCO Plans Faster Expansion Than Wal-Mart in India," *Business Standard,* August 16, 2008, http://www.business-standard.com/india/news/tesco-plans-faster-expansion-than-wal-mart-in-india/331536/.

34. Prime Minister Manmohan Singh spelled out the advantages of the nuclear deal in which access to dual-use technology figured prominently and suggested that if the agreement required tweaking India's policies with Iran, to which the US objected, that was something India might have to consider as long as it did not compromise the goal of strategic independence. Author's interview with Prime Minister Manmohan Singh, January 2006, New Delhi.

35. "Don't Go Ahead with Nuclear Deal: CPI(M)," *The Hindu,* August 19, 2007, http://www.hindu.com/2007/08/19/stories/2007081961920100.htm.

36. Ajay Vaishnav, "Counterview: India Growth Story Is Over," *Times of India*, May 1, 2012, http://articles.timesofindia.indiatimes.com/2012-05 -01/edit-page/31526665_1_india-growth-story-indian-economy-fiscal -deficit.

37. "Ruchir Sharma's New Book Gives India a 50:50 Chance to Emerge as a Breakout Nation," *Times of India,* May 1, 2012, http://articles.timesof india.indiatimes.com/2012-05-01/edit-page/31526665_1_india-growth -story-indian-economy-fiscal-deficit.

38. Ibid.

39. Ibid.

40. Ibid.

41. Tyler Cowen, "Never Mind Europe: Worry About India," *New York Times,* May 5, 2012.

42. Although the nature of the state as it has evolved since the early 1990s is important to the debate about India's power potential, it has not been the focus of inquiry here. Instead, this volume seeks to detail the changes wrought through a succession of coalitions that were compelled to act within the limits of formidable domestic and international constraints. It tells us what the coalition governments could and could not do. The larger question about the changed nature of the postreform Indian state is beyond the scope of this investigation.

43. Numbers are calculated at 1998–1999 prices.

44. These figures are cited in E. Sridharan's study of sectoral mobility among India's growing middle classes. See his "The Growth and Sectoral Composition of India's Middle Class: Its Impact on the Politics of Economic Liberalization," *India Review* 3, no. 4 (October 2004): 405–428. Leela Fernandes, *India's New Middle Classes: Democratic Politics in an Era of Reform* (Minneapolis: University of Minnesota Press, 2006), offers a useful discussion on the politics of the middle classes based on fieldwork in 2003.

45. The National Center for Applied Economic Research, India Market Demographics Report, New Delhi, 2003, No. 2002, Table A6.21.

46. Union Budget speech by Minister of Finance P. Chidambaram, 2008, http://indiabudget.nic.in/ub2008-09/bs/speecha.htm.

47. The center demands utilization certificates from the states. See budget speeches in *Union Budget and Economic Survey* (New Delhi: Ministry of Finance, Government of India, various years), http://indiabudget .nic.in/.

48. In December 2009, former chief economic adviser to the prime minister Professor S. D. Tendulkar submitted the "Report of the Expert Group to Review the Methodology for Estimation of Poverty," bringing the whole controversy into focus once again. He noted that the existing all-India rural and urban official poverty lines were originally defined in terms of per capita total consumer expenditure at 1973–1974 market prices and adjusted over time and across states for changes in prices, while keeping unchanged

the original 1973–1974 underlying rural and urban all-India reference poverty-line baskets (PLBs) of goods and services. These all-India rural and urban PLBs were derived for rural and urban areas separately, anchored in the per capita calorie norms of 2,400 (rural) and 2,100 (urban) per day. They, however, covered the consumption of all the goods and services incorporated in the rural and urban reference PLBs. Tendulkar finds that in 2004–2005, 37 percent of the Indian population was living below the poverty line. This figure is significantly higher than the figure given by the Planning Commission, according to which 27.5 percent were living below the poverty line. Tendulkar's figure is "higher largely because of the larger basket of consumption, which includes expenditure on education and health by the poor." The Tendulkar report recommends that the Planning Commission and the National Sample Survey Organisation (NSSO) should make suitable changes in their approach to defining the poverty line. Interestingly, the NSSO, which undertakes sample surveys of consumer spending, estimated people living below poverty line to be only 28.3 percent in 2004–2005. In contrast to this figure, "the Arjun Sen Gupta Committee constituted by the government for the unorganized sector in the country revealed that more than 77 percent of people are forced to live on INR 20 [less than $2] or less per day, which is insufficient even for the minimum requirement of one person's food, health, shelter and clothing. One may say that more than 77 per cent of people in the country cannot meet their basic needs." See Ashwani Mahajan, "Dilemma of the Poverty Line," Shvoong.com, January 1, 2010, http://www.shvoong.com/business-management /1960075-dilemma-poverty -line/.

49. Left-leaning commentators such as Prabhat Patnaik would believe that the liberalization and opening of India to international capital have caused it to develop in a direction that excludes the poor and petty producers who created livelihoods for millions in rural India. Based on his presentation at the Plenary, South Asia Conference, New York University, New York, New York, February 16, 2013.

50. James Lamont, "Infrastructure Deficit Chokes India," Rediff India Abroad, March 18, 2009, http://www.rediff.com/money/2009/mar/18ft -infrastructure-deficit-chokes-india.htm, reports that "the Indian government has identified the need for $500bn (385bn, 357bn) in infrastructure spending between 2007 and 2012."

51. In 2010, India already had two years of fiscal deficit exceeding 10 percent of the GDP, and not all of it was on account of the fiscal stimulus. The government's debt waiver scheme for farmers, the Sixth Pay Commission awards, and fuel and fertilizer subsidies are some of the reasons behind India's ever rising fiscal deficit. See "Fiscal Deficit a Party Spoiler?" *Economic Times,* February 11, 2010, http://economictimes.india times.com/news/economy/policy/Fiscal-deficit-A-party-spoiler/article show/5558493.cms. However, as India heads into 2014, its fiscal deficit is expected to come down to 4.89 percent or even 3.7 percent according to several reports in news and media; see "FY 13 Fiscal Deficit," *Economic*

Times, October 9, 2013, http://economictimes.indiatimes.com/fullcoverage
/fy-13-fiscal-deficit.

52. Anoop Singh, "Policy Environment and Regulatory Reforms for Private and Foreign Investment in Developing Countries: A Case of the Indian Power Sector," Research Policy Discussion Paper No. 64 (Asian Development Bank, Manila, Philippines, April 2007), Tables 12 and 13, http://202.4.7.101/files/dp64.policy.environment.power.sector.pdf.

5

India in
World Politics

Unlike domestic policies, which often alter with changes in government, foreign policy usually displays a much higher degree of continuity. This has been true of most countries, and India is no exception. Since independence, two broad themes have guided India's foreign policy: awareness of itself as a great country with much to contribute to the shaping of the postwar world and an unflinching determination to retain strategic autonomy.[1]

India's perception of its rightful place in the world stems from the continuity and depth of its civilization. Colonial subjugation, however, taught India that these characteristics did not translate automatically into military power. It therefore sought to establish a position for itself by assiduously propagating the strengthening of international institutions and the rule of law.

If we filter these goals through Eric Ringman's frame, we need in this chapter to ask these three questions. First, did India's successive leaders develop a vision for realizing these goals that would enable concrete, effective domestic and foreign policies? Second, did they back these policies by creating appropriate instruments of diplomacy, entering alliances, and creating a base of military power to support them? Third, did they display an ability to learn from their experiences as they experimented with methods of exerting influence? An answer to all three is in the affirmative, although there were occasions when critics accused the leadership of having missed

137

opportunities or having failed to interpret the intensity of threat correctly. In practice, these aspirations were constrained by India's economic underdevelopment and the turbulence in its immediate neighborhood. This was a product of the vivisection of what had historically been a single economic and cultural space into five separate countries and regions, which left the subcontinent with truncated economic relations and cross-border ethnic divisions that became fertile sources of conflict. These three constraints and New Delhi's aspirations to great-power status set the stage for the evolution of foreign policy. These constraints unfolded differently as India shaped its response to the United States and China and to developments in South and Southeast Asia. This chapter and the next discuss key arenas of India's changing foreign and security policy.

The interplay of aspirations and constraints led to shifts of emphasis between the goals and strategies of foreign policy. We can break these shifts into five different periods:

1947–1962: a period of principled internationalism combined with assertive nonalignment. This began with independence and lasted until the Sino-Indian border war in the Himalayas in October 1962.

1962–1971: a period of regional conflict and passive nonalignment. These years were dominated by regional preoccupations, principally two wars with Pakistan, the first in 1965 and the next in 1971. The second of these led to India's victory and the dismemberment of Pakistan with Bangladesh's secession. But domestic challenges from ethnic separatists prevented India from capitalizing on its victory. In fact, India was gradually marginalized within the nonaligned movement.

1971–1990: a period of defensive regional dominance and international retreat. The Bangladesh war established India's position as the dominant military power in South Asia. But India played no role in the events that led to the end of the Cold War.

1990–1998: a period of searching for a new foreign policy. India was adjusting to the end of the Cold War, reconfiguring the economy, and coping with the end of the political system dominated by the Congress Party.

1998–present: a period of return to a calibrated internationalism via strategic alignment with the United States.

Throughout these five periods (the first three of which are combined in the subsequent discussion), successive governments in India made adjustments to its foreign policy that were required by changes in the regional and international environments and did so without losing sight of the basic goals of strategic autonomy and international recognition. The end of Congress Party dominance in 1989 was therefore not accompanied immediately by any new departures in foreign or defense policy. But this significant break with the past in domestic politics did make it easier for India to adapt to the end of the Cold War and, after a short hiatus, to take advantage of the country's growing economic strength.

Congress Party Dominance: The First Three Phases, 1947–1990

Continuity in shaping foreign policy was evident even when the leaders of independent India took over from the British colonial authorities in 1947.[2] India's first prime minister, Jawaharlal Nehru, built on the British perceptions of India as a key to power in the region and as a gateway to the East. He was aware of India's military weakness and economic backwardness and the pressing need to concentrate on social and political consolidation in the aftermath of the partition. Even though India's weakness and vulnerability required him to design a policy that would be defensive, he did not hesitate to claim a voice for India in world forums consonant with its great size and ancient civilization.[3]

To generate power for the nation in the arena of world politics,[4] Nehru's government upheld and acted on behalf of international law to buttress collective security. India sent its troops to participate in several UN peacekeeping operations stretching from Egypt to Congo. Its presence pretty much saved Congo from descending into absolute chaos and bought the international community time to craft a response to the imminent disintegration of political order there. Although Nehru was very cautious and guarded India's sovereignty jealously, he was also anxious to advance India's cause by participating in the establishment of successful precedents, procedures, and instruments for maintaining order in the world. In Nehru's view, these precedents added up to real power in the international arena.

The doctrine of nonalignment sought to reconcile the gap between India's hard and its soft power. India would not join in the military and ideological rivalry that was dividing the world into two camps. Instead, India would attend to political and territorial consolidation first. For Britain, India had been the fulcrum of its political and economic empire, which stretched from the oil fields of Arabia, to Singapore, Malaysia, and Hong Kong. Nehru's nonaligned India rejected the imperial design but asserted the nation's role in maintaining regional peace and stability. Nonalignment was meant to give India international influence by making it the voice of the newly free countries in Asia and Africa.

Nehru's design was, however, frustrated by India's two large neighboring states: Pakistan and China. Not only did Pakistan challenge India's regional claims, but also to counterbalance India's superior size and military advantage, Pakistan turned to the United States and joined the Baghdad Pact (consisting of Iran, Iraq, Pakistan, Turkey, and the United Kingdom, all under a US alliance umbrella) in 1955. (The pact subsequently became the Central Treaty Organization in 1958.[5]) This brought the Cold War into South Asia. China also challenged Nehru's leadership of the nonaligned nations and rejected the boundary between India and Tibet that British cartographers had drawn up in the heyday of imperial power.[6] The two disputes led to indecisive wars with Pakistan (first in 1948 and again in 1965) and an ignominious defeat at the hands of China in 1962 that weakened India's claims to the leadership of the nonaligned movement. Disappointed by the turn of events, Nehru died a broken man in 1964.[7]

The change of leadership from Nehru to Lal Bahadur Shastri (June 1964 to January 1966)—the first change in leadership after independence—should have led to a reconsideration of foreign policy. Although no such thing happened, by the mid-1960s nonalignment had lost its charm.[8] Behind an increasingly empty façade of continuity, India began to redefine its priorities. Alignment with either of the Cold War camps was ruled out for fear that joining a camp would compromise the country's independence and, even more importantly, India's ability to integrate and consolidate its nationhood. This domestic purpose ensured the continuation of India's nonaligned foreign policy through the decade between defeat at China's hands in 1962 and victory over Pakistan in the war for Bangladesh's independence in 1971.

In the eyes of the world, India's defeat in the 1962 war wholly undermined its claim to regional preeminence.[9] By exposing India's military weakness, the war cast doubt on the viability of India's nation-building model. The country therefore ceased to be regarded (even potentially) as an alternative to the communist or the emerging East Asian models of development. This impression of failure was compounded by India's economic woes: two great droughts in succession in 1965 and 1966 revealed the extent to which the nation was unable even to feed itself. In both years, widespread famine was avoided only by the importing of huge quantities of wheat from the United States under the US Public Law (PL) 480 program. By the end of the 1960s, it had become almost normal to refer to India as a "basket case."[10] The sustained humiliation of those years helps to explain Indira Gandhi's determination to build India's military capability and move still further toward economic autarchy.

While the world was preoccupied with the Vietnam War, India was quietly building its military strength, but unlike in the heyday of nonalignment and voluble opposition to military pacts, Gandhi refrained from voicing India's views on every international crisis.[11] New Delhi's continuing criticism of the US war in Vietnam led President Lyndon Johnson to suspend food exports under PL 480, but India felt compelled to defend its views of a war against an Asian country that had been the victim of both colonial occupation and ill-defined imperial ambition.[12] Gandhi's determination to make India self-reliant in the spheres of economy and defense brought it progressively closer to the Soviet Union. The latter was only too willing to meet India's needs because unlike the United States, which expected India to join its military pact, the Soviet Union was happy with a minimal promise that India would keep out of the Western camp.[13] The USSR welcomed India's desire for self-reliant growth and extended long-term economic and military assistance, including colicensing agreements for the production of weapons and equipment. Such military deals with the Soviet Union had the added advantage of technology transfer to India and coproducing agreements meant to make India self-reliant. This involvement further compromised India's policy of nonalignment and weakened it as a shield against external interference, although spirited arguments are still being made that a close relationship with the Soviet Union did not mean alignment and that, in any event, nonalignment did not foreclose India from acting in its own interests.

India's victory in 1971 and the splitting of Pakistan reversed the impotence generated by the 1962 defeat.[14] These events, too, can be traced to the partition of India in 1947 and the creation of an East and a West Pakistan divided by a large swath of Indian territory. Although a largely Bengali-speaking Muslim community populated East Pakistan, it chose to vote on the basis of Islam and join Pakistan. The relationship between the two halves of Pakistan was troubled, however. The East Pakistanis complained that Pakistan regarded their part as a colony to be subjugated to the interest of the Punjabi elites who dominated the western half. Throughout the 1960s, the tensions between East and West Pakistan had steadily increased until a civil war became inevitable, needing only a trigger to break out. That trigger was the overwhelming victory of the Awami League, a political party headed by Shaikh Mujib-ur-Rehman, who represented East Pakistan's nationalist aspirations.

When the Awami League won the majority of seats in the 1970 national elections, West Pakistan elites were confronted with the possibility of submitting to a government formed by the Bengali-speaking majority in East Pakistan. Unable to face the outcome, the Pakistani Army declared the election null and void; rejected the demands for greater autonomy put forward by the Awami League; arrested Awami League leaders, including Mujib and his supporters; and clamped down on rising civilian protests. These actions prompted East Pakistan to declare independence, in response to which West Pakistan's army moved into East Pakistan. When millions of refugees began to flood into West Bengal, India was sucked into the conflict. In fact, anticipating a rapid deterioration to its east, India had started providing military and guerrilla training to a growing number of East Pakistanis (East Pakistani military, paramilitary, and civilian elements) who had constituted themselves in March 1971 into a liberation army called "Mukti Bahini." In response, Pakistan launched a preemptive attack on the western border of India, which started the Indo-Pakistan war of 1971. Having failed in her appeal to Pakistan to release and reinstate Shaikh Mujib, and to the international community to aid in his reinstatement, Prime Minister Indira Gandhi dispatched armed forces on December 3, 1971, to support the uprising.[15] The Indian military operation ended with the surrender of Pakistani forces on December 16.

From India's point of view, the results were spectacular. Bangladesh was formed, and Pakistan was cut down to half its original size. India had captured close to 93,000 Pakistani prisoners of war, which obviously constituted a great bargaining card in any negotiations that were bound to follow. The balance of power in the subcontinent drastically shifted in India's favor. In a fine display of diplomatic finesse, Gandhi secured a promise from the Kremlin to neutralize China if it attempted to move against India in support of its strategic ally Pakistan.[16] Outmaneuvered by India and the Soviet Union, the United States could do little except send a carrier fleet into the Bay of Bengal. Its ostensible purpose was to intimidate India and prevent it from expanding the war to West Pakistan, but India ended the war well before the Seventh Fleet arrived, rendering the whole thing a futile foray.[17] The war did in fact spread to the western front, but it was started by Pakistan Air Force attacks on Indian airfields. There is no substantial evidence to suggest that India had any plans to leverage its military success in the east to attempt an armed takeover of the Pakistani-occupied areas of Kashmir. Pakistan sued for peace, and the war moved to the negotiating table.

The signing of the Indo-Soviet Treaty of Peace, Friendship, and Cooperation in August 1971 revived again charges that India had abandoned nonalignment, although there is still no agreement on whether India did align with the Soviet Union.[18] The treaty did, however, explain the larger international developments to which India was responding. First, there were growing tensions between China and the Soviet Union in Central Asia with the mobilization of tactical nuclear weapons on the Soviet side and with the deployment of more than 3 million troops on the Chinese side, which eventually led to an armed clash in mid-1969. Second, there was a thaw in Sino-American relations in which Pakistan had played a key role. Third, there was a further deepening and widening of Sino-Pakistani relations.

These developments had already begun wheels turning in Moscow and New Delhi toward some sort of military relationship. The Bangladesh war proved to be the catalyst. The treaty allowed the Soviet Union to provide India with detailed high-resolution monitoring of both Pakistani and Chinese military force movements. Most important perhaps was the real-time human and electronic intelligence the Soviet Union supplied to concerned agencies of the Indian government. These frontline surveillance intelligence inputs played a critical role in India's gaining advantage over the Pakistan Army.[19]

The Bangladesh war had three important consequences. First, India became a regional power able to impose its will on countries in

South Asia.[20] Second, helping Bangladesh liberate itself from the clutches of a military dictatorship put India on the right side of democracy and self-determination and mitigated the criticism that it had violated the principle of noninterference in the domestic affairs of a sovereign state. This added a dimension of soft power to India's image. Third, other countries began to reassess India's future role in international politics. The Bangladesh war proved that India was prepared to use force if events in the region jeopardized its national security. New lines had to be drawn and new equations written.

The Quest for Regional Dominance:
The Fourth Phase, 1990–1998

The Bangladesh war inaugurated a new phase of India's foreign and military policy.[21] Under Nehru, India had pursued a globally oriented and largely cooperative foreign policy in an attempt to retain a degree of independence for its own actions. Nehru's approach maintained distance and avoided entanglement in the Cold War by emphasizing diplomacy over force, but under Indira Gandhi the approach changed. India now sought to consolidate and protect its advantage in size and military superiority and lay claims to preeminence in South Asia. Part of this objective was to deny Pakistan's long-standing claims to parity with India. To this end, under Indira Gandhi India sought to structure interstate relations, shape ideology and regime type, and oppose any military presence in South Asia by outside powers. The Bangladesh intervention was a classic example of India's quest to acquire relational control in South Asia. Subsequent years show more disappointment than success on this score, but India's leaders continued to use it as the guiding theme of their foreign policy. The strategy of national integration and territorial unification India had adopted from the very beginning determined the continuity of its foreign policy.

Sri Lanka

In the two decades after the war, India steadily consolidated its credentials as a regional power that would not hesitate to use a variety of diplomatic and coercive means to safeguard its own security and maintain stability in South Asia. In 1983, India provided safe haven and training to Sri Lankan Tamil rebels to exert pressure on the J. R.

Jayewardene government in Colombo to find an acceptable solution to the ethnic crisis in that country and to discourage Sri Lanka from giving extraregional powers a toehold in South Asia. As the civil war escalated, India initially offered to mediate a peace agreement and even succeeded briefly in getting both sides to agree to a power-sharing plan. The agreement, however, fell apart.[22] Subsequently, under Rajiv Gandhi India tried a stick-and-carrot policy to force Velupillai Prabhakaran, leader of the Liberation Tigers of Tamil Eelam (LTTE), to honor a commitment made in 1987 to surrender arms to an Indian peacekeeping force (IPKF) and take part in elections. When this failed, India mounted a military effort to disarm the LTTE.[23] The critical point of both operations—the one in Bangladesh in 1971 and the one in Sri Lanka in 1987—was to demonstrate that India would intervene. It would use military force to support secession or prevent it from happening based on how and to what extent the separatists affected India's political and territorial integrity and kept South Asia free from extraregional interference.

The Maldives

The IPKF operation was not a success. New Delhi's mandate expired the day that Prabhakaran reneged on his agreement to disarm. In the operations that followed, the need to avoid civilian casualties hamstrung India, and little had been accomplished when India pulled out in 1990. In sharp contrast, India's intervention against rebels in the Maldives in 1987 was an unqualified success. In the Maldives, India demonstrated an impressive rapid deployment capacity, arriving in Malé within twelve hours of the LTTE-backed attempted coup against the elected government of Maumoon Abdul Gayoom.[24] A foray so far into the Indian Ocean drew considerable comments from military analysts, who began yet another reappraisal of India's capacity to project power. At about the same time as the Maldives intervention, India signed a secret treaty with Mauritius to protect it from invasion. These interventions were a forerunner to a far more coercive use of economic power against Nepal in 1989.[25]

Nepal

India has had a close and special relationship with Nepal since 1950 when the Nehru government helped King Tribhuvan regain the throne in Kathmandu. The king subsequently signed a trade and transit treaty with India. Indo-Nepalese relations since then have been based on two treaties, which have witnessed many modifications but have for the most part stood the test of time. First was the Treaty of Peace and Friendship, ratified in July 1950, respecting mutual sovereignty, territorial integrity, and independence and granting the same rights to each other's nationals that each gave to its own. The friendship treaty and accompanying letters included the provisions that "neither government shall tolerate any threat to the security of the other by a foreign aggressor" and obligated both sides "to inform each other of any serious friction . . . with any neighbouring state likely to cause any breach in the friendly relations" between India and Nepal.[26] The second was the Treaty of Trade and Commerce, ratified in October 1950, providing Nepal free transit for its commerce through Indian territory and ports. For landlocked Nepal, a friendly India was necessary for access to the rest of the world, which the treaty provided through Calcutta for goods and the Reserve Bank of India for foreign exchange. The Indo-Nepalese border became an open border as India's influence over Nepal increased throughout the 1950s. In 1952, an Indian military mission was established in Nepal. In 1954, a memorandum provided for the joint coordination of foreign policy, and Indian security posts were established in Nepal's northern frontier. These were withdrawn in the late 1960s.

Over the next five decades, however, relations between the two countries gradually soured, sinking to a low point in 1988 when King Birendra, grandson of King Tribhuvan, signed an agreement with Beijing to purchase weapons and gave China a contract to construct a road in its western sector to connect to Nepal. New Delhi saw these moves as a deliberate attempt to violate the intent of the earlier agreements by jeopardizing India's security. India was also annoyed with the high volume of unauthorized trade across Nepal's border and Nepal's imposition of a 55 percent tariff on Indian goods entering Nepal.

In March 1989, when the Treaty of Trade and Commerce came up for renewal, the two countries were unable to agree over the precise terms of transit for Nepalese goods. Instead of extending the old treaty until the differences could be resolved, Rajiv Gandhi put Nepal under a virtual trade embargo by closing all but two transit points into Nepal. The transit embargo created shortages of Indian imports such as transport fuel, salt, cooking oil, food, and other essential commodities. The resulting inflation caused a wave of popular discontent. The hardships endured by the Nepali people during more than a year of embargo acted as a catalyst for the democratic revolution that ended the earlier system of "guided democracy" and replaced it with a liberal variant in 1990.

The Gujral Doctrine

The intervention in Sri Lanka and the regime change in Nepal consolidated India's claim to regional preeminence. While India's leaders saw these as necessary measures to shield India's political and territorial integrity, the rest of the world, particularly small countries in South Asia, saw India as an expansionist hegemon. The truth lay somewhere in between. The two interventions smacked of gunboat diplomacy, but at the time Indian leaders were addressing a multiplicity of ethnic upheavals within the country: in Kashmir, Punjab, and the Northeast. They were convinced that the first two were aided and abetted by Pakistan. They wanted to make sure that new threats would not arise because of the actions of other neighboring states, notably China.

In fact, throughout the post–Cold War period but particularly after 1990, building a network of economic and strategic ties with Southeast Asia became increasingly important both to counter China and to build a platform that would help extend India's presence in Asia. But for this strategy to succeed, it was necessary to change the dynamics of India's troublesome relationship with the smaller states in South Asia. These strategic calculations gave birth to the Gujral Doctrine in 1997, which envisaged unilateral concessions on India's part to build close and friendly ties with Nepal, Bangladesh, Myanmar, and Sri Lanka.

India's domestic compulsion—namely, the need to promote interlocking ethnic peace—propelled its responses to the crises in Bangladesh, Sri Lanka, and Nepal. But in the post-1990 period, these countries became increasingly important as gateways to Southeast Asia, where India planned to build a thick network of economic and trade relations that could eventually host important military ties.

Pakistan

Pakistan remained the only neighboring state in South Asia that actively contested India's quest for relational control in the region.

Indira Gandhi tried to use India's Bangladesh victory to settle the Indo-Pakistani border dispute but failed.[27] According to Indian diplomats present at the 1972 Simla summit, Prime Minister Zulfikar Ali Bhutto had agreed to turn the cease-fire line into a Line of Control (LoC) in Kashmir and eventually into a permanent border, but he later reneged on the promise and denied ever having made it.[28] Despite being halved in size in 1971, Pakistan continued to maintain a military establishment that was capable of taking on the Indian armed forces. It also embarked with a rarely seen single-mindedness on a quest for nuclear weapons capability as a counter to India's own nuclear weapons program. India had exploded a nuclear device in 1974 but had deliberately refrained from turning its capability into a full-fledged weapons program. Pakistan felt no such inhibition. When it announced in 1987—semiofficially—that it had acquired the capacity to build nuclear weapons, it provided India with a reason for resuming its own abandoned weapons program.

India's rise as a regional power was, however, more than offset by its increasing marginalization in world politics. India's utter failure to get its way with Pakistan stemmed, at least in part, from its complete inability to influence the actions of great powers in the region, which was brought home vividly when the Soviet Union invaded Afghanistan in 1979 and turned that country into the latest battleground in the renewed Cold War. The Ronald Reagan administration in the United States immediately decided to support the Afghan mujahidin to entrap the Soviets in a Vietnam-type quagmire. Pakistan's full involvement was critical to this operation. As a result, it was promoted as a US frontline ally in the new Cold War. From 1982 to 1987, the United States provided Pakistan with $3.2 billion in arms and economic assistance and made it a conduit for even more weaponry to the Afghan mujahidin.[29]

As the war escalated, a large number of Afghans, including those who had been waging guerrilla warfare, crossed the border into Pakistan and began to organize stiffer resistance to the Soviet occupation. The US aid was handled entirely by Pakistan's intelligence agencies, which had trained and armed a whole range of guerrilla groups to roll back the Soviet occupation of Afghanistan. The United States provided arms, ammunition, intelligence, and even sophisticated weapons, such as Stinger missiles, which eventually broke the back of any Soviet determination to continue with the conflict. The Soviet Union finally withdrew its troops from Afghanistan in May

1989. But the war was not over. No sooner had the Soviet troops withdrawn than Afghanistan plunged into a bloody civil war that eventually led to the victory in 1997 of the Southern Pashtuns, supported by the Taliban, an organization established with the support and help of Pakistan's Inter-Service Intelligence (ISI) in the refugee camps of Pakistan.

India was deeply disturbed by the emerging new relationship between the United States and Pakistan. In July 1980, Indira Gandhi had sent her foreign minister, Narasimha Rao, to Islamabad to dissuade it from getting embroiled in the Cold War, warning Pakistan's leaders that they were making a commitment over which they would have little or no control, but his warning fell on deaf ears.[30] Three days after he left Islamabad, the United States and Pakistan jointly announced the details of the military-cum-economic package outlined above in what was meant to be a calculated rebuff to India and a reminder of its impotence in the big-power game.

These events were to have far-reaching and dangerous consequences for Afghanistan and Pakistan in the next two decades. The collapse of the April 1992 Peshawar accord among fighting Afghan factions following the Soviet withdrawal was to plunge Afghanistan into a bloody civil war that became a breeding ground for Islamic extremists and chronic tribal warfare. By 1997, the Taliban had finally vanquished all opposition and gained control over most of the country. The three years of Taliban rule, aided and abetted by Pakistan and then al-Qaeda, established a fertile ground for all manner of Islamic extremists. These developments adversely affected India. Traditionally, governments in Kabul had been friendlier to India than to Pakistan. The unraveling of the Afghan state, with Pakistan and the United States in charge of post-Taliban developments, left India out in the cold. With little influence over the events that were to have the most dangerous consequences for its own security, India watched helplessly from the sidelines as Islamic extremists widened the scope of their activities beyond Afghanistan and the United States poured money and arms into Pakistan.[31] Pakistan spent the funds to back the most rabid Islamist groups in Afghanistan, first the Hizb-e-Islami and then the Taliban; to buy weapons that could be used only against India; and to pay China and North Korea for nuclear weapons technology and a credible delivery system.[32] What the United States sowed, it then reaped in blowback in the decades to follow.

Pakistan's new strategic relationship allowed it to harden its stance toward India. The immediate consequence was a more active support of the mini-insurgency in Punjab. Pakistan offered Sikh separatist groups headquarters in Lahore and bases in places such as Faisalabad, where, in close cooperation with the ISI, it picked from among the Sikh youths who were crossing the border to avenge the Indian Army's attack on the Golden Temple in Amritsar.[33] By 1985, the ISI was also giving small-arms training and logistical support to dissidents from the Kashmir valley who had begun crossing the LoC as a consequence of a series of wrongheaded decisions taken by Indira Gandhi in the early months of 1984. These events climaxed in the outbreak of a full-blown uprising in 1989.

Foreign Policy Under Coalition Rule: The Fifth Phase, 1998–Present

When the Congress Party lost the 1989 election and a minority National Front government came to power, India was dangerously isolated. Nepal seethed under a trade embargo; the new president of Sri Lanka, Ranasinghe Premadasa, was determined to make India pull the IPKF out of the country; and Pakistan, having acquired nuclear weapons capability and a formidable arsenal of conventional weapons, was fomenting insurgency in the two most sensitive parts of India.[34] The United States and other Western nations knew what Pakistan was doing but turned a blind eye to its anti-Indian activities, preferring to believe the fiction that Pakistan was supplying only "moral and diplomatic" support to insurgents in the two Indian states. Worst of all, the Soviet Union was dissolving before the world's very eyes. All the elaborate trade and credit arrangements that had existed between it and India were suspended because with the ruble in free fall, no one knew what price to attach to new purchases. This not only disrupted trade but also brought weapons purchases to an abrupt halt. India thus lost its main backer just when it needed that backer most.

And yet within two decades, India had ended its international isolation; developed a comprehensive economic and military relationship with the United States, the sole remaining great power; and signed a nuclear deal that permitted it to become the sixth recognized nuclear nation in the world, albeit with some additional restrictions.

India also had resuscitated its military and diplomatic ties with Russia under Vladimir Putin, even as it diversified its access to the global arms market, deepened its trade and economic cooperation with the European Union, and expanded trade with China.[35] As the world plunged into a new war against stateless enemies, India's enhanced defense capabilities, especially its much stronger navy and acknowledged expertise in low-intensity conflict, gave it a new status in the post–Cold War international order. In this new world India was regarded as a force for stability in a turbulent region wracked by civil wars and Islamic extremism.

How was India able to achieve this turnaround in an era of shifting and initially short-lived coalition governments?

The Search for a Post–Cold War Foreign Policy

The post–Cold War transition falls, conveniently, into two roughly equal parts: the first, from 1989 to 1998, and the second, from 1998 to present. During the first phase, India slowly extricated itself from the mind-set of the Cold War and began to search for a new anchor for its foreign policy. In the second phase, it asserted its growing economic and military power to claim what it felt was its rightful place in the emerging international order.

Extricating itself from its Cold War mentality was no easy task. The United States was determined to consolidate its global hegemony. Throughout most of his presidency, Bill Clinton focused on dealing with China, the Arab-Israeli conflict, and the fallout in Europe of the disintegration of the Soviet empire. India did not figure in his global perspective, except as a country unwilling to sign the US-led Non-Proliferation Treaty (NPT).[36] The withdrawal of Soviet forces from Afghanistan had all but ended US engagement with the subcontinent.

Clinton's advocacy of a new liberal international order threatened India on at least two counts. The first was his aggressive assertion of human rights and insistence that these had to be protected even at the expense of the rights of sovereign states. The second was his willingness to intervene in defense of the rights of minorities, including their right to self-determination. The former, fuelled by India's failure to adhere to the NPT,[37] provided Pakistan with an excuse to criticize India on Kashmir in international venues, while the latter made Clinton's first administration in particular turn a blind eye to Pakistan's arming and giving logistical support to militants in Kashmir. India felt vulnerable because its long-drawn-out process of nation-building through democratic participation was still not complete, especially in areas with cross-border, ethnic minorities.

From 1989 to 1988, India's foreign policy was therefore essentially defensive. It concentrated on warding off criticism of its suppression of the Kashmir insurgency by insisting upon Kashmir's legal status as an integral part of India, emphasizing its ethnic and religious diversity, and characterizing the insurgency as no more than a proxy war by Pakistan. At the same time, India deepened its economic relations with the United States and more generally with the developed market economies, using the lure of its large home market to attract foreign investment to the country. Market-friendly economic reforms had opened the gates of the Indian economy to the industrialized world, and American companies were the first to enter. For the US government to develop a stake in India, however, New Delhi needed to make more far-reaching changes in policy.

A Cautious Course Under the Rao Government

These adjustments began with Prime Minister Narasimha Rao. India had not signed the NPT and was developing a missile technology program, which made marked advances during the Rao period. In 1992, it successfully tested an augmented satellite launch vehicle and a polar satellite launch vehicle. "In 1994, India test fired 'Prithvi' and 'Agni,' two indigenously built ballistic missiles that could carry nuclear warheads. Plans to launch Surface-to-Air Missiles (SAM)."[38] This was in the background of the Clinton administration's efforts to effectively install an international nonproliferation regime through the passage and acceptance of the Comprehensive Test Ban Treaty (CTBT) in September 1996, the Fissile Material Cut-Off Treaty of May 2009, and the Missile Technology Control Regime in April 1987.[39] From the perspective of the nonproliferation regime (NPR) that the Clinton administration hoped to achieve, India's missile technology program was a destabilizing factor in the regional context.[40]

India's opposition to the CTBT in the Conference on Disarmament in the summer of 1996 also went against American interests. The U.S.

viewed India's opposition to the CTBT as an infringement of the non-proliferation regime. Since the NPR was a major focus of U.S. foreign policy during the Clinton presidency, India's missile programme put Indo-U.S. relations under strain during the Rao premiership.[41]

Rao tried to placate the United States by calling off the thirteenth test of the short-range surface-to-surface missile Prithvi and postponing underground nuclear weapons testing, which scientists had been preparing for during the previous eight years.[42] He had been warned that tests would lead to immediate and potentially crippling US economic sanctions on India. (Rao did not do this willingly and asked for a full assessment of India's capacity to withstand the shock of sanctions.) While stopping short of conducting tests, Rao stepped up development of the missile and nuclear weapons program. In a marked turnabout in India's posture, he established full diplomatic relations with Israel in 1993 and voted along with the United States in the Security Council to extend UN sanctions on Iraq in June 1990. He also endorsed a US-backed West Asian peace plan that Palestinian leaders had rejected. Rao was attempting to safeguard India's strategic autonomy, a principle that had guided India since independence, while at the same time adjusting to the new realities of the post–Cold War international order.

These gestures failed to elicit an overt response from the Clinton administration. India remained stubbornly hyphenated with Pakistan. The Clinton administration bore down on Prime Ministers H. D. Deve Gowda and Inder K. Gujral to sign the NPT and the CTBT. In an unguarded moment, President Clinton's assistant secretary of state for South Asia, Robin Raphael, echoed Pakistan's claim that the "instruments of accession," which joined Kashmir to India (and the anchor of India's legal claims on Kashmir), did not reflect the final status of Kashmir.

Yet beneath this surface continuity, Rao's initiatives began to change perceptions about India as an irredentist, potentially unfriendly country, a perception that had persisted since the Cold War. A key moment in this change was Rao's visit to the United States in April 1994. Previsit briefings on India gave Clinton a glimpse of India's unique achievement: using democracy to construct Indian nationhood instead of postponing democracy until the nation had been constructed by other means. In his joint press conference with Rao, Clinton specifically mentioned this and called India's achievement "breathtaking." Not all of it was hyperbole.

Three contemporary developments changed perception. First, in sharp contrast to Russia and Eastern Europe, India did not suffer a decline in gross domestic product after shifting from a planned to a market-guided economy. Beginning in 1993, its growth rate exceeded 7 percent a year and India experienced one of the fastest-growing economies in the world. Second, India was rapidly emerging as a software writing and development center for the American information technology (IT) industry. Not only were India's exports of IT-enabled services to the United States growing at up to 60 percent a year, but also economic links were being formed with some of the most powerful companies in the most important new sector of American industry. This gave birth to a business-cum-political lobby in the United States that favored India for the first time. Indo-US trade and business collaborations edged upward after Rao's economic reforms.

In 1996, the actual FDI [foreign direct investment] inflow to India was US $2383 million, which constituted 21.4 per cent of the FDI approval to India. In 1997, the actual FDI inflow was US $3330 million, and it constituted 21.1 per cent of the total FDI approval to India. It must be mentioned in this context that in 1995, the actual FDI inflow into India was only 18.7 per cent of the total FDI approvals. Most of the FDI to India came from the US during this period.[43]

Third, the Indian American community—the Indian diaspora—in America was on the rise. By 1991, Indian-born scientists had become the backbone of the IT revolution being hatched in Silicon Valley. By the mid-1990s, they formed the core staff in universities ranging from MIT to Carnegie-Mellon and companies ranging from Intel to Texas Instruments. Sabeer Bhatia, an Indian, developed Hotmail; another, Vinod Khosla, was the cofounder of Sun Microsystems and partner at Kleiner Perkins. The list of successes was long and growing.[44] By the end of the 1990s, the Indian diaspora had been recognized in the United States for its invaluable contribution to America's progress and prosperity. An unequivocal indication of the change was Robin Raphael's statement before the US Senate in November 1994 that the UN resolutions of 1948 were no longer a viable basis for the solution of the Kashmir problem because too much water had flowed under the bridge since then.[45] Nevertheless, the Clinton administration had not given India the most-favored-nation status that it had conferred on China (at this point Indo-US trade was small).

The Janata-Led Coalitions: An Uncertain International Focus

The later years of the Clinton administration were marked by a definite turn for the better in Indo-US relations, partly because the CTBT was bogged down in the US Congress and opposition to it from within the United States put it on the back burner in foreign policy. This had a salutary effect on Indo-US relations. Beginning in April 1997 when Gujral assumed the prime ministership, India and the United States signed several important memorandums of understanding and exchanged visits of high-level officials and leaders. Undersecretary of State Thomas Pickering and Foreign Secretary K. Raghunath signed the Agreement to Combat Terrorism in New Delhi, which preceded the 9/11 events and signaled growing concern about terrorist activities. Although India was eagerly pursuing close ties with the United States, it adhered to principles vital to its national security: Indian advances in nuclear weapons and missile technology continued unaffected, India still refused to sign the CTBT, and relations with Pakistan remained tied to the latter's willingness to rein in jihadi infiltration into Indian Kashmir.[46]

The most important contribution of the Janata-led governments was the introduction of the Gujral Doctrine as a guideline for relations with smaller neighboring states: Bangladesh, Bhutan, the Maldives, Nepal, and Sri Lanka. At the time, India did not have the economic surpluses to give full scope to this new doctrine. The logic behind it was to build nonreciprocal friendly relations in which India would not seek a quid pro quo for every concession it made. Instead, as the largest and most powerful country in the region, India would extend unilateral concessions to build confidence and mutual goodwill. The aim was to gather the smaller South Asian states to its side and to make it more difficult for China and Pakistan to play in troubled waters. This was a major departure from the more hardheaded, realpolitik approach employed by Indira and Rajiv Gandhi.

Under the new approach, India made a generous agreement with Bangladesh on sharing of the Ganga waters, suspended a border dispute with China to pursue instead confidence-building measures, and opened up diplomacy with Pakistan to increase cultural and people-to-people contacts. In signing the water agreement, the Indian government dispensed with complex calculations and measurements in favor of a formulation that was simple and easy to implement and monitor. India agreed to remove tariff and nontariff barriers in trade with Bangladesh, which is widely acknowledged to have contributed to gainful employment in that country. A less widely known contribution of the Gujral Doctrine was the consolidation of India's "look east" policy, which had been initiated while Rao was in office. During the Janata coalition, particularly under the guidance of Gujral, India became a dialogue partner in the Association of Southeast Asian Nations (ASEAN) and a member of the ASEAN Regional Forum.

The NDA's Vision of a Muscular India

The second phase in the development of India's foreign policy began in 1998. Three events ushered in a new era in Indo-US relations. The first was the Pokharan test of nuclear weapons, the second was Atal Bihari Vajpayee's visit to Lahore in February 1999, and the third the Kargil war of May 1999.

On May 11 and 13, 1998, India carried out five underground nuclear tests in the Rajasthan desert. Two weeks later, on May 28, Pakistan carried out six nuclear tests in the Ras Koh Hills of the Chagai District of Baluchistan. The United States responded right away by imposing economic sanctions on both countries. The sanctions, which resulted in an immediate suspension of bilateral and multilateral foreign aid, brought the Pakistani economy to its knees within weeks because the country had been running on borrowed time, using new loans to pay off old ones.[47] In contrast, the sanctions had little impact on India's economy, and it soon became evident that the India of 1998 was not the India of 1975 or earlier. On April 1, 1998, India's foreign exchange reserves amounted to $116 billion, sufficient to cover a year's imports. Two years later, despite UN sanctions, they had risen to $155 billion. India was therefore able to brush off the effects of the sanctions with only a few minor changes in domestic economic policies. Within months of the imposition of sanctions, the Clinton administration came to the conclusion that the nuclear genie was out of the bottle and sanctions would be ineffective, which led to a security dialogue at the highest level with India.[48]

Given that it had failed to prevent India and Pakistan from acquiring nuclear weapons, the United States acted to prevent the conflict in Kashmir from escalating into a nuclear war. This led to Indo-US talks whose immediate purpose was to ascertain India's intentions and forestall a nuclear arms race with Pakistan. The result was the most intensive dialogue on nuclear and security concerns that the United States had ever held with India. Deputy Secretary of State Strobe Talbott and Minister of External Affairs Jaswant Singh met fourteen times in seven different countries over a two-year period to discuss how to bring New Delhi's new nuclear status in line with Washington's arms control and nonproliferation goals. Even though the United States failed to achieve this immediate objective, the two officials soon engaged in broader discussions on the entire scope of Indo-US relations.[49] Insights gained during these talks were the most probable reason for the stand that the United States took and the role it played in defusing the 1999 Kargil crisis. It also laid the groundwork for Clinton's landmark visit to India in 2000.

Vajpayee's decision to get onto the first passenger bus to cross the border between India and Pakistan and to meet Prime Minister Nawaz Sharif in Lahore took the Pakistani government by surprise. But it reassured the world that even a hard-line Hindu nationalist government was capable of making a sincere overture for peace in a supercharged atmosphere. Washington saw the Lahore visit as a sincere offer on India's part to build confidence and begin a serious discussion to resolve the Indo-Pakistani dispute. Thus, when Clinton learned that Pakistan had not reciprocated India's gesture but instead had even then been planning a military operation in Kashmir, he was convinced that the time for equating Pakistan with India in American policy had passed.[50]

There were other reasons that Clinton might have drawn closer to India. After India's nuclear tests, the United States made all possible efforts to stop Pakistan from going nuclear. These attempts failed, causing much embarrassment to the administration. Of greater significance, perhaps, was Pakistan's support for the Taliban regime in Afghanistan, which had extended a safe haven to Osama bin Laden, whose al-Qaeda cells had already bombed US embassies in Kenya and Tanzania. Pakistan was also one of the three countries that had recognized the Taliban regime in Afghanistan. The differences between Pakistan and the United States became evident when Washington launched a missile attack targeting bin Laden. The attack violated Pakistani airspace, but the administration ordered it without informing or consulting Pakistan. Furthermore, a military coup by Pervez Musharraf in 1999 did not endear Pakistan to the Clinton administration.

The outbreak of the Kargil war also helped change the direction of Indo-US ties. Washington's changing perceptions were to no small degree responsible for the US response to the crisis. Clinton's extraordinary pressure on Pakistan played a key role in keeping the conflict localized to Kargil. He insisted on Pakistan's full withdrawal from Kargil and warned Prime Minister Sharif that the United States would pin the blame for the war on Pakistan if he did not agree. Sharif withdrew, and the crisis ended in vindication of India's position in Kashmir, reinforced the LoC as an inviolable boundary, and created considerable warmth and convergence in Indo-US relations.[51]

These events marked a turning point in Indo-US ties, which were cemented when President Clinton visited India in March 2000. In a joint statement with Vajpayee, he pledged to "deepen the Indian-American partnership in tangible ways." Clinton's stop for a few hours in Pakistan contrasted with his longer, highly publicized sojourn in India. Vajpayee returned the visit later in 2000 and addressed a joint session of Congress. The two leaders issued a second joint statement, this one agreeing to cooperation on arms control, terrorism, and HIV/AIDS. Throughout the visit, however, the Indian prime minister stressed India's fast-growing economy and the business opportunities India offered to the American corporate sector.

A Return to Internationalism: The UPA's Vision for a Great India

Burgeoning strategic ties between India and Washington had to wait another seven years before making the next qualitative leap. This occurred in 2008 when the two countries finalized and signed the Indo-US civil nuclear agreement. Most observers ascribed President George W. Bush's readiness to allow India into the nuclear club to his vision of a US-dominated Eurasia that could effectively meet the challenges of China's meteoric rise and of Islamic radicalism. In reality, however, the agreement was the culmination of a continual upgrading of relations since the days of the Clinton administration.

Three aspects of Bush administration policy facilitated the transformation. The first was the dominance in the Bush administration of neoconservatives who were believed to be close to the American pro-Israeli lobby or to the Israeli government and who viewed the development of Indo-Israeli relations with obvious approval. The second, and even more important, was the administration's decision to seize the moment and consolidate US dominance in the world as its sole superpower. Two threats to this dominance were the rise of China and the rise of Islamist terrorism. India appeared the ideal counterpoise to these threats, being a natural rival to China and counting among its citizens 150 million Muslims who participated in little or no terrorism. Key to both these achievements was the success of India's participatory democracy. As a result, when President Bush found himself leaning more and more heavily on his championship of democracy to justify US interventions in Afghanistan and Iraq, India became the cynosure he wanted the world to emulate.[52]

The al-Qaeda attacks on the World Trade Center towers in New York City and the Pentagon in DC on September 11, 2001, brought about a dramatic new change in Indo-US ties and propelled the South Asian subcontinent to the center of Bush's war on terrorism. Pakistan, Afghanistan, and India became inextricably intertwined in the new US strategy, but each state played a different role. Taliban-ruled Afghanistan became the target of America's war against al-Qaeda. Although Pakistan had aided and abetted the rise of the Taliban, its cooperation was critical to the US war in Afghanistan and to operations against bin Laden, but in the long run the prize in South Asia was India, with its enduring democracy, rapidly expanding economy, and impressive arsenal of conventional and nuclear capabilities. From the Bush perspective, strong and comprehensive Indo-US ties would form a protective shield for US interests in the region.

India condemned the attacks on the World Trade Center and took the immediate and unprecedented step of offering the United States its full cooperation and use of its bases for counterterrorism operations.[53] The United States took the Vajpayee government's help and support when it launched Operation Enduring Freedom to depose the Taliban in Afghanistan. The Indian Navy escorted high-value US ships carrying oil and other precious cargo through the Straits of Malacca, and US naval ships used Indian ports for rest and refueling. Access to Indian ports and logistical support greatly eased the strain on American naval forces conducting transoceanic operations. India also permitted the US Air Force to fly over Indian airspace and offered refueling facilities. The United States worked with India, Russia, and Iran in concert to support the anti-Taliban Northern Alliance. New Delhi supplied the Northern Alliance with military equipment, advisers, and helicopter technicians.[54] India's unhesitating support of the United States galvanized US-Indian military ties.

During a November 2001 Bush and Vajpayee meeting, both leaders pledged to build comprehensive ties of cooperation in a wide range of fields, including regional security, space and scientific research, civilian nuclear safety, and the economy. Joint exercises between the army, navy, and air forces of the two countries became a routine activity after 9/11, as did meetings of the Indo-US Defense Policy Group, which had lapsed following India's nuclear tests.

In late 2001, President Bush lifted the remaining economic sanctions on India, making no reference to the CTBT. The Bush administration, which had taken a pragmatic approach to nonproliferation, certainly had no desire to sacrifice a strategic partnership with India at the altar of the NPT.[55] There was also far greater sympathy for the Vajpayee government's repeated complaints about externally sponsored terrorism. The United States banned terrorist groups such as the Lashkar-e-Toiba and condemned the pro-Pakistan leader Dawood Ibrahim for masterminding the 1992 Mumbai attacks. In the 2002 "National Security Strategy" report, the Bush administration called for a "transformation in its bilateral relationship with India based on a conviction that its interests require a strong relationship with India"[56]

America's need for Pakistani cooperation, however, became increasingly evident as the United States became involved in prosecuting the war on terrorism in Afghanistan. As US dependence on Pakistan increased, so did the Bush administration's reluctance to fully endorse India's stance on terrorism and criticism of Pakistan. The administration sought to delink Indo-US ties from the war on terrorism in Afghanistan and from US relations with Pakistan.

In 2004, India and the United States announced the Next Steps in Strategic Partnership (NSSP) between the two countries. Under the NSSP, the National Democratic Alliance (NDA) government of Vajpayee and the Bush administration agreed to expand cooperation in three specific areas: civilian nuclear activities, civilian space programs, and high-technology trade. In addition, the two countries agreed to expand their dialogue on missile defense. These areas of cooperation were designed to go forward in a series of reciprocal endeavors, including a joint implementation group, under the NSSP, to address proliferation concerns and ensure compliance with US export controls. Washington made modifications to American export licensing policies that would encourage cooperation in commercial space programs and permit exports to power plants at safeguarded nuclear facilities. India agreed to compromise its strategic autonomy by submitting its nuclear program to external supervision and verification.

Bush administration officials had privately argued that strong security ties with a militarily powerful India could counterbalance China in Asia. There was no official statement suggesting such a link, but there was growing evidence that many in the Bush administration thought that the United States should hedge its bets by backing India while at the same time cultivating friendly ties with China. India was invited to join the United States, Australia, Japan, and Singapore in joint naval exercises held in the Bay of Bengal between September 4 and 7, 2007, to coordinate efforts to prevent piracy and terrorism and provide safe passage to high-value ships from the Far East to the Persian Gulf and beyond. Manmohan Singh's United Progressive Alliance (UPA) government readily complied. China, which had held similar exercises with Russia and Central Asian oil-rich countries in the Shanghai Cooperation Organization, could not have failed to comprehend the implications of its exclusion.[57] Given India's friendly relationship with Russia and the Central Asian countries, it was unlikely that India would have taken an obviously hostile stance toward any of the above, but as far as China was concerned, India and the United States were not averse to curbing and containing its influence in Asia. The Bush administration was issuing a subtle warning to Beijing not to overreach its military capabilities, and the UPA government for its part was not averse to exhibiting India's newly acquired military power. Neither Washington nor New Delhi, however, wished to openly anger Beijing or scuttle the expanding trade relationships they had developed in the post–Cold War period.

In July 2005, Prime Minister Manmohan Singh paid a landmark visit to Washington, where the early contours of the nuclear deal were hammered out. In March of the following year, President Bush visited India and declared that the United States would develop a strong "global partnership" with India and "help India become a major world power in the 21st century." President Bush's 2002 "National Security Strategy" stated that a strong relationship with India was in the interest of the United States. A 2006 report to the US Congress underscored that "India now is poised to shoulder global obligations in cooperation with the United States in a way befitting a major power."[58]

Faith in New Delhi's rising capability and importance to US global objectives was reflected in the determination with which the administration pursued the nuclear deal with India. Critics of the deal argued that the potential benefits of nuclear energy to the environment were grossly exaggerated and the dangers of turning the Indo-Pakistani conflict into a nuclear one remained high. Such a conflict would damage US security interests, not to mention the global nonproliferation regime to which the United States had been committed since the 1960s. Proponents of the deal, in contrast, pointed to the business contracts and jobs the deal would generate. The US Chamber of Commerce estimated that the deal could produce close to $100 billion in contracts and 27,000 jobs. The Bush administration for its part argued that the deal would assure India that Washington was a dependable ally. In turn, the United States would gain a rising economic and military power as a permanent ally in Asia.

The Singh government could not deliver on the deal, although the framework agreement for it was provisionally signed in July 2005. For two years, Singh's Left Front partners held up the deal, charging him with succumbing to American pressure and compromising India's independence and security. In October 2008, the Indian government formally approved the deal, commonly called the 123 Agreement, assuring India help in developing a strategic reserve of nuclear fuel and fuel for its civilian sector.[59] In early 2008, Minister of External Affairs Pranabh Mukherjee reassured the Indian Parliament of his government's view that the 2006 Hyde Act, which imposed restrictions on India's strategic nuclear program, had internal relevance only for the United States and that only the provisions of the 123 Agreement would be binding upon New Delhi. Assistant Secretary of State Richard Boucher echoed this distinction during his visit to New Delhi at that time.[60]

True to its word, the Bush administration urged the Nuclear Suppliers Group (NSG) to make an exception in favor of India, and after considerable resistance the NSG finally agreed in 2005 to grant India a waiver from existing rules that members sign the Nuclear Nonproliferation Treaty, which was a precondition for membership in the NSG.[61] The United States had gone out of the way to get India to become a member of this exclusive club of countries. In the view of most observers, with the conclusion of the nuclear deal, India had become the sixth de facto nuclear weapons state.[62]

The elements that had persuaded President Clinton to seriously reassess India had only strengthened during the next ten years. The Indian economy was strong, and immigrants of Indian origin had expanded their reach and influence. In fact, the "India caucus" was the largest country-specific caucus in the US Congress. The well-organized lobbying efforts of the Indian American community, which had grown to 2.5 million, played a huge role in the passage of the nuclear deal.

Within a decade and a half of the economic reforms and the end of the Cold War, coalition governments in India had settled on a new direction for foreign policy that was not only more openly pragmatic, as evidenced in closer ties to Israel, a businesslike relationship with China, and strategic and defense-related ties with the United States, but also more assertive. In South Asia, India's more pragmatic stance persuaded Nepal to include Maoists in its government in a reconciliation process (based on a 2005 twelve-point agreement to bring the Maoists into Nepal's political mainstream) that ended the civil war there. Instability and suspicion of India undermined the relationship with Nepal, but the Singh government supported political parties in Nepal that were likely to favor India over China. And since Myanmar's transition to a democracy, New Delhi has made a volta-face to reinstate its traditional support for the democracy movement.

Myanmar is critical to India for at least three reasons: the country is rich in gas and mineral resources, it has developed close economic ties with China, and Myanmar has been used as a sanctuary by Naga and Mizo separatists to wage a war against India. This consideration persuaded Prime Minister Singh to develop the Northeast Region Vision 2020, which seeks to integrate India's Northeast region (it adjoins Bangladesh and Myanmar) with robust infrastructure development and eventually to connect it to India's look east policy and growing trade with the ASEAN countries.

In the second term of Manmohan Singh's government (2009 to the present), India's ties with Bangladesh have progressed to building road and rail projects that will create a transit corridor to facilitate trade with Bangladesh and beyond, an agreement to allow India the use of the Chittagong and Mongla seaports, and an exchange of 115 Indian enclaves in Bangladesh for 51 Bangladeshi enclaves in India. In this swap India will lose close to 10,000 acres of land but it will gain in building trust and trade connectivity with Bangladesh, which will help in controlling India's strife-ridden Northeast. Currently, Indo-Bangladeshi trade in 2012 was close to $524 million, up from $309 million in 2011.[63] Private-sector investment in Bangladesh is growing rapidly. Under the two UPA terms, India began to implement the Gujral Doctrine with greater vigor. Much the same was true with the look east policy initiated a few years previously.

The UPA's assertiveness came from a growing confidence in India's economic growth and ability to compete in world markets and in the efficacy of a host of economic and trade agreements with countries in Southeast Asia, Africa, and the Middle East. While terrorism, Kashmir, and China's growing encroachment in South Asia continued to occupy India's leaders, the nation's approach to Pakistan moved beyond bilateral calculations to include regions of Central Asia. Expanding military capabilities and acquisition of new weapons fuelled, to a large extent, India's aspirations to extend its influence beyond the immediate neighborhood.

Assessing Post–Cold War Changes

Despite some initial confusion and an erratic foreign policy course, coalition governments from V. P. Singh to Manmohan Singh oriented Indian diplomacy to include economic imperatives and trade and investment considerations and took India successfully through a rapidly changing and increasingly dangerous regional environment. It evolved a vision that matched new post–Cold War developments: the collapse of the Soviet Union and the emergence of the United States as the sole great power, the rise of China as an economic and military rival, the rise of Islamic radicalism and wars in Iraq and Afghanistan, the growth of competition for energy and natural resources, and, finally, the danger of links between homegrown and Pakistan-based terrorist attacks on India. Responding to those challenges, India entered into strategic cooperation with the United States and Israel, constructed a network of trade and security ties with several East Asian and Central Asian states, maintained watchful but friendly ties with China, and repeatedly attempted to open a meaningful dialogue with Pakistan.

In an attempt to gain greater control over the changing political environment in Asia, India entered into a whole range of trade and economic ties that have progressively assumed significant security dimensions. It institutionalized these ties with bilateral and multilateral arrangements and pacts. Its relations with Bangladesh, Myanmar,

Thailand, Malaysia, and Singapore, not to mention Vietnam, point to its growing presence in the region. These new initiatives underline India's success in creating an institutional base for its postreform, post–Cold War foreign policy. India's decision to acquire nuclear weapons, forge close ties with the United States, and win US support in a bid to gain a seat in the Security Council point to a convergence of vision, power, and policy. A 2011 Indo-Afghan agreement is a particularly telling instance of India's attempt to project influence beyond South Asia. India not only forged close ties with Afghanistan but sponsored Afghan entry into the South Asian Association for Regional Cooperation with the objective of easing trade with Central Asia and gaining leverage over the region as the United States prepared to withdraw from Afghanistan. Although these initiatives point to enormous changes in India's foreign policy, the path to advancing status and interest was anything but smooth.

New Delhi was frequently forced to resolve conflicting interests and reorder priorities. For example, ties with Iran ran afoul of closer strategic relations with Washington. New Delhi's Pakistan policy frequently conflicted with Washington's "Af-Pak" policy, which has regarded Pakistan and Afghanistan as a single theater for its military and diplomatic operations, but Indian diplomacy did not permit those disagreements to jeopardize relations with the United States. At the same time, India persevered in its dialogue with Pakistan, even though repeated terrorist attacks sent relations into a deep freeze for periods of time. Even though caution and pragmatism characterized post–Cold War policy, India did not hesitate to defend the homeland, meet challenges to its regional dominance, and continue to pursue its quest for influence and recognition. The first was evident in its determined waging of the Kargil war and mobilization of troops along the India-Pakistan border in response to 2002 terrorist attacks on Parliament. India's quest for equality with the other major powers was reflected by the way in which it projected its nuclear capability. It conducted tests knowing full well that it would be subject to sanctions and condemnation by Washington and Beijing. Its success in securing a nuclear agreement with the United States was another triumph for Indian diplomacy. What remained to be seen was whether it had gained enough international influence and military capability to extend these beyond its immediate neighborhood. It is to this question that we turn next.

Notes

1. For broad assessment of India's foreign policy, see Sumit Ganguly, *India's Foreign Policy: Retrospect and Prospect* (New York: Oxford University Press, 2012); Sumit Ganguly and Rahul Mukherji, *India Since 1980* (New York: Cambridge University Press, 2011); David Malone, *Does the Elephant Dance? Contemporary Indian Foreign Policy* (New York: Oxford University Press, 2011); Arndt Michael, *India's Foreign Policy and Regional Multilateralism* (New York: Palgrave Macmillan, 2013); and Jayanta Kumar Ray, *India's Foreign Relations, 1947–2007* (New Delhi: Routledge, 2011).

2. Adda B. Bozeman, "India's Foreign Policy Today: Reflections upon Its Sources," *World Politics* 10, no. 2 (January 1958): 256–273, argues that Indian policy was shaped by Nehru's left-leaning view of world history. Others trace it to the historically derived traditions of Mahabharata and Kautilya or to the post-fourth-century amalgam of Hindu-Buddhist civilization that reigned over India. For discussion of the historical roots of India's foreign policy, see Jaswant Singh, *Defending India* (London: Macmillan, 1999), 1–61. More interested in the operational logic of India's foreign policy, I have argued that the best sources were the "reading" of history by the nationalist leaders and their understanding of how India was to be consolidated as an independent international entity.

3. Alan De Russett, "On Understanding India's Foreign Policy," *International Studies* 4, no. 2 (April 1962): 212–240, quoted in A. Appadorai and M. S. Rajan, *India's Foreign Policy and Relations* (New Delhi: South Asian Publishers, 1985), 17.

4. Ibid.

5. The US-Pakistan alliance in fact began in 1954, which eventually led to unforeseen domestic consequences: the destruction of democracy and the establishment of military dominance in Pakistan's politics. See Appadorai and Rajan, *India's Foreign Policy,* 87.

6. For early discussions of convergence and differences between China and India, see Shao Chuan Leng, "India and China," *Far Eastern Survey* 21, no. 8 (May 21, 1952): 73–78. For the impact of the 1962 Sino-Indian border war, see Ralph J. Retzlaff, "India: A Year of Stability and Change," in "A Survey of Asia in 1962: Part II," *Asian Survey* 3, no. 2 (February 1963): 96–106. See also Margaret W. Fisher, Leo E. Rose, and Robert A. Huttenback, *Himalayan Battleground: Sino-Indian Rivalry in Ladakh* (New York: Praeger, 1963), 136–138; and Margaret W. Fisher, "India in 1963: A Year of Travail," *Asian Survey* 4, no. 3 (March 1964): 737–745.

7. Defeat in the 1962 war with China produced intense debate about the merits of nonalignment and Nehru's successes and failures. J. N. Dixit, G. S. Bajpai, Rana A. Thomas, and Raju Thomas admired Nehru's far-sighted thinking. Ashok Kapur and Kumarswami condemned Nehru's idealism as having no place in the real world of power politics. See G. S. Bajpai, "Ethical Standards on World Issues: Cornerstone of India's Foreign Policy," in

Foreign Policy of India: A Book of Readings, ed. K. P. Misra (New Delhi: Thomson Press, 1977), 91–96; J. N. Dixit, *India's Foreign Policy, 1947–2003* (New Delhi: Picus, 2003); Ashok Kapur, "Eclipsed Moon and Rising Sun," in *Security Beyond Survival: Essays for K. Subrahmanyam,* ed. P. R. Kumar Swami (New Delhi: Sage, 2004), 52–82; and A. Rana, *The Imperatives of Non-Alignment: A Conceptual Study of India's Foreign Policy Strategy in the Nehru Period* (New Delhi: Macmillan, 1976).

8. For defense of Indian nonalignment, see A. Appadorai, "India's Foreign Policy," *International Affairs* 25, no. 1 (January 1949): 37–47; Vincent Sheehan, "The Case for India," *Foreign Affairs* 30, no. 1 (October 1951): 77–90; K. M. Panikkar, "Middle Ground Between America and Russia: An Indian View," *Foreign Affairs* 32, no. 2 (January 1954): 259–270; and B. K. Nehru, "Ambassador Nehru on India's Policy of Non-Alignment," *India News* 1 (April 27, 1962): 8. For critical appraisals, see A. D. Gorwala, *India Without Illusions* (Bombay: New Book Co., 1953); and Winston L. Prouty, "The United States Versus Unneutral Neutrality," speech to the US Senate, September 19, 1961, *Congressional Record,* vol. 107, 87th Congress, 19015–19028.

9. Stanley A. Kochanek, "India's Changing Role in the United Nations," *Pacific Affairs* 53, no. 1 (Spring 1980): 48–68; Charles Heimsath and Surjit Mansingh, *A Diplomatic History* (Bombay: Allied Publishers, 1971), 516–527.

10. President Richard Nixon and his officials had originally referred to Bangladesh as a basket case, but the expression came to signify all of South Asia. See Christopher Hitchens, *The Trial of Henry Kissinger* (London: Verso Books, 2001), 50.

11. Stephen P. Cohen, *India: Emerging Power* (Washington, DC: Brookings Institution Press, 2001), 134.

12. Rahul Mukherjee writes, "At a time when India needed cheap food-grain imports the most, suppliers were unwilling to oblige. Dismayed by the war between India and Pakistan, the U.S. terminated the four-year agreement for food aid to India and Pakistan under the PL 480 program in June 1965. Subsequently, the Johnson administration implemented a policy of 'short tether,' making stocks available for only a few months. Against an estimated need of 8 million tons, the U.S. released only 2 million tons between September and December 1965. The failure of seasonal monsoons in 1965 was followed by another such failure in 1966. In December 1966, President Johnson agreed to commit only half of the 1.8 million tons of PL 480 grains for the February and April shipment." See his "India's Aborted Liberalization—1966," *Pacific Affairs* 73, no. 3 (Autumn 2000): 380.

13. Dietmar Rothermund, "Protagonists, Power, and the Third World: Essays on the Changing International System," *Annals of the American Academy of Political and Social Science* 386 (November 1969): 78–88.

14. For a succinct summary of the 1971 Bangladesh war, its origins, conduct, and, especially, India's role in it, see Maya Chadda, *Ethnicity,*

Security, and Separatism in India (New York: Columbia University Press, 1997), 84–97.

15. For a well-researched summary of the episode, see Richard Sisson and Leo Rose, *War and Secession: Pakistan, India, and the Creation of Bangladesh* (Berkeley: University of California Press, 1990).

16. Rajan Menon, "India and the Soviet Union: A New Stage of Relations?," *Asian Survey* 18, no. 7 (July 1978): 731–750.

17. Sumit Ganguly, *The Origins of War in South Asia: Indo-Pakistani Conflict Since 1947* (Boulder: Westview Press, 1994), 106–110.

18. The treaty was meant to hold both China and the United States at bay while India completed its intervention objectives in East Pakistan. But the signing of the treaty led to a fierce international debate about India's nonaligned claims and the United States held it up as a positive proof of India's hypocritical stance on neutrality.

19. See Nikhil Chakravarty, "Reflections on Indo-Soviet Treaty's Abiding Significance," *Mainstream* 39, no. 33 (August 6, 2011), http://www.mainstreamweekly.net/article2938.html; and Ashok Parthsarathy, "Forty Years of Indo-Soviet Treaty: A Historic Landmark at Global Level," *Mainstream* 39, no. 34 (August 13, 2011), http://www.mainstreamweekly.net/article2951.html.

20. John W. Mellor, ed., *India: A Rising Middle Power* (Boulder: Westview Press, 1979), 147.

21. The more assertive phase of India's policy is referred to as the Indira Doctrine. For elaboration, see Devin T. Hagerty, "India's Regional Security Doctrine," *Asian Survey* 31, no. 4 (April 1991): 351–363. For a Pakistani scholar's perceptions of the Indira Doctrine, see Pervaiz Iqbal Cheema, "What Is the Indira Doctrine?" *The Post,* June 17, 2007.

22. Chadda, *Ethnicity,* 151–159.

23. Ibid., 159–187.

24. Prime Minister Rajiv Gandhi dispatched 1,600 troops by air to restore order in Malé. Less than twelve hours after the request for assistance from President Gayoom, Indian paratroopers arrived on Hulhule, causing some of the mercenaries to flee toward Sri Lanka in a hijacked freighter. The operation started on the night of November 3, 1988, as the Indian Air Force airlifted a parachute battalion group from Agra and flew them nonstop more than 2,000 kilometers (1,240 miles) to the Maldives. The Indian paratroopers landed at Hulhule, secured the airfield, and restored government rule in Malé within hours.

25. "India Shuts Key Nepal Routes in Trade Dispute," *Los Angeles Times,* March 26, 1989, http://articles.latimes.com/1989-03-26/news/mn-1011_1_trade-routes. See also Ramjee Parajulee, *Democratic Transition in Nepal* (Lanham, MD: Rowman and Littlefield, 2000), 194–195.

26. For the text of the 1950 Indo-Nepal Treaty of Peace and Friendship, see http://en.wikipedia.org/wiki/1950_Indo-Nepal_Treaty_of_Peace_and_Friendship#Text_of_the_Treaty.

27. Inder Malhotra, "Revisiting Shimla," *Indian Express,* July 26, 2012, http://www.indianexpress.com/news/revisiting-shimla/969063/4.

28. In a last-minute private meeting between Prime Minister Bhutto and Indira Gandhi, the former had promised to convince his colleagues in Pakistan to settle the Kashmir dispute along the agreed upon LoC. Pakistani diplomats and Bhutto himself denied ever having made the promise. According to T. N. Kaul, India's then foreign secretary and a key member of the Indian delegation in Simla, Gandhi had accepted Bhutto's verbal promise and agreed not to include the language of the promised settlement in the agreement. Bhutto had argued that a promise to settle without proper preparation would endanger his government. For a full account of the summit, see Victoria Schofield, *Kashmir in Conflict* (London: I. B. Tauris, 2003), 118. For a detailed account, see M. P. Ajith Kumar, *India-Pakistan Relations: The Story of Fractured Fraternity* (Delhi: Kalpaz, 2006), 146–152. See also Sumit Ganguly, *The Crisis in Kashmir: Portents of War, Hopes of Peace* (Cambridge: Cambridge University Press, 1997), 46; and Stanley Wolpert, *India and Pakistan: Continued Conflict or Cooperation?* (Berkeley: University of California Press, 2010), 37–46.

29. Peter Levoy, "Pakistan's Foreign Relations," in *South Asia in World Politics,* ed. Devin Hagerty (Lanham, MD: Rowman and Littlefield, 2005), 54.

30. For a brief note on Indo-Pakistani relations in the wake of the Afghan war, see Chadda, *Ethnicity,* 190–195.

31. For India's marginalization during the Afghan war, see ibid., 190.

32. Sharon A. Squassoni, "Weapons of Mass Destruction: Trade Between North Korea and Pakistan," Congressional Research Service, updated November 28, 2006, http://fpc.state.gov/documents/organization /30781.pdf.

33. Author's interviews with Sikh militants in Amritsar, winter 1988 and 1990. For findings, see Chadda, *Ethnicity,* 175–290.

34. For an account of the tensions between Prime Minister Rajiv Gandhi and President Premadasa, see Chadda, *Ethnicity,* 170–174.

35. K. K. Nayyar, "Indo-Russian Strategic Cooperation," in *New Trends in Indo-Russian Relations,* ed. V. D. Chopra (New Delhi: Kalpaz, 2003), 78–79.

36. "Progress Toward Regional Nonproliferation in South Asia" (Washington, DC: Congressional Research Service, February 8, 1994), http://www .fas.org/irp/threat/940216-327448.htm.

37. J. N. Dixit, "Indo-American Relations," *World Focus* (New Delhi) 20, nos. 12–13 (October–November 1999): 41–42.

38. Pavan Gupta, "The Evolution of India's Foreign Policy—Part IX," April 16, 2009, http://pavanblog.com/2009/04/16/the-evolution-of-india %E2%80%99s-foreign-policy-part-ix. For subsequent developments see "India's Missile Chronology," Nuclear Threat Initiative (NTI), James Martin Center for Non-Proliferation Studies, Monterey Institute of International

Studies, Monterey, California, July 2011, http://www.nti.org/media/pdfs/india_missile.pdf.

39. Aneek Chatterjee, "India's U.S. Policy After the Cold War: Sustained Inconsistency," 2008, www.wiscnetwork.org/ljubljana2008/papers/WISC_2008-320.doc.

40. Barbara Leitch LePoer, "India-U.S. Relations," Report No. IB93097 (Washington, DC: Congressional Research Service, December 31, 2001), http://fpc.state.gov/documents/organization/7930.pdf.

41. Chatterjee, "India's U.S. Policy."

42. "Weapons of Mass Destruction: Prithvi," GlobalSecurity.org, http://www.globalsecurity.org/wmd/world/india/prithvi.htm (accessed January 15, 2013). In an interview with K. Subrahmanyam, Prime Minister Rao argued that he did not buckle under US pressure but wanted to wait for the technological development to arrive at an appropriate stage. See K. Subrahmanyam, "Commentary: Narasimha Rao and the Bomb," *Strategic Analysis* 28, no. 4 (October 2004), http://idsa.in/strategicanalysis/NarasimhaRaoandtheBomb_ksubramanyam_1004.

43. Chatterjee, "India's U.S. Policy," 4.

44. Among the leaders were Romesh Wadhwani, who founded Teleca Corporation, MSC Software, Symphony Health Solutions, and Shopzilla; Suhas Patil of Cirrus Logic; K. B. Chandrasekhar of Sun Microsystems, Exodus Communications; Pradeep Sindhu of Juniper Networks; Ramp Networks; Internet Access Solutions; Raj Jaswa, the founder of two tech companies: Selectica and OPTI; Vivek Randive of Tibco Software; and Naren Bakshi, the founder of Versata, which went public in 2000, and of Xpede, CEOJumpStart, Harbinger Real Estate, and the International Venture Group.

45. Schofield, *Kashmir in Conflict,* 191.

46. Besides Gujral's official visit to the United States, Minister of Industry Murasoli Maran went to America to participate in the Destination India program, organized to promote US investment and tourism in India. From the American side, Secretary of State Madeleine Albright, Secretary of Commerce William Daley, and Undersecretary of State for South Asian Affairs Thomas Pickering visited India. Albright's visit was the first by a US secretary of state in fourteen years. As a result of these visits, several important agreements and memoranda of understanding were signed between the two countries.

47. "Weapons of Mass Destruction: A. Q. Khan," GlobalSecurity.org, http://www.globalsecurity.org/wmd/world/pakistan/khan.htm (accessed November 13, 2012).

48. A partial lifting of US economic sanctions began within a year of their imposition, partly because the Singh-Talbott talks were progressing satisfactorily and partly because the sanctions also hurt US exports to India and Pakistan and thus affected American economic interests. By the middle of 1999, relations were back to normal.

49. Strobe Talbott, *Engaging India: Diplomacy, Democracy, and the Bomb* (Washington, DC: Brookings Institution Press, 2004), details the talks and the slow change in US perceptions of India.

50. Seshadri Chari, "Happy and Friendly Ties Ahead," *Organizer* (New Delhi) 51, no. 16 (November 14, 1999): 3, suggests that this was the first time Washington had extended unequivocal support to India in a conflict with Pakistan.

51. Adrian Levy and Catharine Scott-Clark, *Deception: Pakistan, the United States, and the Secret Trade in Nuclear Weapons* (New York: Walker, 2007). According to the authors, Sharif was not aware of the Kargil adventure, nor did he know about preparations for using nuclear weapons. Pakistan's withdrawal led to a falling out between civilian leadership and the armed forces in Pakistan. The impasse ended with Pervez Musharraf seizing control of the government in a coup. There are several versions of the Sharif-Clinton meeting and what may have transpired. In his biography, Musharraf states that Sharif knew about both Kargil and the nuclear weapons. Sharif denies this. See Pervez Musharraf, *In the Line of Fire* (New York: Free Press, 2006), 95–97.

52. Remarks by President George W. Bush at the Twentieth Anniversary of the National Endowment for Democracy, Washington, DC, November 6, 2003, http://www.ned.org/george-w-bush/remarks-by-president-george-w-bush-at-the-20th-anniversary.

53. Foreign Minister Jaswant Singh issued a statement immediately following the 9/11 attacks supporting the United States and condemning the attack. He said, "We stand with the US and the rest of the international community in our commitment to defeat terrorism." See Brigadier Ashok Mehta, "Indo-US Relations: The Way Ahead," USAWC Strategic Research project (Carlisle Barracks, PA: US Army War College, 2008), 8.

54. See *Jane's Intelligence Review,* March 15, 2001, quoted in Northern Alliance Profile, Center for Grassroots Oversight, http://www.history commons.org/entity.jsp?entity=northern_alliance&printerfriendly=true.

55. Surjit Mansingh, "India and the US: A Closer Strategic Partnership?" *Economic and Political Weekly* (Mumbai) 40, nos. 22–23 (May 28–June 10, 2005): 2221.

56. Robert Blackwill, "U.S.-India Defense Cooperation," *The Hindu,* May 13, 2003, http://www.hinduonnet.com/thehindu/2003/05/13/stories/2003051301101000.htm.

57. *Times of India,* September 7, 2007, 1.

58. K. Alan Kronstadt, "U.S.-India Bilateral Agreements and 'Global Partnership,'" Report No. RL33072 (Washington, DC: Congressional Research Service, April 6, 2006), http://assets.opencrs.com/rpts/RL33072_20060310.pdf.

59. "India, US Sign Landmark 123 Agreement," *Times of India,* October 11, 2008, http://timesofindia.indiatimes.com/India_US_sign_landmark_123_Agreement/articleshow/3582223.cms.

60. See "We Can Move Forward with Hyde Act and 123 Agreement: Boucher," *Hindu* (Chennai), March 4, 2008, http://www.indianembassy.org/newsite/press_release/2008/Mar/1.asp. In a move that angered many nonproliferation advocates in the United States who opposed the deal, the State Department requested that congressional staff adhere to unusually strict con-

fidentiality restrictions and not share the answers to congressional inquiries with the general public. Some observers called this a "virtual gag order," a strong indication that the answers contained information harmful to the deal's prospects. See "State Department Asks Congress to Keep Quiet About Details of Deal," *Washington Post,* May 9, 2008.

61. "U.S. Seeks Way Out of India Nuclear Deal Impasse," Reuters, August 29, 2008, http://www.indianexpress.com/news/us-seeks-way-out-of both-india-nuclear-deal-impasse/354986/.

62. Ministry of External Affairs, Government of India, "Statement by the Prime Minister," September 6, 2008, http://pmindia.nic.in/prelease/p content.asp?id=803; Lisa Curtis, "U.S.-India Civil Nuclear Deal: A Sprint to the Finish," Heritage Foundation Web Memo 2054, September 9, 2008, http://s3.amazonaws.com/thf_media/2008/pdf/wm2054.pdf; Seema Sirohi, "Raised to the Power of N," *Outlook* (Delhi), September 22, 2008, http://www.outlookindia.com/article.aspx?238447.

63. Md Jawaid Akhtar, "Engaging Bangladesh: Beyond Confidence-Building Measures," Institute for Peace and Conflict Studies, New Delhi, May 26, 2011, http://www.ipcs.org/article/india/engaging-bangladesh-beyond -confidence-building-measures-3386.html.

6

The Extended Strategic Perimeter

The first of Eric Ringman's measures of a country's power potential is the ability to evolve a vision, defined by broad goals of national policy that reflect an understanding of the changes within and beyond the country's borders. In signing the Indo-US civil nuclear agreement, India was making precisely such an adjustment to the emerging post–Cold War balance of power. The convergence of interests between it and the United States did not, however, change the focus on preserving and enhancing India's strategic autonomy. India did not toe the US line in its attempts to isolate Iran. Mindful of India's own large Shia population and the need for steady access to the light crude for which three-quarters of the nation's oil refineries were designed, India's leaders advocated a negotiated containment of Iran's nuclear program.[1] They did not support the US 2011–2012 interventions in Libya and repeatedly criticized US policy for being overly tolerant of Pakistan-sponsored terrorism against India. The United States and India also differed sharply on the rules of global trade, which largely explains why the 2011 Doha round of trade talks to reform the World Trade Organization (WTO) failed. On climate change, India, along with China, opposed the imposition of carbon dioxide emission caps by international fiat.

These differences highlight India's firm desire to protect its independence and carve out an autonomous space for itself in global

173

politics. As India's economy expanded between 2003 and 2010, the defensive mode of its security and foreign policy began to change into a more assertive, capacity-building effort. India began to vie for leverage in areas that were the key to its continued economic growth. Trade and economic agreements became the leading edge in its look east policy, an important new initiative under coalition governments. Initiated originally by the National Democratic Alliance (NDA) government of Atal Bihari Vajpayee, a thickening network of foreign trade agreements, investments, and economic collaborations came into being under the next government of the United Progressive Alliance (UPA). India forged close economic and security ties with Vietnam and Singapore, joined the Shanghai Cooperation Council with a view to strengthening access to energy-rich Central Asia, and promoted regional organizations such as the Bay of Bengal Initiative for Multi-Sectoral Technical and Economic Cooperation (BIMSTEC). Envisaged as a bridge between South and Southeast Asia, BIMSTEC will forge close economic ties between India and countries to its east: Bangladesh, Myanmar, Thailand, Sri Lanka, Bhutan, and Nepal. Farther afield, India sought out Brazil, Russia, China, and South Africa (as the BRICS forum) to forge a common front among emerging-markets countries.

There was a threefold purpose to India's peripatetic search for economic ties: (1) it would provide Indian policymakers greater room for maneuver in the region; (2) it would give new direction to troublesome relationships with South Asian states, especially Nepal, Bangladesh, and Myanmar; and (3) it would establish a broad set of economic-cum-security ties for future assertions of power. China had successfully followed this strategy since the 1990s, as had the United States during the entire sixty years of the Cold War. Aspiring to great-power status, India could not do better than to follow in their footsteps to success. This required India to move away from a bilateral approach to a multilateral, collective approach to forging ties. In a speech before the Indian Institute of Strategic Studies in 2007, Foreign Secretary Shivshankar Menon observed, "The key to ensuring long-term stability and security in Asia lies in the collective ability of Asian countries to build mutual economic stakes in each other, and to construct an open regional security architecture," as the ASEAN Regional Forum and other organizations are trying to do.[2]

India's Expanding Security Perimeter

Promoting a multipolar world order was nevertheless a distant goal. If India were to sustain its rate of growth, there were more pressing needs to satisfy: protection of borders; secure, steady supplies of energy and raw materials; and access to markets. China's double-digit growth and successful quest for markets and oil had made imperative the extension of India's reach to similar sources. In many instances, these sources were located in unstable and often violence-prone regions of the world. India needed to develop a corresponding strategic and military capacity to ensure access.

In this regard, Central and West Asia were particularly important. "The Gulf forms a part of our strategic neighborhood and an important source of energy, home to over 3.5 million Indians, and a major trading partner," observed Pranab Mukherjee, then India's defense minister. But that was not all. "Parts of it are . . . a source of ideology, funding and recruits to the cause of Islamic radicalism and terrorism. Iraq remains volatile. Iran's nuclear intentions and the response of the international community have introduced a new factor of uncertainty in an already highly disturbed region."[3]

This realization spawned the idea of an extended neighborhood, an expanded perimeter of strategic space that would stretch from the Suez Canal to the South China Sea, including West Asia, the Gulf, Central Asia, Southeast Asia, Asia Pacific, and the Indian Ocean. Jaswant Singh, the NDA minister of external affairs, who argued that India needed to break out of the confines of South Asia, had mooted this idea in the late 1990s.[4] Since then, it has figured regularly in all official statements about India's global and regional concerns. In 2012, the concept of the extended neighborhood was replaced with an Asia-reintegration initiative, but change in the name signaled no change in the purpose for which it had been formulated.[5]

India's intentions to project power beyond the defense of borders have not, however, gone unchallenged. Within India, many commentators have condemned the idea as hegemonistic and alien to the country's core values and interests. They argue that the real security threats for India are not external but domestic—from the discontented poor and oppressed ethnic groups. Therefore, the quest for great-power status is not only a misguided but also a wasted effort. It will not make India safe or serve the interests of its poor. On the contrary, such ambition will trap the country in a dangerous arms race with its adversaries.[6] But successive Indian governments have ignored these warnings.

During its five years in office, the Vajpayee government laid the foundation for the extension of power beyond South Asia by dispatching diplomats to East and Southeast Asia, the Middle East, and Central Asia. Success in developing a defense relationship with Israel was particularly noteworthy because all previous Indian governments had refrained from ties with that country for fear of displeasing the Arab world and the Muslim community at home. But the most important demonstrations of India's new security and foreign policy posture were the testing of nuclear weapons in May 1998 and the development of close ties with the United States, culminating in the Indo-US nuclear agreement a decade later. The UPA government that followed in 2004 eagerly espoused the idea of the extended neighborhood and fleshed it out with huge expenditures on weapons, trade agreements, and networks of economic ties backed by a range of strategic partnerships involving security and military cooperation. The growing Indo-Vietnamese trade ties backed by Vietnam's support for a UN Security Council seat for India, India's Strategic Partnership Agreement with Afghanistan in October 2011, and the Strategic and Global Partnership Agreement with Japan in May 2013 are a few recent examples of success in these efforts.

By any account, India had drastically reoriented the instruments of its security and foreign policy in the post–Cold War period. Traditionally, its external policies had been characterized by a defensive posture, but as its economy expanded and the strategic partnership with the United States bore fruit, India began to be more assertive. In the following, I will provide a brief overview of India's existing military capabilities and plans to acquire more in the near future. But military capabilities need to correspond with likely threats. Therefore, I analyze the threats and the military's ability to meet them, as well as the outcome of these assessments for India's desire to become a preeminent regional power.

Military Budgets

India is the tenth largest military spender in the world.[7] With real economic growth exceeding 6 percent between 2008 and 2011, India had not only largely escaped the ill effects of the 2008 recession but had also increased its tax revenue by more than 40 percent between 2008 and 2011, allowing it to spend increasing amounts on defense through 2010.

The 2012–2013 budget allocated $38.5 billion to defense (see Table 6.1). The lion's shares of these funds went to paying salaries and maintaining the armed forces in good fighting condition. According to the London-based Institute of Strategic Studies 2012 report on worldwide military balance, expanded budgets have nevertheless allowed for substantial expenditures—close to 25 percent of allocated funds—on the purchase of weapons and equipment.[8] "India's capital expenditure on procurement of military hardware is expected to grow from USD 13.1 billion in 2010–2011 to USD 19.2 billion by 2014–15."[9] (See Table 6.2.) Indian armed forces are expected to spend $150 billion (Rs 750,000 crore) during 2013–2023 on arms imports. "The long-term defence acquisition plans include substantial procurement of land, air and naval war fighting systems in order to field highly mobile, lethal, and networked conventional forces in the future."[10] The extensive shopping list includes, among

Table 6.1 Comparative Defense Expenditures, 2004–2012

	India		China		Pakistan	
Year	Millions US$	% of GDP	Millions US$	% of GDP	Millions US$	% of GDP
2004	31,657	2.8	57,542	2.1	5,365	3.6
2005	33,690	2.8	64,726	2.0	5,572	3.4
2006	33,692	2.5	76,065	2.0	5,636	3.3
2007	34,374	2.3	87,739	2.1	5,660	3.0
2008	38,987	2.6	96,663	2.0	5,342	2.8
2009	45,903	2.9	116,666	2.2	5,504	2.8
2010	46,084	2.7	121,064	2.1	5,661	2.8
2011	36,100	1.98	136,700	1.98	5,685	2.6
2012	38,500	1.98	102,436	1.98	5,878	2.5

Sources: The data for 2004 to 2010 are drawn from Stockholm International Peace Research Institute (SIPRI), SIPRI Military Expenditure Data Base, Stockholm, 2012 http://milexdata .sipri.org/result.php4; data for 2011 and 2012 are drawn from International Institute of Strategic Studies, *Military Balance 2013* (London: Routledge, 2013), 550, Table 25.
Note: Totals in millions of US constant 2005 dollars.

Table 6.2 Forecast Expenditures on Defense Services (in US$ millions)

Expenditure Breakdown	2011	2012	2013	2014	2015
Capital expenditure	13,110	14,421	15,863	17,451	19,194
Army	6,948	7,643	8,407	9,249	10,173
Navy	2,098	2,307	2,538	2,792	3,071
Air force	4,064	4,471	4,918	5,410	5,950

Sources: Indian Thirteenth Finance Commission Report, December 2009; Union Budget and Economic Survey, 2003–2011; and Confederation of Indian Industry, "Prospects for Global Defense Export Industry in Indian Market," EUROSATORY, 2010, http://www.deloitte .com.br/publicacoes/2007/Prospects_for_global_defence_export_industry_indian _defence_market.pdf.

others, military transport aircraft, artillery guns, and attack and heavy lift helicopters.[11]

In absolute terms these expenditures look very large, but when measured against the military spending of India's principal adversaries, the bulk of this expenditure is clearly intended to buttress an essentially defensive, not offensive, military posture. China, with which India has a long-standing border dispute in terrain that puts it at a severe disadvantage, has embarked on an extensive program of military modernization and greatly ratcheted up its capacity to build weapons domestically. Between 2001 and 2011, its expenditure added up to an average of 10.9 percent (in real terms) of its annual budget, rising by 10.7 in 2013 over the previous year.[12] China's defense expenditure, however, adds up to less than 2 percent of gross domestic product (GDP) since 2011.[13] India's defense expenditure, after it is discounted for inflation, adds up to about 2.7 percent of GDP in 2010 and then falls to less than 2 percent for the next two years.[14] Comparable figures for Pakistan from 2008 to 2010 are 2.8 percent, declining slightly in 2011 and 2012. Pakistan has managed to spend large amounts on defense because of the close to $29.9 billion that the US Congress has appropriated (between 2002 and 2014) for that purpose.[15] Although the scheduled US withdrawal from Afghanistan in 2014 might reduce these amounts somewhat, in all likelihood Pakistan will continue to figure prominently in US security calculations.

Pakistan's military ties with the United States and China have seriously negative implications for India's key defense goals: management of the nation's borders, control over Indian Kashmir, and the ability to project power in its extended strategic space. It is against these that India's military capability needs to be measured. A thumbnail sketch of actual capabilities will enable us to better understand how far India has progressed toward this goal.

Indian Armed Forces: Military Capabilities

The Army

The Indian Army consists of close to 1.3 million active personnel and 960,000 in reserves, making it the second largest army in the world in terms of manpower. The army is regarded generally to be highly professional and well trained.[16] It is structured into six commands: the Northern, Western, Southwestern, Central, Eastern, and Southern. Eighty percent of troops and corresponding weapons and equipment are under the Northern, Western, and Southwestern Commands—that is, in Jammu and Kashmir and along the border with Pakistan. The Indian Strike Corps conducts exercises and plan war games and simulations for attack and defense in southern Punjab and Rajasthan and in the Thar Desert.[17] The army has eighteen corps with thirty-four divisions, including four Rapid Action Divisions, which have been constituted to spearhead ground offensives. India is one of the largest providers of personnel for UN peacekeeping operations.[18]

Indian ground forces are equipped mostly with domestic and Soviet-made equipment, such as infrared (IR)-guided 9K35 Strela-10 surface-to-air missiles and third-generation IR-guided Nag antitank missiles. In recent years, however, India has acquired a complement of force multipliers such as unmanned aerial vehicles, and weapon-locating radar. Given India's preoccupation with Pakistan, Indian strike forces consist mainly of a large inventory of tanks and support vehicles, backed by acknowledged numerical superiority in the air. In numbers and equipment, the Indian military dominates Pakistan's ground forces.

Having to guard a border of more than 10,000 miles, a substantial portion of which passes through high mountains or difficult terrain, is a demanding task. Close to 4,500 miles are disputed by Pakistan and China and are the frequent scene of cross-border shelling and skirmishes, not to mention terrorist infiltration. The Indian Army has also mustered an impressive capacity in mountain warfare and rapid deployment of moderate numbers of troops, as the Kargil miniwar and engagements on the Siachen sector of the Indo-Pakistan border have demonstrated.[19] In addition, ethnic insurgencies in areas bordering Pakistan, Kashmir, and Punjab have forced the army to engage in low-intensity warfare, requiring it to combine constabulary functions with counterinsurgency and counterterrorism operations.

Two significant features of these low-intensity operations are a strict avoidance of the use of weapons that blur the distinction between civilians and combatants, such as artillery, bombs, rockets, and missiles whether launched from the ground or the air, and a corresponding willingness on the part of the defense forces to accept higher levels of casualties. While some experts fear that frequent domestic deployment will affect troop morale (as is evident with the Border Security Forces in Kashmir), others stress the expertise the army had gained from engaging in jungle and urban warfare.[20] This experience has been put to good use in the scores of UN-led peace-keeping missions to which India has contributed generously, which underscores its ability to operate in regions that are neither contiguous nor friendly, albeit as peacekeepers under a UN mandate. According to security experts, India's considerable involvement in these missions demonstrates its willingness to contribute to the common good, an attribute of aspiring great powers, and its ability to project power well beyond its borders.[21]

The Cold Start Doctrine

For the first five decades after independence, India's security policy and therefore its military posture was almost always defensive. Its 1971 intervention in Bangladesh was largely, if not entirely, triggered by an insupportable inflow of refugees from what was then East Pakistan. The 1987 intervention in Sri Lanka was designed to prevent a Tamil nationalist upsurge there from reigniting Tamil nationalism in Tamil Nadu. But Pakistan's increased use of jihadis in Kashmir and elsewhere after unveiling its nuclear weapons and rapidly maturing missile capability in 1998 forced India to revise its doctrine. The result was a counterinsurgency doctrine named Cold Start (CS).

Even though India's conventional forces are more than a match for Pakistan's armed forces, asymmetrical warfare as typified by terrorist attacks from groups based in Pakistan has been more problematic. India's policymakers felt frustrated after the hijacking of an

Indian airliner by Jaish-e-Muhammad operatives in 1999. At the time, no military option was available to rescue or extract the plane with its passengers intact. India had to acquiesce to the terrorists, who were supported by Pakistan's intelligence agencies and granted safe haven in Pakistan. Subsequent terrorist attacks on the Indian Parliament and failure to subdue the Pakistan military in the 2001–2002 standoff led to initiation of India's Cold Start doctrine. The 2008 terrorist attack on Mumbai only further strengthened India's resolve to induct it as a doctrine.[22]

CS presumes that a limited conventional war can be fought as a via media between two distinct orders of threat: nuclear exchange and terrorist-based, proxy war. The purpose of CS is to calibrate retaliation in a way that will allow India to punish Pakistan but not push it to the point where it would feel compelled to respond with nuclear weapons; CS also requires blitzkrieg mobilization and rapid response. It envisages a massive but limited thrust using rapid reaction force to move across the border and hold small territories that can be used as bargaining chips in subsequent negotiations.[23]

> Rather than seek to deliver a catastrophic blow to Pakistan (i.e., cutting the country in two), the goal of Indian military operations would be to make shallow territorial gains, 50–80 kilometers [31–50 miles] deep that could be used in post-conflict negotiations to extract concessions from Islamabad. Some commentators have emphasized the ability to quickly amass ground and air power to deliver a punishing blow to the Pakistan Army, perceived to be the source of much of Pakistan's aggressive foreign policy, while not harming civilian centers.[24]

Even though CS was fashioned as an answer to Pakistan's use of jihadis as an active tool of state policy, there was no way to test the doctrine's assumptions. Nor was it possible to know for sure how Pakistan would respond to a humiliating defeat in a clash with India. The Cold Start doctrine therefore marked a break with the fundamentally defensive posture that had guided the responses of the Indian military to Pakistan's aggressiveness since 1947.

Pakistan's response to Cold Start was to increase its own rapid reaction response. To this end, it mechanized its infantry divisions and created several independent brigades composed of armor, artillery, and mechanized infantry. Its preoccupation with Cold Start, however, severely restricted its capacity to deal with the growing Taliban and Islamist menace in its western border regions, thereby frustrating the US objective of denying al-Qaeda and the Taliban a base within Pakistan. India therefore encountered considerable US criticism of Cold Start as unnecessarily provocative. In October 2010, under enormous pressure from the United States, India's chief of army staff general, V. K. Singh, announced that the army has not implemented the CS doctrine, meaning that India had no plans to launch unprovoked attacks and that its armed forces continue to maintain a defensive posture.[25] But the army had no intention of allowing the capacities that it had built up under CS to atrophy. On May 12, 2011, India launched Operation Vijayee Bhava (Blessed to Win), a massive defense exercise involving 50,000 troops in Bikaner and Suratgarh, which is close to the Pakistan border in Sindh. The purpose was to boost the synergy among the defense forces and to cut down the mobilization time of the military, which had been twenty-seven days during Operation Parakram in 2002. This, Indian military leaders knew, was too long. In exercises held May 12, 2011, the mobilization time was drastically reduced to forty-eight hours.[26]

The Air Force

In the view of India's chief of air staff Norman Anil Kumar Browne, withdrawal of NATO forces from Afghanistan in 2014 was likely to trigger new threats to India in addition to the ongoing tensions over border disputes with China and Pakistan. These threats have sent India in search of building its long-range preemptive and retaliatory capabilities, particularly for its air force and navy.[27] As of 2013, the Indian Air Force (IAF) had more than 127,200 personnel and 1,473 aircraft, of which 798 were combat aircraft operating from sixty-one airbases—making it one of the largest air forces in the world. India's strike fighters were of Russian and French origin, including the Mikoyan MiG-29, the Dassault Mirage 2000, and the Sukhoi Su-30. In addition to these, the IAF also owns ground attack aircraft, reconnaissance aircraft, unmanned aerial vehicles, and support helicopters—a majority of these of either Soviet or French origin.[28]

The 230 fourth-generation Sukhoi Su-30s give the air force a long-range strike platform, which includes an ability to strike in the immediate neighborhood. To operate at distances, however, the air force needs in-flight refueling capabilities, which it has to some extent. Acquiring more will require buying more aircraft, which are prohibitively expensive. To circumvent these costs, India plans to introduce surface-to-surface missiles that will give it the ability to strike deep into enemy territory and against heavily defended targets such as airfields.[29]

The IAF's prize possession is the first of three airborne warning and control systems (AWACS), which was introduced in 2012. The AWACS, or "eyes in the sky," will help the IAF detect incoming hostile cruise missiles and aircraft much earlier than ground-based radars can detect.[30] India is likely to buy two additional AWACS aircraft to strengthen its air defense and is set to acquire four more Israeli Aerostat radars, at a cost of around $300 million, which will bolster its ability to detect hostile low-flying aircraft, helicopters, spy drones, and missiles.

The Navy

The Indian Navy is the principal instrument for projecting strategic power in the extended neighborhood. The navy has received special attention and a greater slice of the defense expenditure pie. According to Vice Chief of Naval Staff Admiral Suresh Mehta, by 2020 the Indian Navy will be capable of influencing the outcome of land battles and performing a constabulary role in the Indian Ocean region.[31] However, the Indian Navy will need substantial upgrades and replacement of its current "brown water navy" (which has the ability to operate along the coastline) with a true "blue water navy" (which has the ability to project power far from the home country). In 2011– 2012 it possessed fifteen submarines, twenty-one principal surface combatants, one aircraft carrier, ten destroyers, ten frigates, and sixty-one coastal combatants. It has also acquired seventeen amphibious vessels including one LPD Jalashawa, ten landing ships, and forty-nine supporting logistical crafts, which can spearhead a rapid response operation.[32] The Indian Navy has two operational fleets— the Eastern Naval Command and Western Naval Command. Eventually the navy plans to build three carrier battle groups, each around an aircraft carrier. The navy's modernization plans formulated initially in 2005 have only since 2012 begun to be implemented. This Maritime Capability Perspective Plan (2012–2027) seeks to expand the navy to a fleet of 150 ships, with 50 warships now under construction and 100 new vessels in the acquisition pipeline. If these plans go as intended, the Indian Navy will have the ability to join key strategic partners such as the US Navy or navies of Japan and Australia. In the words of Defense Minister A. K. Antony, the objective is to "balance our resources with a strategy that is responsive across the full range of blue and brown water operations. . . . The maintenance of a strong and credible navy and strengthening cooperation and friendship with other countries to promote regional and global stability is the need of the hour."[33] The Indian Navy is also engaged in setting up forward-operating bases and naval air capabilities in order to enhance India's surveillance efforts in the Indian Ocean region. To this end it has begun induction of Boeing 737 P-8I maritime reconnaissance aircraft and plans to add five additional Kamov Ka-31 AEW helicopters to the existing fleet of eleven helicopters. Further, "the navy's amphibious landing capability has been enhanced considerably by the acquisition of the INS *Jalashwa* (ex–USS *Trenton*) and other landing ships, and additional capabilities for amphibious warfare are being rapidly developed."[34] Clearly, India plans to become a key maritime player in the Indian Ocean. In addition to protecting sea-lanes and trade routes, the Indian Navy will be capable of launching expeditionary operations from its shores in cooperation with other friendly states in the Indian Ocean region.

Into the foreseeable future, its capabilities are likely to remain modest. Similarly, having performed largely rescue operations and naval exercises, the navy's combat capabilities also remain untested. In the view of some experts, however, the navy will acquit itself well against the current naval power of Pakistan and China.[35]

Expanded Neighborhood and Naval Power

There are several scenarios with respect to the future expansion of India's naval power, which is slated to be the main vehicle of the country's power projection capabilities. India's future navy could serve several missions to this end. Each mission would entail a different kind of strategic reach. India's naval power could be treated as an adjunct to its land-based security focus, shaped by concerns over Pakistan and China, and therefore equipped with weapons to match the arsenal of these two states.[36] Alternatively, the Indian Navy could expand in function with at least three additional roles in the future. First, it could act as a sea-denial navy. In which case, it would have to be strong enough to deny China the ability to coerce India, a capacity that India does not currently possess. Second, it could become a sea-line communication stability navy, meaning a navy that ensures the safety of global commerce in the Indian Ocean. This is the opposite of a denial navy, and the Indian Navy is far from planning for such a role. Third, the navy could function as an international coalition navy, a role even more distant. Currently, India is developing a sea-based leg for its nuclear deterrent force, aimed at Pakistan and China, each a nuclear power with which it has an ongoing territorial dispute.[37]

To sum up, the pattern of recent weapons acquisitions suggests that India's first concern is deterring Pakistan and China from launching attacks, but India is also laying the foundations for becoming a prominent naval force in the Indian Ocean. The launch of India's first domestically produced nuclear-powered submarine on July 26, 2009, was a major step toward closing the gap with China's underwater offensive capability.

The audacious terrorist attack on Mumbai on November 26, 2008, in which the terrorists landed on the shores of South Mumbai in an inflatable craft launched from a hijacked fishing trawler, highlighted a new responsibility for the navy: to prevent terrorist operations by the sea and interdict and forestall future attacks. In the view of India's defense planners, the entire Indian Ocean seaboard, including Africa's eastern shores, will become a vast web of energy trade, rendering India more vulnerable to piracy, terrorism, and other hostile acts. India therefore wants to extend its naval and economic presence from the Plateau of Iran to the Gulf of Thailand—an expansion west and east that would approximate the colonial defense perimeter of the British Raj in the early twentieth century.[38]

The reasons for this extension of India's strategic space beyond the borders are not hard to see. Close to 89 percent of oil imports arrive by sea. India is therefore seeking to secure the sea lines of communication defense for its own ships and other countries as well. Protecting international shipping trade and commerce is a common concern.[39] In the past, supplies from this region have been disrupted on several different occasions—beginning with the 1973 Arab oil embargo, including the Iranian revolution in 1979, the first Gulf War in 1991, the US-led war in Iraq to depose Saddam Hussein, and during the US- and UN-imposed oil embargo on Iran—all of which were due to political causes and have not been driven by the market. In one highly credible assessment, "An expanding economy, increasing maritime capability and security ties with Japan, Australia, and the

United States, as well as key Southeast Asian nations, are positioning India to have an impact on the distribution of power in the Asia-Pacific. This is a role that successive Indian governments have actively cultivated—ambitiously expanding their strategic focus over the past two decades from South Asia to the Pacific."[40]

Nuclear and Strategic Defense

The 1998 Pokharan tests underscored India's indigenous capacity to develop nuclear weapons, although it remains modest. Pakistan immediately conducted its own tests and stepped up the production of nuclear weapons. According to one estimate, China had close to 240 active nuclear warheads in 2012.[41] In comparison, India is estimated to have stockpiled about 100 nuclear warheads, while Pakistan is known to have between 90 and 110 nuclear weapons.[42] "The most powerful warhead tested by India had a yield of 0.05 megatons, which is quite small compared to China's highest yield of 4 megatons."[43] India has sufficient fissionable material to produce about 400 bombs.[44] Its strategic doctrine, however, calls for "no first use," which presumes that nuclear weapons serve only as a credible but minimum deterrent. Pakistan has understandably not subscribed to no first use and has warned that if threatened, it will retaliate with nuclear weapons.

While content with minimum deterrence, India has expended considerable energy in developing delivery system and missile defense since 1970s. Its nuclear delivery system consists of bombers, supersonic cruise missiles, and medium-range ballistic missiles. Agni-2, India's longest-range *deployed* ballistic missile, is capable of a range of 2,500 kilometers (1,550 miles), whereas Agni-5 is known to have a range of 5,000 kilometers (3,100 miles). To further augment its missile capabilities, India is introducing the BrahMos, a supersonic cruise missile with a range of 290 kilometers (180 miles) that can be launched from land, aircraft, ships, or submarines.

Pakistan has matched India's missile development weapon for weapon. Its first-generation HATF (43-kilometer-range [27-mile]) missiles were planned to counter India's Prithvi missiles. They were built for operations in the border region, where they would be effective in targeting Indian weapons aimed at Pakistan. As India diversified its missile program, Pakistan moved on to the Ghauri series (close to a 1,500-kilometer [930-mile] range), which will put all parts of India within reach. Experts say the main target of this series would be peninsular India.

But it is China that is way ahead of India in most aspects of missile development. To begin with, China's nuclear delivery system has the capacity to carry multiple warheads, in contrast to India's single-warhead carrying capacity.[45] China has reorganized its launch facilities recently in Tibet and along its northern border with Russia. Among China's major India-specific missiles are the Dong Feng 21. With a range of 2,500 kilometers (1,550 miles), it is comparable to Agni-3, which is still not operational. China also has long-range intercontinental ballistic missiles—the Dong Feng 31 and Dong Feng 11—that are known to have a strike range of 8,000 to 10,000 kilometers (4,960 to 6,200 miles). What worries India most is China's effort to militarize the Tibetan region, which will bring most of North India within easy range of the Chinese missile system.

Rapid Deployment Capabilities

To project power beyond its borders, India needs expeditionary abilities that can launch rescue, defensive, or preemptive operations. This would entail substantial air- and sea-lift capabilities and a specially trained force to land and fulfill military objectives in the face of hostility. In June 2010 *India Today* reported that the navy and army had proposed to the government that their capacity for rapid deployment of forces within the neighborhood be raised to an independent brigade strength. This meant the capacity to ferry 5,000 heavily armed infantry and special forces troops, along with tanks and weapons, to distant locations for military operations.[46] The army had already created an independent brigade group for amphibious assault operations in 2011. But the Indian Navy can only transport less than half of these new forces currently. That effort must be doubled if India is to defend the "1,200 island territories . . . energy investments worth thousands of crores across the seas . . . [and the] huge diaspora in the Middle East," asserted Admiral Arun Prakash. "If there was a Kargil-like situation on any of our island territories, we would need adequate boots on the ground for combat. There are also . . . piracy and potential hostage situations."[47]

India has already demonstrated a substantial airlift capability: it airlifted troops to the Maldives in 1988 to stop the coup attempt by rebel forces, during the 1991 Gulf War it airlifted close to 100,000 Indian ex-patriots from Iraq, during the 2005 tsunami, and during the 2006 Lebanon crisis troops were airlifted to perform rescue operations. Although certainly extensive, these operations were not carried out under fire. To further enhance this capability, India has signed a contract with Boeing for ten C-17 transport planes. By October 2013, three had been delivered and inducted into the armed forces. As the *Defense Industry Daily* notes, even though this order will still fall short of what is needed to airlift an entire brigade, the C-17s will beef up India's ability to quickly lift larger numbers of troops when necessary to its borders with China and Pakistan and to develop effective responses to terrorism and low-intensity warfare.

In addition, India is looking to increase its amphibious lift capacity by augmenting the INS Jalashwa, a 16,900-ton American-built landing platform dock (LPD), which can transport nearly 1,000 soldiers and six medium helicopters. This will address "the lack of heavy sea lift and mass-landing capability, while also providing the ability to function as a command and control platform for fleet operations in an amphibious landing or emergency response scenario."[48] India plans to acquire more LPDs to complement its Magar-class landing ship tanks, which can transport 500 personnel or fifteen armored vehicles. And in line with these future plans, India's integrated defense staff has developed an amphibious warfare doctrine, which was tested in naval exercises conducted since 2005–2007.

Since the late 1990s, the Indian Navy has joined in numerous naval exercises with a whole host of nations and participated in expeditions against piracy as well as in rescue operations. It has begun to organize naval exercises for the Indian Ocean region, the first of which took place in February 2012 close to the Andaman and Nicobar Islands, India's island territories.[49] On balance, then, the post–Cold War decades have seen a steady and impressive expansion of India's military arsenal.

Future Acquisition of Arms and Weapon Systems

With plans to modernize and build capacity, India is therefore set to acquire in the near future "160 plus ships by 2022, including three aircraft carriers, 60 surface and sub-surface combatant vessels and close to 400 aircraft. The Coast Guard too is set to triple its manpower and force levels over the next decade or so."[50] The navy intends to buy and induct two more aircraft carriers with the flotilla of seventy-one ships by 2016.[51] In September 2011, it deployed Boeing P-81 maritime patrol and antisubmarine warfare aircraft for the first time. The navy is scheduled to lease the INS *Chakra,* a Russian Akula-class ship, and commission its first ballistic missile submarine, the INS *Arihant,* although it will not become operational for some time. The *Arihant* will be equipped with a 700-kilometer-range (434-mile) Sagarika missile, which is still being tested. *Military Balance 2012* explains, "Should the Arihant and its missile complement become operational, and should its vessel's missiles be equipped with nuclear warheads, India will have a triad of nuclear delivery systems."[52]

India is also reported to be working on a subsonic cruise missile, *Nirbhaya.* Its air-launched version is to be integrated with the air force's multirole combat aircraft, which are on order. With the April 19, 2012, successful firing of Agni-5, a missile with a 5,000-mile range, India has China within striking range. The Agni-5 can carry a nuclear warhead as well.[53]

The Indian Army's acquisition plans include upgrades and purchases of artillery, tanks, vehicles, missiles, and other items such as infantry upgrades. These upgrades and purchases will create

> eight divisional-sized armoured battlegroups, comprising artillery, armour and motorised infantry, with state of the art communications equipment and coordinated air support. Many acquisitions outlined appear to be part of the USD 8 billion artillery modernisation program, the FARP [Field Artillery Rationalisation Plan], originally formulated in 1999. The program aims to induct around 2,184 guns over 20 years, at a minimum rate of 100 units per annum. In its 11th Defence Plan, spanning 2007–2012, the Indian Army has designed around 600 modernisation schemes, amounting to around USD 1.44 billion.[54]

To build its air force capabilities, India upgraded its 63 MiG-29s and 51 Mirage 2000s and acquired 40 Su-30 MKI 80s. Purchase of an additional 140 Su-30 MKIs and 126 medium multirole combat aircraft is planned for 2015, with the option of buying 64 to 74 more. India will also purchase and introduce 120 LCAs (Tejas) by 2013–2014.[55]

These acquisitions are likely to fill most of the current gaps in India's security architecture. Experts are skeptical, however, about how far these would take India in coping with a two-front war. They also question the priority given by successive coalition governments to the acquisition of offensive capabilities when in fact the real security threats emanate from domestic sources such as the spreading Maoist insurgency and ethnic separatism. But those who argue priorities need to explain how any government in New Delhi can ignore the unresolved boundary disputes with China and Pakistan and the frequent cross-border skirmishes, which could escalate into a war. Improved ties with China and Pakistan might diminish the danger of conflict, but it is unlikely to disappear in the foreseeable future.

Threats and Concerns

India's most problematic security relationship is with Pakistan, a country that shares history and border with India. Neither wars nor negotiations have settled the boundary dispute over Kashmir, which has bedeviled their relationship since partition in 1947. The Indo-Pakistani conflict has remained largely impervious to war as a way to settle differences. This is evident in the long record of clashes and wars, the first of which broke out in 1948; others followed in 1965 and in 1971. In 1990, India and Pakistan came close to a war, which was avoided because of US diplomatic intervention. By May 1998, following Pakistani incursions into the Kargil sector of Kashmir, the two fought a short war, but its limited nature still carried the terrible danger of a nuclear exchange, making Kashmir, in the words of President Bill Clinton, the most dangerous flashpoint in the world. President Clinton's apprehensions were understandable in view of the warning issued by Pakistan's foreign secretary, Shamshad Ahmed, at that time. He had declared that Pakistan would "not hesitate to use any weapon in our arsenal" should its territorial integrity be threatened.[56] The terrorist attacks in Jammu and Kashmir on October 1, 2001, and two months later on the Indian Parliament in New Delhi again impelled India and Pakistan to mobilize their armies in a confrontation mode. The dispute over Kashmir still remains unresolved.

Paradoxically, there is also a thick record of negotiations, although it is yet to produce results. President Pervez Musharraf and Prime Minister Manmohan Singh, according to 2007 press reports, had reached a breakthrough agreement to make the India-Pakistan border in Kashmir a soft border with some territorial modification and joint management of the disputed territory, all within the framework of an autonomous Kashmir. Domestic turmoil in Pakistan and procrastination in New Delhi put paid to that agreement, and soon the 2008 terrorist attack on Mumbai pushed the dialogue into a deep freeze. Beginning in April 2012, India and Pakistan began to again explore confidence-building measures, boost cross-border trade, and ease visa restrictions to promote travel. Sadly, by January 2013 border clashes in Kashmir and belligerent rhetoric on both sides led to the suspension of talks. Domestic events in Pakistan created new uncertainties, which put a damper on the negotiations.

Pakistan as a Threat

For India, many levels of security concerns converge in the matter of Pakistan because of its unmitigated hostility and its geopolitical location as a gateway to India's strategic neighborhood. Pakistan shares borders with China and enjoys a close relationship with Beijing, which makes India vulnerable to a two-front war. Located athwart India's trade routes to the Persian Gulf and Central Asia, Pakistan is important to any Indian efforts to secure borders, maintain control in Kashmir and Punjab, and promote trade and economic ties with Iran, Afghanistan, and oil-rich states in Central Asia. Commenting on Pakistan's ability to stymie India, David Robinson writes,

> Pakistan . . . has been a key supporter of the Taliban in Afghanistan, factions of which the Pakistani Army is now fighting in a de facto civil war; elements within the state support Islamic terrorist organisations that periodically attack India, provoking regional crises; and, the Pakistani Army has a growing nuclear arsenal, which could be vulnerable to misuse by malicious elements within the state. . . . Pakistan has adopted an asymmetric nuclear escalation posture [that has deterred Indian conventional military power and enabled Pakistan's] aggressive strategy of bleeding India by a "thousand cuts" with little fear of significant retaliations.[57]

Pakistan pursues asymmetric warfare against India largely because it fears defeat in a protracted conventional conflict. India is four times larger and has a more powerful military machine. Scholars who have studied possible war scenarios between India and Pakistan conclude, however, that any future war between them is likely to be a complex and unpredictable affair, particularly because armed clashes harbor the potential to escalate into full-scale war and that into a nuclear exchange.[58] The war game scenarios enacted by the US military point to just such an outcome.[59]

Even though conventional or nuclear weapons have failed to give India the power to compel Pakistan to yield Kashmir, the US military presence in Afghanistan, instead of facilitating resolution, has only further complicated the mission to project power in the extended neighborhood. The abandonment of Cold Start was a case in point. Washington had stridently opposed any escalation of tension between India and Pakistan, urged New Delhi to exercise restraint, and pressured Islamabad to rid itself of Islamic radicals. US advocacy, however, vacillated with the fortunes of the Afghan war and the escalation of violence in Pakistan's tribal areas.

The US Factor

For the United States, defeating the Taliban and neutralizing Islamic radicals from Pakistan's Federally Administered Territories adjacent to Afghanistan took precedence over the Kashmir dispute and Indo-Pak tensions. Shored up by quantities of US military and economic aid, the Pakistani military had little incentive to settle on Kashmir. Needing a cooperative Pakistan in its war against the Taliban and al-Qaeda, the United States was reluctant to push Pakistan to abandon its jihadi ploy against India. Even when the United States withdraws from Afghanistan in 2014, the need to retain leverage in Pakistan is likely to steer it into a neutral stance on the Kashmir dispute.

On balance, then, Pakistan has an effective deterrent against India because of its ability to wage a complex mix of conventional and unconventional warfare with nuclear weapons as a first-strike option. As long as distrust of and hostilities toward India remain deeply embedded within Pakistan's national ideology, Indian leaders cannot gain advantage regardless of whether Pakistan is weak or strong. Each scenario poses a danger for India. A strong and ambitious Pakistan can push with vigor on Kashmir; a weak and ambitious Pakistan can still push on Kashmir with proxy forces while avoiding confrontation, as it has been doing since the late 1980s. India can neutralize these threats by reaching out to the moderate elements within Pakistan, or it can limit and contain Pakistan by building ties with key states in the extended neighborhood and bypass

Pakistan completely. Indeed, under the United Progressive Alliance (UPA) I and II India pursued both options simultaneously.

Containing and Circumventing Pakistan

As a part of this larger strategy, India has committed close to $2 billion to build hospitals, schools, roads, and infrastructure in Afghanistan. These projects have brought it political goodwill and a degree of leverage with the government of Hamid Karzai in Kabul. By signing the India-Afghanistan Strategic Partnership Agreement on October 4, 2011, India turned its soft power leverage into a security relationship that will have long-term implications for its regional role. India's primary interest there is to stabilize the Karzai government and deny the Taliban control over Afghanistan. Indian leaders fear radical Islam spilling over into India via Pakistan. Even if the Karzai government is deposed following the US withdrawal, India hopes it can retain some leverage from the goodwill it has earned from investing in the people of Afghanistan.

For India, Afghanistan is a land bridge to energy-rich Central Asia.[60] A close relationship with Central Asia can strengthen India's security against Pakistan, weaken Islamic fundamentalism in the region, and provide access to markets and vast new sources of energy that could enable India to break through China's strategic and economic encirclement of India. The United States shares these objectives and therefore beginning in 2012 it not only withdrew opposition to Indian presence but also began to urge India to actively participate in stabilizing Afghanistan, including committing troops to defend Afghanistan against the Taliban takeover. India, however, refused to put a military face to its involvement in Afghanistan. Ironically, this earned it high praise from the most unexpected quarter: Mullah Omar, the leader of the Afghan Taliban, who had declared India an enemy state.[61]

To circumvent Pakistan, India has built alternative routes to Afghanistan via Iran. At the cost of $150 million, it built a 220-kilometer (136-mile) road in the southwest Afghan province of Nimroz. This road runs from "Delaram in Nimroz to Zaranj on the Iranian border, which connects to the Iranian port of Chabahar. It opens up an alternate route into Afghanistan," which has had to otherwise rely "mostly on goods transported overland from ports in Pakistan."[62]

India's growing presence in Afghanistan triggered fears of encirclement in Islamabad.[63] Pakistan regards Afghanistan and Central Asia as its strategic hinterland in a war with India; India regards Afghanistan as a land bridge to "building strategic space . . . to encircle Pakistan."[64] A Pakistani military spokesman warned the International Security Assistance Forces fighting against Taliban insurgents in Afghanistan that the situation could get "ugly" should India acquire a significant military presence in Afghanistan. The strategic stakes in the outcome of the Afghan war rose even higher when China offered Pakistan a civil nuclear deal along the same lines as the Indo-US nuclear agreement.

Extending India's presence in this northwestern quadrant has another strategic objective: countervailing China. India believes that China's investment in Pakistan and Kazakhstan is meant to deny India access to oil and gas while China builds a transit corridor to Central Asia that would tie this energy-rich region firmly to the Chinese economy. In a countermove, India has sought membership in the Shanghai Cooperation Organization, but with mixed results. It lost out to China in a bid to gain exploration rights for Kazak oil and trade; it was more successful in a bid for an oil-producing bloc in the Tomsk region of western Siberia in Russia, although China and Pakistan tried to deny India access. New Delhi has developed strong security links with Tajikistan, and in 2007 Indian engineers reopened the Ayni airbase, which can be used by India, Russia, and Tajikistan.

Indian companies have begun to reach into and beyond Central Asia. For instance, India's Oil and Natural Gas Corporation (ONGC) has acquired a 10 percent stake in the Caspian bloc Kurdish fields. In partnership with Turkey, Punj Lloyd, an Indian construction company, will participate in building the Baku-Tiblisi-Ceyhan pipeline. These regional initiatives reflect India's desire to gain a foothold in the extended neighborhood and access to sources of energy. Even though Washington's Afghanistan-Pakistan priorities and Islamabad's distrust of New Delhi remain major "transit obstacles" to Central Asia, in the long term India, not Pakistan, is the prize in South Asia. It has the wherewithal—military, economic, and technological—to encourage stability in the region.[65] "With its energy companies well positioned to take advantage of the three-million-strong . . . diaspora in the energy and service industry of the Persian Gulf economies, India can become the preeminent actor in the region "extending across Eurasia and beyond."[66] But for now, it is not ready to fulfill this role.

India has had a difficult time competing with China's economic diplomacy. The latter is building a deepwater port in Gwadar, Pakistan, to provide China a firm foothold in the Arabian Sea. In response, under the UPA I and II India has sought a strategic relationship with Iran. But in this effort it has had to walk a tightrope strung between jeopardizing ties to its new great-power ally, the United States, and forgoing oil from its long-term trade partner, Iran. India had agreed since 2003 to work on joint infrastructure projects that will link Iran's Chabahar port to the network of Garland Road bordering Iran and Afghanistan. When completed, Chabahar will become the main port for energy and trade among the Central Asian states, Afghanistan, and the Caspian region. Iran, the Central Asian states, and India have found a common interest in securing a stable Afghanistan free of excessive Pakistani and jihadi influence.

India and China: Competition or Cooperation?

In the long term, a "rising China" is the main threat facing India, not only because of the unsettled border dispute but also because China has made deep inroads into South Asia. According to Brigadier Harinder Singh, dealing with Pakistan requires India to have operational readiness and dealing with China demands structural readiness.[67] To counter China, India will have to build roads, airports, and means of communication all along the disputed border. In addition, it will need to forge alliances with states that are as keen as India is to limit China's expansionist ambitions. Broadly, the India strategy in the post–Cold War era has been to both engage and compete with China: engage it in border talks and compete with it in gaining access to resources, oil and gas, and minerals. This strategy hopes to ward off a military conflict by giving China a stake in talks while ensuring India's options to forge a widening circle of ties with Southeast Asia and the United States.

Indian Views of China

India's foreign policy community is divided on how to view China and its growing international influence and, even more urgently, its growing inroads in areas traditionally within India's strategic space.

India's former foreign secretary Nirupama Rao argues that many in India's foreign policy community are exaggerating the China threat and oversimplifying India-China relations by defining them in terms of a single, military/security dimension. Rao and others who see China as open to cooperation underscore the growing trade between the two countries, which reached $66 billion in January 2013 and was expected to grow substantially in the next decade.[68] They moreover argue that trade will provide an incentive for both countries to solve their differences peaceably instead of going to war. General Deepak Kapoor, a former chairman of India's Chiefs of Staff, disagrees: "From an Indian perspective, China's 'string of pearls' policy, its strategic relationship with Pakistan, the extensive infrastructure development in Tibet, an increasing footprint in the Indian Ocean and Pakistan-occupied Kashmir (PoK) and its aid to fledgling insurgent movements in India are some of the irritants that are not conducive to good relations."[69] In his view, war between India and China is inevitable. At a minimum, he comments, China is "opposed to India's rise and recognition."[70]

Chinese Views of India

Throughout the 1990s and until India tested its nuclear bomb, China was dismissive of India's claims to great-power status. This view changed when in 2005 the Bush administration began to build a long-term strategic partnership with India and signed the agreement that institutionalized the Indo-US defense ties.[71] Beijing suspected that India was being recruited as a junior partner in a US cordon sanitaire to contain China. This suspicion turned into a conviction when the Bush administration twisted arms to pressure the Nuclear Suppliers Group (NSG) to admit India into its ranks. China's apprehensions solidified as India and the United States conducted more than fifty joint military exercises between 2002 and 2013, which has led to considerable progress in integrating some aspects of operations in the Indian Ocean region. India has also signed deals in excess of $8.2 billion for the purchase of US arms, which alarms China.[72] The apprehension in Beijing about the Indo-US strategic partnership can be measured by the concern expressed by China's Ministry of Foreign Affairs, which "pressed India for an explanation, even suggesting that an Asian NATO was in the offing. This exaggerated response coincided with a much more aggressive Chinese claim to the disputed northeast border along the McMahon Line on the Himalayan frontier and the Line of Actual Control."[73]

China's greatest worry is India's support of a growing rebellion in Tibet, an area annexed by China in 1959 against Indian objections. To forestall any hostile Indian move, China has put in place, according to Mohan Malik, "a sophisticated military infrastructure . . . five fully operational air bases, several helipads, an extensive rail network, and thirty thousand miles of roads—giving them the ability to rapidly deploy thirty divisions (fifteen thousand soldiers each) along the border, a three-to-one advantage over India." In addition, Malik writes, "the PLA's [People's Liberation Army] strategic options against India are set to multiply as Chinese land and rail links with Pakistan, Nepal, Burma, and Bangladesh improve."[74] China had also shored up "an east-west strategic corridor in Tibet across India's northern frontiers, as evident in the building of a $6.2 billion China-Tibet railway from Gormu to Lhasa that opened in July 2006. This link is to extend to the Napali capital of Kathmandu,"[75]

China has aggressively sought energy-related opportunities overseas, frequently at India's expense. It persuaded Myanmar's military government in 2006 to sell "China gas from the partly Indian-owned A-1 and A-3 offshore blocks via a planned 2,380-kilometer [1,479-mile] pipeline to Yunnan."[76] China concluded deals for gas fields with Bangladesh, another state adjacent to India; forged oil and gas deals with Iran; and promised to build a 386-kilometer (240-mile) oil pipeline that will directly link the Atasu-Alashnkou pipeline to Kazakhstan and Xinjiang. China is pushing forward with construction of a north-south Karakoram strategic corridor stretching to Pakistan's new Chinese-built Gwadar port. This corridor links the Irrawaddy corridor to the Yunnan province by road, river, and rail.

India's Response

Belatedly, India has stepped up its efforts to countervail China's encroachment across the Indian border into Eastern Ladakh. It has expanded military and economic ties with Myanmar to the east, which required "cozying up" with Myanmar's military junta before the 2010 opening to democracy in that country. Myanmar possesses abundant natural resources—oil, natural gas, coal, zinc, copper, uranium, timber, and hydropower—in which China is heavily invested. Fortunately, the democratic opening in Myanmar eased the need to focus on the military rulers and allowed India to resolve the earlier contradictions in its Myanmar policy. India "hopes that a network of east-west roads and energy pipelines will eventually allow it greater play in the regions stretching from Iran to Myanmar."[77]

Most alarming for India are Chinese claims to the Indian state of Arunachal and an offer of a nuclear reactor to Pakistan, including a promise to sponsor the latter for membership in the NSG.[78] Therefore, in 2008 India officially adopted a two-front war doctrine to prepare for a limited war with Pakistan and China simultaneously. To counter China's widening economic-cum-security network, India has invested in building strategic ties with countries on China's periphery: Afghanistan, Tajikistan, Mongolia, Vietnam, and Myanmar. Joint defense exercises with the United States, Japan, Australia, Singapore, and Malaysia have been important parts of India's effort to counterbalance China.

Commenting on this rivalry Mohan Malik observes that China's "Malacca paranoia" is matched by India's "Hormuz dilemma": while "China's navy is going south to the Indian Ocean, India's navy is going east to the Pacific Ocean."[79] A naval confrontation between the two, very likely in the Indian Ocean region, is in his view a real possibility. It therefore came as no surprise to hard-liners in India's policy community when a Chinese warship ordered an Indian naval vessel off the waters near Vietnam in September 2011. ONGC had signed a contract with Vietnam for oil exploration, which according to New Delhi was well within Vietnam's territorial waters. China, however, announced that the contract was an illegal, deliberate provocation meant to test China's natural and well-founded claims to the South China Sea.[80] India's look east policy was beginning to irk China.

Justifying the westward naval expansion, China's official news agency, Xinhua, wrote that the country now needed to

> establish overseas strategic support stations for adding ship fuel, resupply of necessities, staff break time, repairs of equipment, and weapons in Pakistan, Sri Lanka, and Myanmar, which will be the core support bases in the North Indian Ocean supply line; Djibouti, Yemen, Oman, Kenya, Tanzania, and Mozambique, which will be the core support bases in the West Indian Ocean supply line; and Seychelles and Madagascar, which will be the core support bases in the South Indian Ocean supply line.[81]

These stations cover the entire Indian Ocean area surrounding India and are precisely the ocean waters in which India is seeking to build its own strategic influence. With this in view, India has entered into a close security arrangement with Singapore, which is India's gateway to Southeast and Far East Asia; with the Maldives; and with the Gulf states of Qatar and Oman. India has signed a bilateral maritime security partnership with Mauritius, Seychelles, Mozambique, and Madagascar. One look at these far-flung points on the map suggests that the Indian Navy means to build a strong and significant presence in the Indian Ocean.

The Purpose of Indian Strategic Policy

The end of the Cold War; the rapid rise of China to the status of a great Asian power, if not a great global power; and Pakistan's involvement with the United States in the war in Afghanistan, its deepening military ties with China and North Korea, and Islamabad's quest for nuclear weapons and missiles forced India to abandon its largely reactive security policy and defense doctrine and adopt more proactive ones that covered not only the South Asian subcontinent but also India's extended neighborhood. The air force was the first to release its modified defense doctrine in 1995.[82] The Indian Army revamped its war-fighting strategy and formulated a new doctrine that sought to leverage "advanced technology to fight short duration conflicts in a nuclear environment."[83] An army counterinsurgency doctrine was promulgated in 2006. This new doctrine includes practices best suited for subconventional operations, including counterterrorism and low-intensity conflicts. Later in the same year, the Indian Navy released its maritime doctrine, which envisions blue water naval capabilities.[84] In 2009, it revised this to develop a fourfold capability to fulfill diplomatic, military, humanitarian, and constabulary missions. Since 1999, India has spent increasing amounts on modernizing its armed forces.

Do these changes meet Eric Ringman's three criteria for measuring a state's potential for expanding power: a coherent vision that responds to changing international threats and opportunities, a demonstrated ability to implement any changes in that vision, and an administrative and political capacity to resolve the conflicts that arise between old and new strategies?

As this chapter shows, changes in military strategy and doctrine have been consciously developed responses to new challenges in what is now regarded as India's extended neighborhood. Policymakers in New Delhi have concluded that India's national interests require reaching beyond South Asia into the Gulf states to the west and the Straits of Malacca to the east. Beginning with the Narasimha Rao government and continuing in later years, India's coalition governments have given a concrete shape to this new thrust in regional policy. Defense analysts generally agree that India has articulated the broad vision of what it wants to be. But in their view, India's strategy lacks coherence. Defense expenditure has been stepped up, but the weapons India already has and wants to acquire in the near future do not match the threats it is likely to face. Analysts believe that India is yet to complete the transition from old to new ways of thinking about war fighting and military procurement and that in the absence of an overarching strategic policy, arms procurements and doctrines fail to dovetail in a meaningful fashion.

This is true. The Ministry of Defense does issue annual reviews, but these are too general and fail to explain how India will meet its security and military objectives. Similarly, Parliament's Standing Committee on Defense debates policy and arms requirements, but these are partisan and therefore a poor guide to defense planning. There have been reviews of military preparedness in the recent past—for instance, a Kargil Committee Report after the Kargil miniwar—but these have focused narrowly on a specific problem instead of carrying out an overall assessment of the ends and means of defense policy.

But critics may be exaggerating the value of a framework document because even if it were to exist, it cannot guarantee a sound defense policy. Strategic documents are written usually to justify defense budgets and frequently to build a case for weapons that an objective assessment might find unnecessary. The annual exercise in defense budgets presented to the US Congress is a case in point. Despite annual reviews, the Bush administration failed to anticipate and was not prepared for the terrorist attack on 9/11; nor did it estimate the expenditures and troop requirements for the Afghan and Iraq wars accurately. Indeed, mistaken assessments in each case have confounded the exit of the United States from these two countries. There is a tendency among defense planners to overspend, prepare for worst-case scenarios, and opt for maximum security by exaggerating external threats.

Nevertheless, in the case of India commentators point to something more fundamental than an absence of an overarching defense document. They argue that India lacks a strategic culture, a habit of thinking about designing a national strategy and planning for defense. George Tanham was one of the early writers to draw attention to India's lack of a strategic culture.[85] Others concurred but explained it by pointing to India's diversity. They argued that collective action was difficult to achieve in such a highly divided society.[86] An ideological preference characterized by avoidance of war was the third explanation offered by some scholars for India's absent strategic culture. Referencing Nehru's anticolonial anti-imperial convictions, Rajesh Basrur, a well-known expert on India's security policies, wrote that strategic restraints, a key characteristic of India's defense culture, reflected the ideological preferences of India's top leaders.[87]

I have argued in this volume that India seeks to exercise relational control—namely, the ability to structure or shape relations within South Asia. India strives for this control because it needs to combine nation-building—unification, modernization, and development—with security planning while also warding off undue external interference. These are largely defensive goals. During the Cold War, India tried but failed to prevent the great powers from structuring Indo-Pakistani relations. Nor did it succeed in preventing China from occupying large parts of border territory that India claimed as its own. Despite those failures, India advanced national integration and expanded the purview of its central state. In the years since independence, the challenge of unification has become progressively less acute, although it has not gone away, and India's democracy and economy have expanded and matured while creating new challenges for each new government. Sustaining an effective supranational state still remains a key goal of relational control, especially because power has accumulated in the regional, ethnic, and caste-based parties since the arrival of the coalition governments. What is more, the stability of India's coalition governments has come to depend on their delivering sustained economic growth and a better life to the country's aspiring millions. This requires integrating the Indian economy into the global marketplace but doing so with caution and prudence so as not to jeopardize the livelihoods of India's people.

The domestic dimension of protecting strategic autonomy has therefore remained unchanged. What has changed is in foreign policy, particularly the instruments and scope of relational control. India needs to now extend its footprint beyond South Asia. This new thrust in its security policy is meant to establish ties beyond and around

Pakistan to bring greater pressure on that country to resolve bilateral disputes, to lay down the economic and diplomatic foundation for a more assertive role in the future, and to create a solid economic and military presence in the extended neighborhood. The overall objective is to make India an important player in the entire arc of countries stretching from Southwest Asia to the Far East. The primary rationale of this policy is to protect India's strategic autonomy and economic interests.

Experts such as Stephen P. Cohen and Sunil Dasgupta concede that there is new thinking in India's defense establishment but nevertheless argue that the proposed arms acquisitions fail to meet the kinds of threats India should be preparing for—namely, Maoist rebellion, ethnic insurgencies, and regional separatism. These pose greater threats than an aggressive Pakistan or an ambitious China.[88] Not everyone agrees with this view, at least not totally. Brigadier Singh rejects the "incoherency" charge as exaggerated and argues that China and Pakistan pose real threats to India's security.[89]

He agrees with Cohen and Dasgupta that the weak institutional coordination that currently exists among the army, navy, and air force is dangerous and that simply issuing new doctrines is not the answer. A proliferation of doctrines might even hinder coordination. Nevertheless, he believes that the armed services are slowly but visibly moving toward that goal. Singh points to recommendations made by the "Group of Ministers (GoM) Committee constituted in February 2001 on reform of the Indian national security system" and acknowledges that since then the armed forces have taken "several important actions" with regard to "higher defence planning structures and planning processes."[90] These include the institution of the Defence Acquisition Council (DAC), which streamlines the process of defense procurement. "Another significant development has been the establishment of HQ Integrated Defence Staff (IDS) to enable joint staff planning among the three services."[91] He reports that the "HQ IDS has also been involved in evolving the long term integrated perspective plan (LTIPP) for the Indian armed forces. LTIPP looks at the tri-service capability development over a fifteen year perspective."[92]

India's foreign policy commentators do not agree on the goals of defense planning. Most agree, however, that counterinsurgencies in Kashmir and the Northeast have eroded the military's "land war fighting capability."[93] And in his study on defense preparedness Harinder Singh concedes that at the moment and in the foreseeable future India will not have the capacity to fight on two fronts (Pakistan and China); nor is it adequately prepared or equipped to fight one adversary on the border while coping with a conflict at sea with the other.[94] A rapprochement with China and resolution of the Kashmir dispute might ease India's defense burden, but neither possibility is close at hand. India needs therefore to maintain appropriate levels of land, sea, and air force readiness to fight on both fronts. A quick, decisive victory against Pakistan is uncertain and in that event a defeated and nuclearized Pakistan would be even more dangerous. India is far behind China in almost all indices of power and military capabilities. It has made progress in laying the foundation for a widening network of trade and economic-cum-security relations with countries in its extended neighborhood, but that still leaves the question of immediate threats open and unanswered.

To sum up, most experts admit that the following goals are still to be accomplished:

1. India needs to make a hardheaded assessment of its own weaknesses and strengths and concentrate on building up aspects of military capabilities that can deter Pakistan and China separately and together should that become necessary.
2. India needs coercive and diplomatic capabilities that will enable it to gain from the changing power equation between the United States and China.
3. India needs to eliminate delays in the procurement of arms and equipment and strengthen indigenous production capacity, which requires, in turn, an expanding industrial base and robust international trade.
4. India needs forward bases and infrastructure to defend its borders and be able to move its forces rapidly to the India-China and the India-Pakistan borders.
5. India needs to develop an effective insurgency doctrine that efficiently dovetails military, political, and diplomatic capabilities.
6. India needs to change the current organization of its armed forces to create a single-point flow of military-strategic advice. Most important in this regard is the integration of the three service headquarters and the appointment of a chief of defense staff to the Ministry of Defense who will participate in the formulation of defense policy and decisionmaking.

India has purchased sufficient weapons and weapons systems to fulfill several aspects of its military requirements, and these may eventually cohere into effective strategic and military preparedness. For now it has a tactical advantage over Pakistan if a war were to remain conventional, although forward bases and roads and other facilities would have to be built to ensure a rapid and effective response to China were it to activate the borders in Arunachal, eastern Ladakh, or elsewhere in the Northeast. It is this preparedness that will give India the capability to defend itself in a two-front war. In applying Ringman's criteria, we can see that India's defense policies show much movement but insufficient focus, forward progress but lack of coordination.

Notes

1. India is one of the few countries that got a waiver (three so far) from the embargo the US imposed on Iran in 2010. This waiver came in exchange for scaling down India's trade and imports from Iran. Continuation of the waiver depended on the state of the triangular relationship among India, Iran, and the United States.

2. Speech by Foreign Secretary Shivshankar Menon, "India and International Security," International Institute of Strategic Studies, New Delhi, India, May 4, 2007, http://meaindia.nic.in/speech/2007/05/04ss01.htm.

3. Speech by Foreign Minister Pranab Mukherjee, "India's Strategic Perspectives," Carnegie Endowment for International Peace, Washington, DC, June 27, 2005, http://www.usindiafriendship.net/viewpoints1/mukherjee.htm.

4. David Scott, "India's Extended Neighborhood Concept: Power Projection for a Rising Power," *India Review* 8, no. 2 (May 2009): 112.

5. Speech by Minister of External Affairs S. M. Krishna, "India's External Environment and Current Foreign Policy Challenges," Institute of South Asian Studies, Singapore, March 9, 2012, http://www.indiablooms.com/NewsDetailsPage/2012/newsDetails090312n.php.

6. Sumit Ganguly doubts that India can rise to great-power status in the foreseeable future. Ramachandra Guha, in contrast, argues that it should not aspire to be one. See Sumit Ganguly, "Think Again: India's Rise," *Foreign Policy,* July 5, 2012, http://www.foreignpolicy.com/articles/2012/07/05/think_again_india_s_rise; and Ramachandra Guha, "Ten Reasons Why India Will Not and Should Not Become a Superpower," lecture at the International Development Research Centre, Ottawa, Canada, video, http://www.youtube.com/watch?v=TVbhB1YjjA0 (accessed September 24, 2012).

7. Harinder Singh, *Establishing India's Military Readiness: Concerns and Strategy,* Monograph No. 5 (New Delhi: Institute of Defence Studies and Analyses, November 2011), 12.

8. International Institute for Strategic Studies (IISS), *The Military Balance 2012* (London: Routledge, 2012), 217.

9. Singh, *Establishing India's Military Readiness,* 130.

10. Ibid., 12.

11. The shopping list includes six Lockheed C-130J Super Hercules military transport aircraft for $1.2 billion (Rs 6,000 crore), 310 Russian T-90 tanks for $800 million (Rs 4,000 crore), eight Boeing P81 Super Hunters for $2.1 billion (Rs 10,500 crore), 250–300 FGFA Sukhoi T-50 PAK FA for $30 billion (Rs 150,000 crore), and 10 Boeing C17 Globemaster III aircraft for $5.8 billion (Rs 29,000 crore). Modernization of INS Vikramaditya will cost $2.33 billion (Rs 11,650 crore). The list further includes 3,000 artillery guns for $4 billion (Rs 20,000 crore), 75 Pilatus trawler aircraft for $1 billion (Rs 5,000 crore), attack and heavy lift helicopters for $2 billion (Rs 10,000 crore), six midair refuellers for $1 billion (Rs 5,000 crore), and 197 helicopters for reconnaissance and surveillance for $650 million (Rs 3,250 crore). Gautam Nalakha, "India: Military Budget 2013–14: Giant with Clay Feet," *Economic and Politics Weekly* 38, no. 24 (June 15, 2013), http://www.epw.in/perspectives/military-budget-2013-14 .html.

12. "China Boosts Defense Spending as Military Modernizes Arsenal," Bloomberg News, March 5, 2013, http://www.bloomberg.com/news/2013 -03-05/china-boosts-defense-spending-as-military-modernizes-its -arsenal.html.

13. IISS, *Military Balance 2012,* 215.

14. See Stockholm International Peace Research Institute, SIPRI Military Expenditure Data Base, http://milexdata.sipri.org/result.php4 (accessed January 21, 2013).

15. Congressional Research Service, "Direct Overt Aid Appropriations for Military Reimbursements to Pakistan, FY2002–FY2014," April 2013, Washington, DC, http://www.fas.org/sgp/crs/row/pakaid.pdf.

16. The combined strength of the army, navy, air force, and paramilitary forces, however, adds up to nearly 2,414,700 troops, the world's second largest military after China.

17. A corps is an army field formation responsible for a zone within a command theater. There are three types of corps in the Indian Army: Strike, Holding, and Mixed. A command generally consists of two or more corps. A corps has army divisions under its command. The corps headquarters is the highest field formation in the army.

18. See the Ministry of Defence, "Security Environment—An Overview," http://mod.nic.in/aforces/body.htm (accessed February 12, 2013). The Ministry of Defence defines the basic responsibilities of the Indian Army as safeguarding the nation's territorial integrity, assisting the civil administration during internal security disturbances, maintaining law and order, and

providing relief operations during natural calamities such as floods, earthquakes, and cyclones.

19. Indian forces engaged Pakistani soldiers from the Northern Light Infantry at altitudes of 14,000–17,000 feet in Siachen. In Kargil, Indian forces were at a marked disadvantage because Pakistan had occupied the higher ground, which Indian troops had to recapture. In order to minimize the risk of escalation to a nuclear level, Indian troops had to recapture their territory, not make diversionary forays into Pakistan, and remain strictly on their side of the Line of Control.

20. C. Christine Fair, "US–Indian Army-to-Army Relations: Prospects for Future Coalition Operations," *Asian Security* 1, no. 2 (April 2005): 162, quotes a US Army foreign area officer saying that the US military (especially in the conduct of military operations other than war) could be informed by Indian approaches to counterinsurgency, which may be more suitable than current US practices.

21. Walter Ladwig III, "India and Military Power Projection: Will the Land of Gandhi Become a Conventional Great Power?" *Asian Survey* 50, no. 6 (November–December 2010): 1167.

22. Masood Ur Rehman Khattak, "Indian Military Cold Start Doctrine: Capabilities, Limitations, and Possible Response from Pakistan," Research Paper 32 (London: South Asian Strategic Stability Institute, March 2011), 6.

23. In line with these ideas, the Indian Army held a number of major military exercises—Divya Astra (2004), Vajra Shakti (2005), Desert Strike (2005), Sanghe Shakti (2006), and Aswamedh (2007)—on the western front applying the operational logic of the Cold Start War Doctrine.

24. Ladwig, "India and Military Power," 165. See also his "A Cold Start for Hot Wars? The Indian Army's New Limited War Doctrine," *International Security* 32, no. 3 (Winter 2007–2008): 158–190.

25. "No Cold Start Doctrine: India Tells the US," *Indian Express*, September 9, 2010, http://www.indianexpress.com/news/no-cold-start -doctrine-india-tells-us/679273/.

26. See "Exercise Vijayee Bhava to Boost Synergy Between Armed Forces," Yahoo! News, May 9, 2011, http://in.news.yahoo.com/exercise -vijayee-bhava-boost-synergy-between-armed-forces-105205242.html.

27. For reference to threats, see "India Faces Twin Threats from China, Pakistan: IAF Chief," CNN-IBN video, April 29, 2012, http://ibnlive.in .com/videos/253189/india-faces-twin-threats-from-china-pakistan-iaf -chief.html.

28. The Pakistan Air Force has about 453 combat aircrafts and 65,000 active personnel operating out of nine airbases. Its strike fighters consist of US, Chinese, and aging French fighters such as the F-16 Fighting Falcon, the JF-17 Thunder, and the Dassault Mirage ROSE-III. The air force also has transport aircraft such as the Lockheed Martin C-130 and Airbus A310. However, unlike India, there are no unmanned aerial vehicles or reconnaissance aircraft in the Pakistan Air Force. For details on Pakistan's number

and types of aircraft, see IISS, *Military Balance 2012*, 274. For Indian Air Force strength and types of aircraft as well as equipment, see IISS, *Military Balance 2012*, 246.

29. B. K. Pandey, "Indian Air Force of the Future," *Indian Defence Review*, March 2009, http://www.indiandefencereview.com/2009/03/indian -air-force-of-the-future.html. The army has approved the Agni-3, a 3,000-kilometer-range (1,864-mile) missile. Agni-4 was successfully tested in November 2011 and Agni-5, an intercontinental missile with a range of 5,000 kilometers (3,100 miles), was tested in September 2013. It is to be inducted in India's strategic command between 2014 and 2015 provided all the tests are successful.

30. For instance, an AWACS flying over the Indian town of Amritsar will be able to detect a Pakistani F-16 fighter as soon as it takes off from the Sargodha airbase in Pakistan. In July, India also signed a $210 million deal with the Brazilian firm Embracer for three aircraft to serve as aerial platforms for its own indigenous miniature AWACS project. "Indian Airforce: Phalcon-AWACS to Be Delivered Jan–Feb 2009," India Defence, September 17, 2008, http://www.india-defence.com/reports-4021.

31. Cited In Rahul Bedi, "Getting in Step: India Country Briefing," *Jane's Defence Weekly,* February 6, 2008, 6.

32. IISS, *Military Balance 2012*, 244–245.

33. Vinay Kumar, "Credible Navy Need of the Hour: Antony," *The Hindu,* July 22, 2012, http://www.thehindu.com/news/credible-navy-need -of-the-hour-antony/article3665741.ece.

34. Gurmeet Kanwal, "India's Military Modernization: Plans and Strategic Underpinnings," National Bureau of Asian Research, September 24, 2012, http://www.nbr.org/research/activity.aspx?id=275#.UliAV2Tk8zE.

35. "The Indian Navy's surface-strike capability centers on the 290-kilometer-range (180-mile) supersonic BrahMos cruise missile. This missile is three times faster than the US Tomahawk cruise missile. The BrahMos is good for an antishipping role, but its capacity for land attack is limited. The Indian Defence Research and Development Organization is currently developing a subsonic cruise missile with a reported range of 1,000 kilometers (620 miles), code-named Nirbhay, which could fill an important gap in the navy's land-attack capability. Although the March 12, 2013, test failed, India is planning to integrate a variant of Nirbhay into the newly acquired Suhkoi Su-30 MKI Flanker strike aircraft, which will give India a long-range—and potentially strategic—strike capability. Although details on the Nirbhay program remain scant, Indian officials confirm the proposed range of 800–1,000 km. (500–620 miles). See "India to Test Nirbhaya Cruise Missile in 2012," November 15, 2011, http://rusnavy.com/news/other navies/index.php?ELEMENT_ID=13620.

36. Thomas P. M. Barnett, "India's 12 Steps to World Class Navy," 2001, Bharat Rakshak, http://www.bharat-rakshak.com/NAVY/History /2000s/Barnett.html. Also see Suryakanthi Tripathi, "The Indian Ocean—Rim, Routes, and Region: An Overview," *Indian Review of Global Affairs,*

November 9, 2012, http://www.irgamag.com/component/k2/item/384-the
-indian-ocean-rim-routes-and-region-an-overview.

37. "India's Navy in $1.8bn Sub Deal," BBC News, September 12, 2005, http://news.bbc.co.uk/2/hi/business/4237578.stm.

38. According to a US Energy Information Administration estimate, the Straits of Malacca recorded a transit volume of 15.2 million barrels of oil per day in 2011. Over 60,000 vessels transit the Straits of Malacca per day. If the strait were blocked, nearly half of the world's fleet would be required to reroute around the Indonesian archipelago through Lombok Strait, located between the islands of Bali and Lombok, or the Sunda Strait, located between Java and Sumatra. See "World Oil Transit Chokepoints," August 22, 2012, http://www.eia.gov/countries/regions-topics2.cfm?fips=WOTC.

39. Sea lines of communication (SLOC) is a term describing the primary maritime routes between ports used for trade, logistics, and naval forces. SLOC refers to naval operations that seek to keep SLOCs open, or in times of war, to close them. Sea-denial navies have the ability to control the chokepoints in the body of water where an adversary is denied passage.

40. Walter Ladwig III, "Delhi's Pacific Ambitions: Naval Power, 'Look East,' and India's Emerging Influence in the Asia-Pacific," *Asian Security* 5, no. 2 (2009): 105.

41. "Nuclear Weapons: Who Has What at a Glance," Arms Control Association, August 2012, http://www.armscontrol.org/factsheets/Nuclear weaponswhohaswhat.

42. Ibid.

43. Dmitri, "India vs China on Military Strength—Conventional and Nuclear," Aby the Liberal, June 5, 2007, http://www.abytheliberal.com /internationalism/india-vs-china-military-conventional-nuclear.

44. Telephonic conversation with Raja Raman, a leading commentator on India's nuclear program and a physicist of international repute, Princeton, New Jersey, June 2009.

45. Dmitri, "India vs China."

46. "Army and Navy Plan to Set Up a Marine Brigade," *India Today,* June 9, 2010, http://indiatoday.intoday.in/story/army-and-navy-plan-to-set -up-a-marine-brigade/1/100770.html.

47. Ibid.

48. "L INS Jalashwa Landing Platform Dock (LPD)," GlobalSecurity.org, http://www.globalsecurity.org/military/world/india/l-jalashwa.htm (accessed September 24, 2012).

49. "14 Countries to Join India in Naval Exercise," *Economic Times,* January 30, 2012, http://articles.economictimes.indiatimes.com/2012-01 -30/news/31005751_1_indian-navy-andaman-and-nicobar-command -exercise.

50. Singh, *Establishing India's Military Readiness,* 207.

51. Ibid., 216.

52. IISS, *Military Balance 2012,* 217.

53. "Agni-V Capable of Reaching China, Test Fired Successfully," *Times of India,* April 19, 2012, http://articles.timesofindia.indiatimes.com /2012-04-19/india/31366912_1_agni-v-inter-continental-ballistic-missiles -wheeler-island.

54. See "Prospects for Global Defence Export Industry in Indian Defence Market," a study produced by Deloitte, with the assistance of Confederation of Indian Industry Mission, EUROSATORY (2010), 30, Table 11, http://www.deloitte.com.br/publicacoes/2007/Prospects_for_global_defence _export_industry_indian_defence_market.pdf (accessed October 22, 2013).

55. Ibid., 31.

56. Devin Hagerty, "The Kargil War: An Optimistic Assessment," in *Nuclear Proliferation in South Asia: Crisis Behaviour and the Bomb,* ed. Sumit Ganguly and S. Paul Kapur (New York: Routledge, 2009), 134.

57. David Robinson, "India's Rise as a Great Power, Part Two: The Pakistan-China-India Dynamic" (Nedlands, Australia: Future Directions International, July 14, 2011), http://www.futuredirections.org.au /publications/associate-papers/145-indias-rise-as-a-great-power-part-two -the-pakistan-china-india-dynamic.html. See also Vipin Narang, "Posturing for Peace? Pakistan's Nuclear Posture and South Asian Stability," *International Security* 34, no. 3 (Winter 2009–2010): 39, http://belfercenter.ksg .harvard.edu/publication/19882/posturing_for_peace_pakistans_nuclear _postures_and_south_asian_stability.html.

58. Christopher Clary, "What Might an India-Pakistan War Look Like?" (Cambridge, MA: MIT Center for International Studies, Spring 2012), http://web.mit.edu/cis/precis/2012spring/india_pakistan.html#.UidiuBasjdl. See also Sumit Ganguly and S. Paul Kapur, *India, Pakistan, and the Bomb* (New York: Columbia University Press, 2010), 61–83.

59. Singh, *Establishing India's Military Readiness,* 76.

60. Shanthie Mariet D'Souza, *India-Afghanistan Strategic Partnership: Beyond 2014?* ISAS Insights No. 142 (Singapore: Institute of South Asian Studies, October 24, 2011), 1.

61. "Taliban Praise India for Resisting US Pressure on Afghanistan," *Times of India,* July 17, 2012, http://articles.timesofindia.indiatimes.com /2012-06-17/india/32281402_1_afghan-taliban-mullah-omar-northern -alliance.

62. "India and Afghanistan Unveil Strategic Road," Reuters, January 23, 2009, http://in.reuters.com/article/2009/01/22/idINIndia-376056200901 22Reuters.

63. The 2008 suicide bombing of the Indian Embassy in Kabul, which killed fifty-eight people, including two Indian diplomats, was suspected to have been instigated by Pakistan's Inter-Service Intelligence (ISI). US intelligence later supported this conclusion. An October 2009 bombing killed seventeen people and injured scores of others outside the Indian Embassy. Although the Taliban claimed responsibility for the 2009 bombing, Indian government circles strongly suspected the ISI's hand behind it.

64. See Stephen Blank, "India's Continuing Drive into Central Asia," *Central Asia Caucus Analyst,* January 14, 2004, 8–9, http://www.cacianalyst .org/?q=node/1758.

65. Juli MacDonald, "Rethinking India's and Pakistan's Regional Intent," *NBR Analysis* 14, no. 4 (2003): 5–26.

66. Ibid., 20.

67. Before the publication of his 2011 monograph on military preparedness written for the Institute of Defence Studies and Analyses, Singh commanded a brigade in the western sector. Singh, *Establishing India's Military Readiness,* 55.

68. Ananth Krishan, "Amid Strains, India, China Look to Push Trade Ties," *The Hindu,* May 27, 2012, http://www.thehindu.com/news /international/article3459857.ece.

69. Deepak Kapoor, "India's China Concern," *Strategic Analysis* 36, no. 4 (July–August 2012): 663.

70. Ibid. See also speech by Nirupama Rao, "On India-China Relations," Observer Foundation, New Delhi, India, December 3, 2010, 7, Vitalspeechesinternational.com.

71. It is noteworthy that China has helped Pakistan build a reactor to produce weapons-grade plutonium at the Chashma nuclear facility. It has transferred M-9 and M-11 ballistic missiles and also facilitated the clandestine transfer of Taepo Dong and No Dong missiles from North Korea to Pakistan.

72. Francine Frankel, "The Breakout of China-India Strategic Rivalry in Asia and the Indian Ocean," *Journal of International Affairs* 64, no. 2 (Spring–Summer 2011): 2.

73. Ibid., 2.

74. Mohan Malik, "China and India Today: Diplomats Jostle, Militaries Prepare," *World Affairs,* July–August 2012, http://www.worldaffairsjournal .org/article/china-and-india-today-diplomats-jostle-militaries-prepare.

75. Brahma Chellaney, "Assessing India's Reaction to China's Peaceful Development Doctrine," *NBR Analysis* 18, no. 5 (April 2008): 26–27.

76. The ONGC and the Gas Authority of India had owned close to a 30 percent stake in Myanmar's gas fields A-1 and A-3.

77. Robert Kaplan, "Center Stage for the Twenty-First Century: Power Plays in the Indian Ocean," *Foreign Affairs* 88, no. 2 (March–April 2009): 16–29.

78. "Analysis: China Pursues Pakistan Nuclear Deal; Dilemma in West," Reuters, December 15, 2010, http://af.reuters.com/article/energyOil News/idAFL3E6NF08Q20101215.

79. Malik, "China and India Today."

80. "India Ignores China Warning over Oil," *Taipei Times,* September 25, 2011, http://www.taipeitimes.com/News/world/archives/2011/09/25/200 3514155.

81. Quoted in Malik, "China and India Today."

82. Rahul Bedi, "Indian Air Force Draft Doctrine Envisions Broader Role," *Defense and Security Intelligence and Analysis: HIS Jane's,* August 8, 2007, http://www.janes.com/products/janes/defence-security-report.aspx?id=1065927009.

83. See "Indian Army Doctrine" (Shimla, India: Army Training Command, October 2004).

84. "Navy Releases 2009 Version of Maritime Doctrine," *The Hindu,* August 29, 2009, http://www.hindu.com/2009/08/29/stories/2009082960571000.htm.

85. George Tanham, "Indian Strategic Thought: An Interpretive Essay" (Santa Monica, CA: Rand, 1992), www.rand.org/pubs/reports/2007/R4207.pdf.

86. Stephen Peter Rosen, *Societies and Military Power: India and Its Armies* (Ithaca, NY: Cornell University Press, 1996).

87. Rajesh Basrur cited in Stephen P. Cohen and Sunil Dasgupta, *Arming Without Aiming: India's Military Modernization* (Washington, DC: Brookings Institution Press, 2010), x.

88. Cohen and Dasgupta, *Arming Without Aiming.*

89. Singh, *Establishing India's Military Readiness,* 104.

90. Ibid., 105.

91. Ibid.

92. Ibid.

93. Ibid.

94. Ibid., 133.

7

Soft Power

Buoyed by rapid rates of growth, the acquisition of nuclear weapons, closer defense and strategic ties with the United States, and inclusion in global forums, India's self-esteem markedly advanced under coalition governments. But the internal debate about India's future course continued. Many within and outside India argued that the country was on its way to becoming a great power. Others disagreed. Much of this debate turned on the moral and material implications of prosperity. For some, growth had little meaning if it did not eliminate poverty; for others, growth was the only way to eliminate poverty. Yet another set of commentators believed that growth could not be sustained if it was not inclusive. India, in this view, had the wherewithal to strike a grand bargain with its people and achieve both; all that was needed was the right balance. And once it had figured out the formula, growth and prosperity would flow more smoothly, making India an internationally influential state.

But in the twenty-first century, international influence is measured by more than building a strong economy and powerful military or successful balancing of political demands within; it is measured, in addition to these, by a state's ability to shape international discourse and world opinion. Whether a country has the potential for greatness is dependent to a large extent on perceptions, that is, how

213

friends and foes regard that country's potential importance in international politics. This is where possession of "soft power"—described by Joseph Nye Jr. as an ability to shape events and opinion by noncoercive means—really counts. Almost all hegemonic powers possess soft power, says Nye, an eminent scholar of international politics. In Nye's view, soft power is "co-optive power," an ability to get "what you want through attraction rather than coercion or payments. It arises from the attractiveness of a country's culture, political ideals, and policies."[1] Culture in the soft power context is a set of practices that create meaning for a society, which may be high culture such as literature and the arts expressed through television, films, and music, or mass culture such as folk forms and popular entertainment markets.[2] If a country pursues ideals that uphold international law and international norms, such as noninterference and human rights, it will be regarded as worthy of emulation instead of as a country that flaunts international norms and goes about committing aggression or oppressing its people. Similarly, stable political institutions, values that respect popular consent, and effective governance will be an attractive model for others. It is also important to remember that in the twenty-first century, states are no longer the sole depository of international power. Global and international networks, civil society groups, nongovernmental organizations (NGOs), multilateral organizations, and even individuals exert far greater influence on international perceptions than ever before. The influence of such networks is visible in shaping policies for transnational collective problems like climate change or single issues like banning landmines.[3] Soft power strategies eschew the traditional foreign policy instruments of carrot and stick and work through using transnational networks to build and communicate compelling narratives about policies and events, forging a coalition of international actors behind a policy or a norm. In short, "hard power is push; soft power is pull."[4]

The concept of soft power is especially appealing to India's foreign policy community because its noncoercive nature fits with their own image of their country as a peaceful democracy. Shashi Tharoor, currently the minister of state for human resources in the United Progressive Alliance (UPA) II and a strong advocate of cultural power, believes that soft power without hard power is an instrument of the weak but hard power alone frequently leads to resentment.[5] Tharoor makes a strong case for India's potential for soft power. In support of Tharoor's advocacy, John Lee, another student of soft power, observes, "India's enormous 'soft power' potential in Asia is based not on the growing popularity of Bollywood movies and Indian cuisine but on the fact that a rising India (unlike China) complements rather than challenges the preferred strategic, cultural and normative regional order."[6] Tharoor notes that in addition to India's civilizational contributions, the Indian diaspora is a critical asset in India's wielding soft power.[7] David Malone, a former Canadian ambassador to India and an author of highly acclaimed books on India's foreign policy, comments that "India's diaspora" is "certainly an asset," but far from the only one. India is attractive also because of its "cultural and civilisational riches, its vibrant (if at times chaotic) democracy, its free media, its mostly independent judiciary, its dynamic civil society, and the impressive struggle for human rights since independence."[8]

This chapter looks at three key instruments (among several that have been cited by experts) to understand the sources of India's soft power and the extent to which India has leveraged these to advance its cause. They are India's civilizational experience, its democracy, and its diaspora. All three fit neatly into Eric Ringman's measures for assessing a country's potential for power, which he defines as a nation's capacity to evolve and implement a vision for change that sets the course of its future policy and shapes international perceptions of a nation's power potential. I argued in Chapter 2 that India's choice of a federal democracy as a tool for nation-building is both a vision and a policy that was culled from a particular understanding of India's history. The pioneers of India's independence saw the country's past as characterized by ethnic and religious accommodation, avoidance of conflict, and a quest for excellence. These characteristics are reflected in India's foreign policy, which shows a marked preference for defensive, rather than aggressive, behavior and for maintenance of the status quo in preference to war. How well has India leveraged its soft power assets? A short answer is that it has begun to leverage its democracy and economic achievements to gain a place among tomorrow's rising powers but the full advantage of its civilizational achievements remains to be exploited. It is yet to develop the foreign policy instruments and required strategies to make full use of its unique developmental model.

Indian Civilization as a Soft Power Asset

As a state that is also a great civilization, India possesses formidable resources to project its culture and to affect by example. India is the birthplace of two great world religions, and its temple arts, sculpture, music, and dance compare with the best in the ancient world. India was a land of fabulous wealth and great empires until the collapse of the Mughal Empire in the eighteenth century. The achievements and glory of the past, however, were insufficient to insure India against the vicissitudes of more recent history. India declined steadily as a new imperial power, this time from Europe, appeared on the horizon. Within a matter of a few decades, a small number of merchants and traders had assumed control over the subcontinent. By 1857, the British East India Company owned most of India. The sun had set on the great Mughal Empire. Dissatisfied with the ways in which the land was governed, the British Crown took over from the East India Company and declared India a crown colony in 1857.

For the next century, as the British Raj put down roots and expanded to all corners of the subcontinent, the world came to see India through a colonial prism. It was a mixed picture. A few British administrators admired and wrote about the cultural achievements of ancient India, its arts and its languages, but for the most part India moved to the periphery of great-power politics, figuring only as a colonial rampart of the British Empire. To the British, India was the land of maharajahs and warring princelings, where religion and traditions held sway and caste discrimination, poverty, and illiteracy predominated. These images persisted in the Western mind even after the British had departed and an independent nation of India was born in 1947.[9]

In a study carried out in the early 1950s based on interviews of US officials and diplomats, Harold Isaacs, one of the first to write about Americans' perceptions of India, observed that they constructed their views with "bits and pieces" gathered from their British cousins across the pond. In the American mind, India came to be associated with "the notion of mystery and fabulousness, the religionists and philosophers, the benighted heathen masses, the varieties of 'lesser breed,' and to this were added the images of Gandhi and Nehru . . . all mingled in the kaleidoscope."[10] Although he found Mohandas Gandhi widely admired by most Americans, they thought the Indian leader impractical. Prime Minister Jawaharlal Nehru, in contrast, elicited sharply negative reactions. A few American officials and people from the media admired his writings, but an overwhelming number resented Nehru's refusal to support the US Cold War "containment" strategy. India's nonalignment was derided as empty posturing and Nehru was condemned in the media and American official circles as arrogant and self-righteous.[11]

These Western assessments were shaped by the ideological stance of the United States, which regarded nonalignment as immoral and opportunistic. But such biased perceptions are no guide to India's soft power potential. They merely explain the nature of dominant discourse at the time. What are important here are India's self-perceptions. Priya Chacko analyzes several instances when India refrained from choosing the conventional response to international challenges.[12] The most dramatic example among the several she cites is India's decision not to develop a nuclear arsenal for twenty-four years after having demonstrated (the 1974 tests) the ability to do so. India was among the first countries to recognize the People's Republic of China and champion its entry into the United Nations in place of Taiwan and continued to do so despite China's annexation of Tibet. After the 1971 war and the birth of Bangladesh, India withdrew without hesitation and repatriated 93,000 Pakistani prisoners of war without demanding an explicit quid pro quo from Pakistan. Lastly, India hastened the withdrawal of its peacekeeping forces from Sri Lanka when asked to do so by the Ranasinghe Premadasa government, although this put Indian soldiers at risk.[13] Had India acquiesced to conventional expectations, according to Chacko, it would have pursued nuclear weapons immediately upon gaining the capability to do so, refrained from supporting China's entry into the United Nations because China was a potential rival in Asia, insisted on a settlement of Kashmir in exchange for the Pakistan prisoners of war, and not given in to Premadasa's insistence on the withdrawal of Indian troops when their original mandate, to which Sri Lanka had agreed, remained incomplete.

Chacko ascribes these choices to the way India understands its own international identity, which is shaped by "a deep ambivalence toward Western modernity which incorporates self-understanding of India's long and rich cultural and civilizational heritage."[14] "This ambivalence," she remarks,

> arises because, on the one hand, Indian nationalists accepted colonial narratives in which the backwardness of "Indian civilization" led to its

degeneration, but on the other hand, they recognized the need to advance a critique of western modernity and its deep imbrication with colonialism. The result is a striving for a post-colonial modernity that is not only imitative but strives to be distinctly different and superior to western modernity by being culturally and morally grounded.[15]

Chacko has based her conclusion on a careful examination of Indian writings of the nationalist era, which agree with some colonial critiques of India's backwardness, but asserts at the same time that Indians can draw on the historical depth of experience to frame their own solutions to the challenge of nation-building.

That is why India consistently opted for the power of persuasion over the use of force. This alternative definition of power was evident in the first decade after independence in India's active mediation to prevent the Korean War if possible; in India's fierce opposition to the formation of military blocs, such as NATO and the Warsaw Pact; in the founding of the nonaligned movement; and in India's advocacy of five principles, known as the Panchsheel, as guidelines for interstate relations. These principles were mutual respect for each other's territory and sovereignty, mutual nonaggression, noninterference in each other's internal affairs, equality and mutual benefit, and peaceful coexistence. But the dominant discourse of the Cold War was hostile to Indian "middle-way" approaches. India's foreign policy declarations were regarded as the empty rhetoric of a weak country claiming a status far higher than what it actually deserved.

At this stage, India could leverage neither its democracy nor its civilizational past, nor was there receptivity to India's advocacy of negotiated settlements for several Cold War conflicts. In the view of many Western commentators, democracy was an unwarranted luxury for a poor and undeveloped India. India's nationalist leaders rejected this assessment while acknowledging that underdevelopment and lack of unity were the reasons for the nation's succumbing to the British colonialism and its consequences, namely, enslavement and poverty.

Keen students of India in the West, such as Selig Harrison Jr., were pessimistic about its future, as was V. S. Naipaul. In his initial assessment, made popular through volumes such as *India: A Wounded Civilization* and *An Area of Darkness,* Naipaul wrote that India and Indians lacked the innate strength to overcome the country's civilizational flaws. Subsequently, however, Naipaul all but admitted that he had been too hasty in his judgments and that the "area of darkness" had turned into a land of a "million mutinies" (*India: A Million Mutinies Now*) that no longer feared disintegration.

India's battle to build a secular democracy, to empower its people, to achieve equitable economic development, and to hew an independent path in foreign policy drew no accolades from a world caught in Cold War rivalries. Its venerable past had little bearing on tense Indo-US relations. Angry at India's nonaligned stance, Washington turned to Pakistan and showered it with economic and military assistance. India was no strategic asset, too weak, too poor, and too independent to be of any use to the United States against the Soviet Union. In fact, George Tanham, a leading scholar of Indo-US relations, observed decades later that India lacked a strategic culture and that its leaders tended to confuse the idea of India as a great power with its civilizational past. India had built a great civilization, but its claims to great power were not credible.[16] As a true realist, Tanham measured power and asked, as perhaps Joseph Stalin might have asked, How many battalions can a temple raise? India had thousands of temples, but on the world stage at that time it was an insignificant military and economic power.

But the end of the Cold War changed the international discourse about war and peace and about sources of power. Even though the fear of a general world war vanished, a growing incidence of civil and religious conflicts soon prompted new fears. These new wars weakened the international order, built, as it was, on the sanctity of sovereign nation-states. Clashes between differing cultures, whether between fundamentalist Islam and the Christian West or between radical and moderate Islam, were considered more probable than interstate conflicts. Victors in the Cold War soon found that devising a workable formula for interethnic, interreligious harmony within a democratic framework was perhaps the greatest challenge they faced. This challenge was highlighted repeatedly throughout the wars in disintegrated Yugoslavia, post-Saddam Iraq, and post-America Afghanistan. Indeed, closer to India, Pakistan faced a similar challenge. Its outcome will have far-reaching consequences for the entire arch of countries from the Persian Gulf to China's western Muslim regions.

Anxiety about these issues took a quantum leap when rebellion against strongly pro-West authoritarian regimes spread throughout the Arab world in January 2011. The West found itself facing a stark choice between the promotion of democracy and the preservation of secular, albeit nondemocratic, regimes. Finding ways to combine both became the West's overriding preoccupation. Against this background, India's success in building a multiethnic, multireligious nation-state gained new salience. Indeed, President Bill Clinton, as Chapter 5 describes, went out of his way to repeatedly stress India's multiethnic nation-building success.

There is another way in which Indian experience has become potentially important—namely, in India's successful absorption of many Western values and institutions by claiming them as quintessentially Indian. There is, of course, a difference between mimicry and absorption. Both are amply visible in India's national life. Several other countries have also successfully absorbed Western values and made them a part of their national life: Japan, South Korea, Malaysia, and Singapore immediately come to mind. The East Asian states adopted modern markets and technology to grow prosperous, but attributed their success to their Confucian ethos and to "Asian" values of discipline, frugality, obedience, and hard work. Whatever the contributions of Asian values, East Asia's authoritarian states and their intervention in facilitating capitalist transformation arguably had a lot to do with this prosperity.

For the arc of Islamic countries stretching from Turkey to Indonesia, modernization has posed a far more complex and difficult challenge. Many in the Islamic world crave cultural authenticity and demand that the state's political identity be rooted in Islam. This, they believe, is the only way to prevent the destruction of their culture and the Muslim way of life. They point to the demeaning consequences of adopting Western values and hold Western imperialism responsible for their countries' multiple failures.[17]

In contrast to East Asia and the Islamic world, India has furrowed a third path. Its post–Cold War transformation has synchronized the gradual expansion of a market economy with a devolution of power away from the center and to the regions and provinces. Although the path has not always been smooth, India has repeatedly shown a capacity for self-correction within democratic constraints. A striking example in the realm of economic policy was India's rejection of the "shock therapy" mode of transformation from a command to a market economy so ardently advocated by the World Bank and the International Monetary Fund and followed to the edge of chaos by Russia. India's democracy, and the fact that when the Narasimha Rao government embarked upon reform it had a wafer thin majority in Parliament, virtually mandated the adoption of incremental change.

India's postreform transformation is more than just a notional pointer to a third path. Like East Asia, India has results to show for it. In the mid-1990s, the economy grew at an average rate of close to 7 percent per year until 2005–2008, when growth edged closer to 9 percent. Even during the 2008 recession, India retained a respectable momentum and continued its upward trajectory in 2010. In the following three years India's growth slowed down and the UPA government of Manmohan Singh, in its second term, faced waves of popular protests as numerous reports of political corruption involving government officials and ministers began to hit the headlines. There was no doubt, however, that over the decades following the economic reforms of 1992, India was a transformed country. And nations around the world saw it as such. India's transformational achievements can be measured by its inclusion in global economic forums for climate change and financial reforms. The Indo-US nuclear treaty adds a great-power imprimatur to India's economic success. The United States has agreed in principle to back India for a seat on the Security Council.

The National Intelligence Council (NIC) projects that Brazil, Russia, India, and China together will match the gross domestic product (GDP) of the original G7 countries by 2050.[18] For the first time since the eighteenth century, the report observes, China and India will become the largest contributors to worldwide economic growth and in all likelihood surpass, by 2025, the GDP of all other economies except the United States. India is projected to become the third-largest economy after the United States and China in 2025.[19] But India's leaders seek to put India's power behind the construction of a multipolar world in which no single country can dominate. That vision of a world order is as much a reflection of their understanding of future realities as it is of their distinctly different worldview. And this worldview is drawn from their understanding of their own history and of human affairs as represented by their civilization.

Indian Democracy as a Soft Power Asset

India's history has provided Indian leaders with an understanding of how best to build a multiethnic democracy. Prime Minister Manmohan Singh echoed previous generations of Indian leaders when, addressing an audience at Oxford University in 2005, he observed,

> The idea of India . . . with its emphasis on the principles of secularism, democracy, the rule of law and, above all, the equality of all human beings irrespective of caste, community, language or ethnicity, has deep roots in India's ancient civilization. Our Constitution remains a testimony to the enduring interplay between what is essentially Indian and what is very British in our intellectual heritage. The idea of India as an inclusive and plural society draws on both these traditions. The success of our experiment of building a democracy within the framework of a multi-cultural, multi-ethnic, multi-lingual and multi-religious society will encourage all societies to walk the path we have trodden.[20]

India's attempt to systematically leverage its democracy and political values has fluctuated with time and circumstance. Until the 1970s, scholarly literature as well as popular tracts considered India an unlikely candidate for an enduring democracy. The country was extremely poor, underdeveloped, and predominantly agricultural. Its heterogeneity raised serious questions about its survival as a unified, single state, while its vulnerability to hunger and famines made a mockery of its planned development. How could a country so large, so diverse, and so poor develop as a secular and pluralist democracy? This question changed into a grudging recognition and, more recently, into an acceptance of the Indian experiment. To arrive at this acknowledgment, however, required betting against a long list of what were perceived as fundamental flaws, some of which resulted from the mechanical application of Western models to Indian progress.

Throughout the 1970s and 1980s, the stress on flaws persisted. In the view of many observers, these flaws—a bankrupt economy and a failing central government—were responsible for the multiple crises of the early 1990s. Popular and scholarly comments pointed to a weakened India and feared that the center might disintegrate. The stormy rise of Hindu nationalism and caste wars in the 1990s precipitated by debates over quotas and reservations for the backward castes and classes reinforced the impression that India's historic characteristics—fragmentation and weakening—had resumed their course.

It was not until economic reforms were well under way in the late 1990s and new foreign policy alliances had been forged that Indian leaders began to think about pointing to the difficulty of their situation and the resilience of their model, which had survived the twin dangers of economic and political collapse. The advent of a responsible coalition government led by the Bharatiya Janata Party (BJP) followed by an equally stable United Progressive Alliance (UPA) coalition changed the tone of international commentary as well. The contrast between India and its neighboring states was too stark to be ignored. Afghanistan and Pakistan had become the cockpit of Islamic extremism, Nepal had succumbed to Maoist insurgency, and Sri Lanka remained trapped in a bloody civil war. Beginning with the Clinton administration, policy circles in Washington began to comment on India as an island of stability. President Clinton was particularly appreciative of India's ability to cope with diversity and religious separatism. Anxious to be seen as a promoter of global democracy, President George W. Bush was even more vigorous in his praise for India's democracy. Western media and official circles routinely commented on the natural links between the world's largest and the world's strongest democracies.

The positive press and shifting perceptions did not appease domestic critics, who pointed to a multiplicity of flaws in India's transformation strategy: a tendency to avoid painful and difficult changes and opt instead for those that incurred few or possibly no political costs, a growing scale of corruption, and huge leaks in the delivery of assistance and subsidies meant for the poor, whose numbers remained stubbornly high. The burst of Maoist violence in the expanding swath of regions from Chhattisgarh to Andhra Pradesh underscored the refusal of the disempowered to accept their fate. Even though their rebellion reflected the failures of the much-publicized growth model, its success in reducing the number of poor and producing a vast new middle class could not be denied.

But most remarkably, and perhaps less well appreciated, was the triumph of a truly multiparty democracy in place of the dominant-party system that had defined Indian politics since 1947. What is more, the multiparty coalition model has been enhanced by the introduction of a third tier of electoral politics, which mandates village-level elections every five years. India pointed to the possibilities of a progressive devolution of power in which the market, democracy, and social welfare were closely interlinked while the state retained the capacity to regulate and intervene. It is true that panchayat (village-level) democracy is uneven and weak in wresting power from the better-endowed and more entrenched ruling circles and that the multiparty system is weak in delivering social justice or account-ability, but it is also true that Indian democracy is a work in progress. Its ability to expand and give voice to a growing number of people is undeniable, as is the visible and real empowerment of those who had no access to power in the past.

An important part of the attraction of Indian democracy is its ability to accommodate diversity. This is especially important as ideas of hard boundaries and homogenous nation-states have given way to the spread of global markets, the Internet, and ethnic and reli-gious nationalism. The Indian nation-building experiment accommo-dates many identities and substitutes the idea of hard sovereignty with a layered one. An Indian can at once be a Muslim, a Bihari, and a citizen. All three identities carry some form of recognition within the Indian legal-political system. India's federal experience has cre-ated a unique mix of order and representative democracy. It has shown a built-in capacity for the lateral devolution of political power so evident in post-1990 coalition governments.

The Indian model of accommodation stands in stark contrast to the solutions employed in Yugoslavia and Kosovo. The United States and the European powers sought to end the civil war in each instance by encouraging partition along ethnic lines. Widespread ethnic cleansing led to the creation of a Croatia for the Croats and a Serbia for the Serbs. A similar line of reasoning motivated proposals for dividing postwar Iraq into three parts: a Kurdish part, a Shia-dominated part, and a smaller Sunni-majority part. In contrast, the Indian experiment, however arguable its success, suggests that a par-ticipatory democracy is possible despite ethnic and religious sepa-ratism, violence, and poverty and that it can endure if the state is structured to accommodate new entrants into the political arena. It is these attributes—the capacity to weave together individual and group rights and balance regionalism, party competition, and minority protection—that have drawn increasing attention in a world besieged by ethnic wars, secessionist violence, and religious fundamentalism. India has managed to remain a democracy despite the presence of all three within its body politic.

Where President Clinton had repeatedly commented on the value of India's democratic experience, President Bush cited it to explain why the United States could trust India, but not Pakistan, with a nuclear treaty. In Bush's view, Pakistan had descended into military dictatorships throughout its history. Pranay Gupte, a well-known journalist, observed that with India and Pakistan in mind, President Bush "signaled that parity isn't a concept to be applied universally in contemporary diplomacy."[21]

Despite a history of Hindu-Muslim violence, the bulk of India's Muslims live within a democracy, vote and elect their representatives, and enjoy freedom of worship. The provision of a separate Muslim personal law offers protection for their customs and traditions while incorporating them in the competitive party system. This is a highly relevant counterexample for those who believe that Islam and democracy are incompatible. The Indian example points to the possibility of peaceful coexistence between Muslims and non-Muslims, but by the same token it also underscores the terrible failures. There have been many such in the Indian experiment; the most infamous among these were riots in Gujarat in 2002 and pogroms against Muslims in Ahmedabad. The Gujarat riots tarnished the image of a vigorous democracy for many years following that terrible carnage, but the UPA government that followed the BJP's defeat in the 2004 elections set out to investigate the deeper causes of Hindu-Muslim divisions and has been considering setting quotas in education and jobs for Indian Muslims as well. In May 2013, the government of India made a decision to grant 4.5 percent reservations for minorities largely targeting Muslims but the constitutionality of this decision is under debate by the Supreme Court. The clamor for an early decision on fixing these quotas has picked up steam as various parties eye the Muslim vote to ensure their win in their particular region.

Commenting on the Mumbai Muslim community's refusal to allow the terrorists killed in the December 2008 attack to be buried in the city's Muslim cemetery, Thomas Friedman, a widely read *New York Times* columnist, writes, "India's Muslims, who are the second-largest Muslim community in the world after Indonesia's, and the one with the deepest democratic tradition, do a great service to Islam by delegitimizing suicide-murderers by refusing to bury their bodies. It won't stop this trend overnight, but it can help over time." He observes that India's Muslims stood up to the attack largely because

they . . . are the product of and feel empowered by a democratic and pluralistic society. They are not intimidated by extremist religious leaders and are not afraid to speak out against religious extremism in their midst. It is why so few, if any, Indian Muslims are known to have joined Al Qaeda. And it is why, as outrageously expensive and as uncertain the outcome, trying to build decent, pluralistic societies in

places like Iraq is not as crazy as it seems. It takes a village, and without Arab-Muslim societies where the villagers feel ownership over their
lives and empowered to take on their own extremists—militarily and
ideologically—this trend will not go away.[22]

India's accommodation of religious differences, in the view of many
observers including Thomas Friedman, serves as an important study
on building from diversity.[23]

How do these domestic characteristics of pluralism, constitution-
alism, and democracy translate into soft power abroad? A short
answer is that they have provided India with moral credibility and a
voice in aligning itself with the prevailing global norms of social justice, human rights, collective security, and democracy.

The connections between soft power and security are hardly
ever direct or obvious, but they do make India more visible and por-
tray its life and culture in a positive light. This is clearly evident in
the example of Afghanistan, where India is trying to protect its
access to oil-rich Central Asia. Even though the Indian government
has given Afghanistan more than $1 billion of aid in building roads
and schools, it is the popularity of Indian television, particularly its
soap operas, that have "won the hearts and minds" of the average
Afghan. (The enormous popularity of Indian music forced the Taliban moral police to ban its sale and distribution in 1992, and the
more conservative faction in the Karzai government forced a partial
ban in 2008, which led to huge public protests against the ban.)
Such popularity permits India to showcase its civilizational attractiveness as well as its modern technological power.[24] India's presence on TV and screens has certainly won goodwill in Afghanistan
and the Arab world that have for decades watched Indian films and
TV soap operas. This ability to transcend formal government-to-
government relations is an important instrument of soft power,
which makes India attractive to other cultures and nations. The
endurance and vibrancy of the Indian democracy, though often characterized as raucously noisy, offers New Delhi the first soft power
advantage to promote its image and claim a moral right to speak
about human and political freedom.

The second soft power advantage of democracy is that, in contrast to China's development, India's rise has created no apprehension within the international community. It is largely viewed as
benign. This could be because India's economy and military have not
grown to the point where established powers feel threatened, but it

is also true that a state committed to the rule of law and regular elections, one that does not violate international norms of public consent and responsive government, is generally regarded as amenable to reason.[25] On the whole, democracies are less inclined to make war, act in an irresponsible manner, or indulge in crass violations of human and political rights. The same cannot be said of an authoritarian state, or, at least, that is the prevailing perception. Democratic norms constrain a state's behavior, even when it might be changing the balance of power and surrounding strategic calculations. The contrast between India and China in these regards is instructive. Although China's economy is miles ahead of India's, and its military power is far short of the Pentagon's, it is still regarded with deep apprehension, and many in US policy circles want China to be contained.

The Indian Diaspora as a Soft Power Asset

The projection of India as a rising power has also been made possible to a large degree by the number of Indians immigrating to the United States, Europe, and the Middle East since the 1970s. The total number of people of Indian origin living abroad is close to 25 million, making it perhaps the world's largest diaspora.

There have been two main phases of emigration from India. The first occurred in the early nineteenth century and may be called the colonial phase. The second, occurring during the postcolonial phase in the twentieth century, saw Indian immigrants arriving in industrially developed countries. Each phase differs in the composition of people who emigrated. During the colonial phase, a great number of Indians were taken to British colonies in the Caribbean, the Middle East, Africa, and Southeast Asia mainly to work on plantations owned by British, French, and Dutch companies. There was also a steady trickle of Indian traders in the wake of the plantation labor. This wave of migration at the time was impelled by the integration of peripheral economies into the emerging world capitalist colonial system. In many countries, people of Indian origin became a sizable minority; in Guyana, Fiji, Mauritius, and Suriname, they became a majority. With the end of the colonial era, and with the passage of time, these communities lost their Indian roots, but their emotional tie to India has remained strong and has strengthened even more with the rise in India's standing.

With the oil boom of the 1970s, a large number of Indians, skilled and unskilled, migrated to the Middle East, particularly to the Gulf states. They have remitted enormous amounts of capital back home since then, providing India with a precious foreign exchange cushion. Indeed, after Mumbai, Abu Dhabi has become a second hub for Indian traders, bankers, and businesspeople, who practically dominate the service sector of that entrepôt economy and use it as a springboard for expansion of businesses to Europe and Southeast Asia. According to Minister for Overseas Affairs Vayalar Ravi, "India received over USD 66.13 billion in remittances in the year 2011–12 as compared to USD 55.62 billion in the previous, a hike of 19 per cent."[26] These remittances have strengthened economic ties between India and global markets and between India's managerial and business classes.

The most important stream of migration, also accelerating since the 1970s, is to the United States, Canada, and England. The initial migrants to these countries were largely professionals from the middle classes of India's large cities and towns. They were soon joined by members of the less-well-educated working classes, whose ubiquitous presence is visible in the form of taxicab drivers and owners or employees of gas stations, grocery and convenience stores, and news kiosks in the cities on the Eastern and Western Seaboards of the United States. In 1975, there were 175,000 Asian Indians in America.[27] Their numbers have grown rapidly since then. According to the US Census Bureau, the Asian Indian population in the United States grew from almost 1,679,000 in 2000 to 2,570,000 in 2007, representing a growth rate of 53 percent—the highest for any Asian American community. In 2012, that figure was 3.18 million, thereby constituting 1 percent of the US population.[28] Indian Americans are the third-largest Asian American ethnic group, after Chinese Americans and Filipino Americans, and are among the fastest-growing ethnic groups in the United States.[29]

The American Dream

Whereas the first generation of immigrants to the United States remained attached to their culture, partly out of a sense of nostalgia but also as a way to build a community, the second generation of Indians, born and raised in the United States, has been far less concerned about building community or showcasing cultural heritage.

They have quickly adapted to the American dream and have ventured forth into politics, business, finance, banking and technology, social activism, and the arts, film, and entertainment—fields that were inaccessible to the first generation of Indians in America. The US motel business came to be synonymous with the Patels, members of a Gujarati-speaking community with close, clanlike ties, while many gas stations in New Jersey are owned and operated by Sikhs and Punjabis. Indian grocery stores and restaurants serve both upscale and less affluent American and British customers. Ambassador from India Mira Shankar pointed out in a 2010 speech,

> There are 50,000 India-born physicians, many of them highly specialized, who are an indispensable part of the U.S. healthcare system. There are 10,000 Indian American owners of hotels and motels, who employ nearly 600,000 people. Around 40% of all hotel rooms in the United States are owned by Indian Americans, driving to a great extent the growth of the tourism industry. The social mobility of the community is also reflected in its diversifying occupational profile.[30]

Both generations of immigrants have faced prejudice and discrimination, sometimes violent, which provided an initial impetus for political involvement and organizational efforts.[31]

A growing number of Indian Americans occupy strategic positions in the corporate world. An equally impressive number of Indian professionals work in universities. Indian immigrants in the United States are concentrated in the fields of information technology (IT), medicine, engineering, and law. Their contribution to biotechnology is particularly impressive. Indian scientists work in sensitive US government laboratories, including in the nuclear field. Boeing and the National Aeronautics and Space Administration (NASA) employ a significant number of Indian Americans as technicians. According to one estimate, close to 35 percent of Boeing's technical workforce is Indian.[32] At Silicon Valley's peak in the 1990s, close to 300,000 Indian Americans worked in technology firms there. They added up to "15% of high-tech start-ups and their average annual incomes were estimated to be $200,000. There are close to 650 to 700 Indian-owned companies in the Silicon valley, with more appearing every day."[33] Vivek Wadhwa notes, "Indians were the most numerous of the high-tech company founders. They had founded more startups than the next four groups (from Britain, China, Taiwan, and Japan) combined." The proportion of Indian-founded startups in Silicon Valley had increased from 26 percent to 33 percent since 2008 although the proportion of migrant start-ups was on a decline.[34]

This history of migration has produced some interesting diplomatic moments in recent Indo-US negotiations such as when an Indian American employed in the State Department took an important meeting with his counterpart in the Ministry of External Affairs, of course another Indian. During the 2010 Barack Obama–Manmohan Singh meeting in Washington, Singh's principal assistant and note-taker was his private secretary, Jaideep Sarkar, a young gun of the Indian Foreign Service. On the opposite side was his counterpart, Anish Goel, a senior appointee at the National Security Council and a rising star of the US Foreign Service. Anish Goel was born of Indian immigrant parents. When Washington engaged New Delhi on Af-Pak issues, the Indian government discovered that in day-to-day dealings with Special Envoy Richard Holbrooke, it had to consult with Vikram Singh, Holbrook's senior defense adviser. Indian American presence has become fairly common in the US government; many work as senior staffers and occupy assistant and deputy secretary positions in the government. The rise of Indian Americans in politics and journalism makes the idea of people-to-people ties between the two countries a physical reality.

The presence of Indian Americans in the US administration does not mean that these individuals can twist and bend US policy or influence legislation to favor India. For instance, Anish Goel, who earned a PhD in chemical engineering from MIT, had no influence on the outcome of the Indo-US nuclear deal, even though that is his area of expertise and he initially served as the desk officer dealing with the subject in the State Department. Similarly, Vikram Singh's influential role in Af-Pak policymaking did not exactly endear his boss, the late Richard Holbrooke, to New Delhi, which balked at efforts to add "In" to Af-Pak. In fact, that these men were of Indian origin may have made them more intent on not being seen as favoring India. Holbrooke's relationship with his counterparts in New Delhi remained wary.

Yet in the long run, the presence of Indian Americans in politics and administration will no doubt benefit India. By accumulating experience in public office and politics, the Indian community in America will learn about the inside workings of the government and develop connections that will outlast any single administration. Journalist Chidananda Rajghatta observes that, even though Chinese

Americans are more numerous, they do not enjoy the same level of
visibility as Indian Americans do in the United States. This may be
because Indian immigrants have better facility with English and are
familiar with the workings of a democracy. Both factors are advantages that have allowed for faster assimilation of Indians in the
American mainstream.[35]

Although many of the fourteen or so Indian Americans currently
in mid- and senior levels of the administration will move back and
forth from public office to academic positions and/or membership in
think tanks, a system that is quintessentially American, a few will
doubtless go on to occupy higher office, as Bobby Jindal did. He
was a policy wonk in health care, working as the principal adviser to
the secretary of health and human services during the first Bush
administration before running successfully for Congress in 2004 and
then for governor of Louisiana in 2007 (he was reelected in 2011).
In the 2008 presidential elections, Jindal came close to the Oval
Office when John McCain short-listed him as a Republican vice
presidential running mate. Although the final choice was Sarah
Palin, knowledgeable politicos believe that Jindal has a bright future
in the Republican Party, particularly if he does well in managing his
governorship (he is currently chairman of the Republican Governors
Association). Nikki Haley, currently governor of South Carolina and
the first woman to hold that position, is the daughter of Indian Sikhs
and is yet another rising star in the Republican Party. And there is a
separate stream of Indian Americans coming up from the grassroots
in the Democratic Party. Currently, Ami Bera (US Congress, California), Kumar Barve (Maryland House of Delegates, majority
leader since 1991), Kamala Harriss (California state attorney general), Prasad Srinivasan (state representative in Connecticut), and
Upendra Chivakula (deputy speaker, State Assembly of NJ) hold
elected public offices. Indian Americans are highly visible in other
fields as well: Dr. Sanjay Gupta of CNN, who, although he declined
it, was offered the post of US surgeon general; and journalist Fareed
Zakaria, who edited *Foreign Affairs,* is now an editor at large for
Time, and hosts a popular international affairs program on CNN.
Indra Nooyi, CEO of Pepsi; Shantanu Narayen, CEO of Adobe Systems; Lakshmi Niwas Mittal, CEO of Arcelor Mittal; and Anant
Gupta of HCL Technologies all head multimillion-dollar multinationals and have made their mark in the public sphere and corporate
world.

The India Lobby

The growing Indian American presence in US political and business life has had an undeniable effect on India and the United States. Two key developments—the post–Cold War economic reforms in India and the nuclear deal with Washington—would not have taken place without the Indian American community's urgings and consistent pressure to move the processes forward. Indeed, an India lobby was already beginning to crystallize in 2002. Frank Pallone, a New Jersey congressman representing the strong and well-heeled Indian business community that had settled in his part of the state, promoted the idea of a congressional caucus to deliberate concerns pertaining to India and Indian Americans.

In spelling out the consolidation of the India lobby and its impact on the success of the nuclear deal, journalist Mira Kamdar writes, "On Capitol Hill, despite deep divisions over Iraq, immigration and the outsourcing of American jobs to India, Democrats and Republicans quickly fell into line on the nuclear deal, voting for it last December [2006] by overwhelming bipartisan majorities. Even lawmakers who had made nuclear nonproliferation a core issue over their long careers, such as Sen. Richard Lugar (R-Ind), quickly came around to President Bush's point of view."[36]

Why did these lawmakers support the proposed deal when they had opposed it earlier? The answer, Kamdar suggests, is that

> the India lobby is now officially a powerful presence on the Hill. The nuclear pact brought together an Indian government that is savvier than ever about playing the Washington game, an Indian American community that is just coming into its own and powerful business interests that see India as perhaps the single biggest money-making opportunity of the 21st century. The nuclear deal has been pushed aggressively by well-funded groups representing industry in both countries. At the center of the lobbying effort has been Robert D. Blackwill, a former U.S. ambassador to India and deputy national security adviser who is now with a well-connected Republican lobbying firm, Barbour, Griffith & Rogers LLC. The firm's web site touts Blackwill as a pillar of its "India Practice," along with a more recent hire, Philip D. Zelikow, a former top adviser to Secretary of State Condoleezza Rice who was also one of the architects of the Bush administration's tilt toward India.[37]

With India expected to purchase weapons and weapons systems worth $100 billion for long-term defense plans (2012–2027), many major US corporations have thought it prudent to support the India lobby and contribute money to it. They are hoping that the nuclear deal will open the path to other lucrative deals, including building more nuclear power plants in India from which they can profit for years to come. According to a recent report by the Press Trust of India, "Nearly 20 United States–based companies and organizations spent more than $200 million last year [2012] to lobby American lawmakers for their Indian business interests and other issues affecting their businesses globally."[38] Lockheed Martin is said to be lobbying for a $4 to $9 billion contract for more than 120 fighter planes that India plans to buy. "The bounty is enormous," announces Ron Somers, the US-India Business Council's president.[39] According to *Indian Express,* in 2012 alone US-based firms spent more than $200 million in Congress to lobby on behalf of their business interests in India and in global markets.[40]

The anticipated profits from the civil nuclear deal, especially from the potential sale of nuclear energy plants and equipment, were estimated to be so large (around $200 billion) that Bonner & Associates, a public relations firm, created a parallel India lobbying group to nudge the US Congress to sign the deal. Renamed the Indian American Security Leadership Council, this organization consisted mostly of business leaders and activists from the Indian community and was funded by Ramesh Kapur, a former trustee of the Democratic National Committee, and Krishna Srinivasa, an ardent supporter of GOP causes. Their strategy was to get the civil nuclear deal and subsequent defense equipment contracts for American defense firms. They proposed to do this by launching a two-pronged approach: the Indian government would make a business case for the deal by suggesting the huge business opportunities it would open up, while Indian Americans would make an emotional case by pointing to India's enduring democracy and the values it shares with the United States, including individual rights, the rule of law, and constitutional government. Nevertheless, the deal would have had a difficult time going through had the Bush administration not been convinced of the need to incorporate India into its global security architecture as a hedge against China and as a force for stability in South Asia.

The political activism of Indian Americans is especially noteworthy among the second generation. Sanjay Puri, who founded the US India Political Action Committee (USINPAC) in 2002, has been particularly effective. In the following five years, USINPAC became a force to be reckoned with. It targeted senators and representatives who were seen to be anti-Indian and ended the Senate career of Virginia Republican George Allen, whose notorious taunt of "macaca" aimed at a young Indian American had outraged the Indian community. Less publicly, USINPAC claims to have brought around a lot of lawmakers, for example, Dan Burton, a Republican congressman from Indiana, who had long been a critic of India.[41] Khalid Chandio comments, "US congress received a personal letter from Sanjay Puri . . . with an online petition signed by over 16,000 citizens calling for [Congress] to cut off funding to Pakistan if it does not shut down the terror training camps. Indian lobby is active in blocking every move that is favourable to Pakistan like sophisticated weapons for countering insurgency in tribal belt of Pakistan."[42]

This same lobby was active in getting the Obama administration to maintain the pro-India tilt achieved during the previous administration. The course of events in Afghanistan and Pakistan, however, made rapid progress in official Indo-US ties more difficult, notwithstanding the extra mile traveled by the White House to welcome Prime Minister Manmohan Singh when he came to Washington in 2010. Misgivings prevail about American priorities in South Asia, and policymakers and leaders of the Indian American community feared that President Obama's commitment to an even-handed approach to South Asia might reverse many of the gains India made under the Bush administration. Nevertheless, Prime Minister Singh's visit to the White House in 2005 was a spectacular occasion showcasing the new dynamism of the Indo-US relationship as were the subsequent visits to New Delhi by President Obama in October 2010 and Secretary of State Hillary Clinton in July 2011.

Obama's large economic and military commitment to Pakistan is, however, troubling to India, and it is trying hard to convince policymakers in Washington that the administration cannot hope for an enduring success in Afghanistan without India's cooperation in South Asia. The next few years will see the India lobby bend its efforts toward neutralizing pro-Pakistani advocacy on this question while the Indian government moves to balance its state-to-state relationship with Islamabad.

The India lobby might find it difficult to sell India if the Indian economy falters and New Delhi advocates a multipolar world order by increasing the distance between it and the United States. These factors explain the growing doubt for the future of Indo-US ties during the second Obama administration when the United States became preoccupied by the 2008 global recession and its aftermath, the doubtful outcome of the 2010 troop surge in Afghanistan, and finally the Arab Spring and its fallout in the Middle East. Many commentators regretted the consequent drift in Indo-US ties and the lack of progress in getting the issue of liability (in the event of a nuclear accident in US-established nuclear plants) resolved.[43] No nuclear energy plants could be sold until the responsibility and legal liability in the event of an accident at a nuclear plant were sorted out. But US-India relations are a work in progress in which the maturing Indian diaspora will maintain substantial leverage.

All things considered, the notion of projecting soft power is relatively new in India, especially when it goes hand in hand with the acquisition of weapons and military strength. Post–Cold War India has nevertheless expanded its soft power repertoire and added new sources of power to the ones it earlier possessed. The new sources are situated in its burgeoning diaspora, enduring democracy, knowledge of markets and business, and expanding pool of educated Indians with facility in English. The latter have already made significant contributions to the global knowledge economy. Bollywood and yoga have a worldwide following. Indian artists are now a regular part of international festivals organized in places as varied as London, Paris, New York, Rome, Abu Dhabi, and Tokyo. Indian novelists and writers—in the diaspora or from India—are highly regarded in the United States and Europe for their contribution to the world of letters. Salman Rushdie, Arundhati Roy, Anita Desai, Shashi Tharoor, Kiran Desai, Jhumpa Lahiri, Bharati Mukherjee, and Abraham Verghese, to name but a few, are followed by a long and glowing list of new and younger writers who populate literary circles in the United States and Europe. Amartya Sen and Jagdish Bhagwati are world-famous economists and Prahlad is a much-sought-after management guru.

To sum up, India's soft power no longer resides in the Nehruvian traditions of socialism, scientific temper, and rejection of military power. In the post–Cold War era, its soft power draws on the acquisition of sophisticated weapons and weapons systems, the ability to project power beyond India, and the productivity of its newly inaugurated market economy. If New Delhi manages to effectively leverage the global connections of 25 million people of Indian origin living abroad, it can emerge as a highly influential presence in global forums.[44]

For now, the links between India's hard and soft power remain largely underdeveloped. Evidence is growing that Indians within and outside the country are transforming India's image and that the Indian nation is now being perceived as strong and vibrant, with the potential to become an important player in this century. But there is no overall diplomatic strategy within which India's soft power assets can be leveraged. The institutional infrastructure required to do this is mostly absent. There are growing numbers of cultural centers and people-to-people exchanges. Indian business has also established some joint forums to boost trade and provide information about laws and regulations affecting investment in India. These efforts are, however, woefully inadequate at this time. There is potential, but it remains unexploited.

Notes

1. Joseph S. Nye Jr., *Soft Power: The Means to Success in World Politics* (New York: PublicAffairs, 2004), x.

2. Jonathan McClory, "The New Persuaders II: A 2011 Global Ranking of Soft Power, Institute for Government (London: Adilson Henrique, 2012), 10, http://www.instituteforgovernment.org.uk/sites/default/files/publications/The%20New%20PersuadersII_0.pdf.

3. Ibid., 8.

4. Joseph Nye, "Power and Foreign Policy," *Journal of Political Power* 4, no. 1 (April 2011): 19.

5. Shashi Tharoor, "Why Nations Should Pursue Soft Power," video of a lecture under the auspices of TEDindia: YouTube, November 2009, http://www.ted.com/talks/shashi_tharoor.html.

6. John Lee, "Unrealised Potential: India's Soft Power Ambitions in Asia," *Foreign Policy Analysis,* no. 4 (June 30, 2010), http://www.hudson.org/files/publications/Unrealised%20Potential%20-%20India's%20Soft%20Power%20Ambition%20in%20Asia.pdf.

7. See the article "The American Desi," Shashi Tharoor's blog, August 3, 2012, http://tharoor.in/articles/the-american-desi/.

8. David Malone, "Soft Power in Indian Foreign Policy," *Economic and Political Weekly* 36, no. 36 (September 3, 2011): 35.

9. V. S. Naipaul, *An Area of Darkness* (New York: Penguin Books, 1968).

10. Harold Isaacs, *Scratches on Our Minds: American Views of China and India* (Armonk, NY: M. E. Sharpe, 1980), 322.

11. Ibid., 312–316.

12. Priya Chacko, "Indian Foreign Policy and the Ambivalence of Post-Colonial Modernity" (PhD diss., University of Adelaide, November 2007).

13. There are alternative explanations based on the realist perspective for India's strategic restraint, but we can accept them only if we ignore the force of ideology, self-image, history, and future imaginings in India's foreign policy behavior. That does not seem reasonable. A realist perspective can offer a valuable but only partial explanation. We need to also take into account India's self-presentation in understanding its response to challenges from beyond its borders.

14. Chacko, "Indian Foreign Policy," v–vi, http://digital.library.adelaide .edu.au/dspace/bitstream/2440/48196/1/02whole.pdf.

15. Ibid.

16. George Tanham, "Indian Strategic Culture," *Washington Quarterly* 15, no. 1 (Winter 1992): 129–142.

17. Cultural and value differences between Asia and the West were for the first time fully articulated by Chinese and Singaporean delegations at the 1993 World Conference on Human Rights in Vienna. Singapore's foreign minister, Won Kang Seng, warned, "Universal recognition of the ideal of human rights can be harmful if universalism is used to deny or mask the reality of diversity." The Chinese delegation made a point of emphasizing regional differences and in making sure that the prescriptive framework adopted in the declarations acknowledged regional diversity. This was essentially a rejection of individual rights and civil liberties as universal values. The spokesman for China's foreign ministry (quoted in W. S. Wong, "The Real World of Human Rights," mimeographed, 1993) went on record suggesting that "individuals must put the state's rights before their own." The former prime minister of Singapore, Lee Kuan Yew, argued vigorously that "Asian values" and the collective freedoms they stressed were effective in promoting economic success. For a full discussion, see Amartya Sen, "Human Rights and Asian Values," Sixteenth Morgenthau Lecture on Ethics and Foreign Policy, Carnegie Council on Ethics and International Affairs, New York, 1997, http://www.carnegiecouncil.org/publications /archive/morgenthau/254.html/_res/id=sa_File1/254_sen.pdf.

18. National Intelligence Council (NIC), "Global Trends 2015: A Dialogue About the Future with Non-Government Experts," December 2000, Washington, DC, http://www.dni.gov/files/documents/Global%20 Trends_2015%20Report.pdf.

19. Ibid. According to the NIC, "A generation of globally competitive companies is emerging from within India, particularly in IT, pharmaceuticals and auto parts. Of the top 100 new global corporate leaders from the non-OECD world listed in a 2006 report from The Boston Consulting Group, 84 were headquartered in Brazil, Russia, China and India." See National Intelligence Council, "Global Trends 2025: A Transformed World," November 2008, 8, http://www.aicpa.org/research/cpahorizons2025/global forces/downloadable documents/globaltrends.pdf.

20. Address by Prime Minister Manmohan Singh, Oxford University, Oxford, England, July 8, 2005, reproduced in *The Hindu*, http://www.hindu onnet.com/thehindu/nic/0046/pmspeech.htm.

21. Pranay Gupte, "President Bush Sets America Right on India," *New York Sun Times,* March 8, 2006, http://www.pranaygupte.com/article.php ?index=457.

22. Thomas Friedman, "No Way, No How, Not Here," *New York Times,* February 17, 2009, http://www.nytimes.com/2009/02/18/opinion/18friedman .html.

23. Ibid.

24. The most obvious example of this is the "Incredible India" campaign in media and print, originally meant to boost the tourist industry and attract more foreign tourists to India. The campaign, rather cleverly showcasing India's rich culture and art forms, has helped join the image of a modern computer-savvy India to its civilizational heritage.

25. The United States is an exception. Although a democracy committed to international laws, the United States has frequently violated them. Its post–Cold War interventions in Iraq and Bosnia are cases in point.

26. "India Remittances at $66 BN in 2011–12," *Indian Express,* September 7, 2012, http://m.indianexpress.com/news/%22india-remittances-at --66-bn-in-201112%22/999493/. According to a *Times of India* report, India has received $71 billion in remittances in 2013. See "India, China Get a Third of Global Remittances," *Times of India,* October 4, 2013, http://articles.timesofindia.indiatimes.com/keyword/remittances.

27. For instance, when US immigration laws tightened, restricting the admission of Indian doctors to the United States, the American Association of Physicians from India (AAPI) was formed. In 1993, Indian doctors constituted close to 4 percent of their profession in the United States. AAPI's growing political clout can be gauged by the fact that President Clinton addressed its annual convention in 1995.

28. US Census Bureau, "Race Reporting for the Asian Population by Selected Categories: 2010," http://factfinder2.census.gov/faces/tableservices /jsf/pages/productview.xhtml?pid=DEC_10_SF1_QTP8&prodType=table.

29. US Census Bureau, "United States ACS Demographic and Housing Estimates, 2008," http://factfinder.census.gov/servlet/ADPTable?_bm=y& -geo_id=01000US&-qr_name=ACS_2008_1YR_G00_DP5&-ds_name =ACS_2008_1YR_G00_&-_lang=en&-redoLog=true.

30. "Ambassador's Address at the People-to-People Conference" (Washington, DC: Embassy of India, October 28, 2010), http://www.indian embassy.org/prdetail1618/ambassadorandrsquo%3Bs-address-at-the -andquot%3Bpeople-to-peopleandquot%3B-conference.

31. In New Jersey, a number of Indians whose success rendered them visible were attacked or murdered by young white men who came to be known as "dot busters," a reference to the cosmetic dot Indian women wear on their foreheads.

32. Anette Ignatowicz, "Indian Diaspora: 10K Club on Fundraising Mission in the USA," Innovation in India, June 15, 2010, http://iii2010 .wordpress.com/2010/06/15/indian-diaspora-10k-club-on-fundraising -mission-in-the-usa/.

33. Report of the High Level Committee on the Indian Diaspora, New Delhi, Government of India, December 19, 2001, 170, http://indiandiaspora .nic.in/diasporapdf/chapter13.pdf.

34. See Tim Devaney and Tom Stein, "Why Are Indians so Entrepreneurial in the US?" Readwrite Small Biz, October 19, 2012, http://readwrite .com/2012/10/19/why-are-indians-so-entrepreneurial-in-the-us#awesm =~oklVoWsUhCeGkM. For a more comprehensive study of Indian diaspora in IT see Vivek Wadhwa, "The Face of Success: How the Indians Conquered Silicon Valley," *INC.*, January 13, 2012, http://www.inc.com/vivek-wadhwa /how-the-indians-succeeded-in-silicon-valley.html.

35. Within months of assuming the presidency, Obama chose a slew of Indian Americans, many of them from his campaign, for important jobs in his administration. He appointed Aneesh Chopra to be first chief technology officer and Vivek Kundra to be federal chief information officer, appointments that endorsed the Indian presence in the technology sector. Obama chose Preet Bharara as the US attorney for New York, a job previously held by Rudy Giuliani, Preeta Bansal was appointed general counsel and senior policy adviser in the Office of Management and Budget, while Georgetown University law professor Don Neal Katyal became principal deputy solicitor general. The most high-profile appointment, however, was the choice of Rajiv Shah to head the US Agency for International Development (USAID), a job that will include disbursing massive foreign aid to Pakistan, a country already worried about who controls US pursestrings. Vinay Thummalapally was appointed US ambassador to Belize, Vikram Singh became deputy assistant secretary of defense for South and Southeast Asia, Subra Suresh got the post of director of the National Science Foundation, Nisha Biswal is assistant administrator at the Bureau for Asia in the USAID, Islam Siddiqui as ambassador is chief agricultural negotiator at the US Trade Representative (USTR), and Priya Aiyar serves as the deputy general counsel for environment and nuclear programs in the Department of Energy. Other Indian Americans currently holding important posts in the Obama administration include Mythili Raman (Department of Justice); Subhasri Ramanathan, counselor to the secretary, Department of Homeland Security; Sri Srinivasan, principal deputy solicitor general in the Department of Justice; Kiran Ahuja, executive director of the White House Initiative on Asian Americans and Pacific Islanders (AAPI); Nealesh Kemkar, deputy counselor to the secretary in the Department of Interior; and Lopa P. Kolluri, who is deputy chief of staff, operations, and strategy in the Department of Housing and Urban Development. "Obama Inducts Record Number Indian-Americans into His Administration," IBNLive, November 19, 2012, http://ibnlive.in.com/news/obama-inducts -record-number-indianamericans-into-his-administration/306285-2.html.

36. Mira Kamdar, "Forget the Israel Lobby. The Hill's Next Big Player Is Made in India," *Washington Post,* September 30, 2007, http://www .washingtonpost.com/wp-dyn/content/article/2007/09/28/AR20070928 01350.html.

37. Indian American Ashley Tellis, who served as a key adviser to Ambassador Blackwill, produced the intellectual arguments for the Indo-US nuclear deal and defense framework. Carnegie Endowment for International Peace, "Ashley J. Tellis: Key Figure in the U.S.-India Nuclear Deal," March 3, 2006, http://carnegieendowment.org/2006/03/03/ashley-j.-tellis-key-figure -in-u.s.-india-nuclear-deal/1ri2.

38. "India-Focused Lobby Bill Reached $212 Million in 2012," Press Trust of India, March 6, 2013, http://www.indiawest.com/news/9486-india -focused-lobby-bill-reached-212-million-in-2012.html.

39. Ibid.

40. "India-Focussed US Entities' Lobby Bill Reach $212 Mn in 2012," *Indian Express,* February 10, 2013, http://www.indianexpress.com/news /indiafocussed-us-entities-lobby-bill-reach--212-mn-in-2012/1072173/.

41. Ibid.

42. Khalid Chandio, "Rising Indian Lobby in US," *Pakistan Observer,* June 16, 2011, http://pakobserver.net/detailnews.asp?id=97876.

43. NDTV, "Is the India-US Relationship in a State of Drift?" YouTube video, July 20, 2011, http://www.youtube.com/watch?v=YarwW4B8hIM.

44. India has established the Ministry of Overseas Indian Affairs with a view to leveraging its diasporic communities abroad. It has also expanded the number of Indian cultural centers. The main purpose of these initiatives is to project India's soft power—the power of its popular and traditional culture—to all parts of the world. In the words of Himachal Som, the direc- tor general of the Indian Council for Cultural Relations, "The new overseas centers fall within the matrix of our overall foreign policy in which soft power (culture) is a major component. The expansion of cultural presence is one of the new goals of India's foreign policy." India now has twenty-four cultural centers in twenty-one countries. It plans to increase the number to forty in the next few years, thereby expanding India's footprint globally. See Madhushree Chatterjee, "India Projecting Its Soft Power Globally," *Enter- tainment Daily,* October 6, 2009, http://blog.taragana.com/e/2009/10/06 /india-projecting-its-soft-power-globally-iccr-chief-interview-39910/.

8

Why India Matters

In this book I have attempted to explain the paradox that India presents today. On the one hand, there can be no doubt that many of its governmental processes are steadily deteriorating. On the other hand, when judged by outcomes rather than processes, India continues to make progress. This is apparent in its expanding democracy, increasingly assertive middle class, and success in building consensus, nurturing plurality, revitalizing the economy, and projecting both hard and soft power abroad as the need arises.

And India has done all this within a unique and unconventional model of a modern state that is grounded in the past while having its eyes firmly fixed on the future. India has demonstrated that democracy can be rooted in a poor, underdeveloped, largely illiterate society; that primordial identities can coexist without the use of force and be subsumed under an umbrella of a single sovereign nation; that a multinational state can be effective in its own defense; and that despite the burden of colonialism, leaders of such a nation are capable of pursuing bold and innovative paths to nation-building. India demonstrates that authoritarianism is not a necessary precondition for rapid economic growth in a developing country and that fundamental political change can be carried out amid social and economic upheaval. These are indeed the reasons that India matters.

The Past as Prologue

The acute foreign exchange crisis of 1990, the near-simultaneous demise of the dominant Congress Party, and the burgeoning power of regional political configurations in relation to the central state all contributed to gloomy forecasts about India's future. The country's historic dilemmas—fragmentation and erosion of the central political authority—seemed to be resurfacing. This economic and political crisis called for a fundamental change, and India's leaders, to their credit, responded to the call. But the resulting departure from time-honored policies of state-led growth, which had protected the masses from the depredations of international markets, produced a fierce controversy. The optimists believed that embracing the market would be a way out of the trap of slow growth, whereas the pessimists predicted that it would increase social inequality and create widespread social unrest. India, they feared, would collapse under the burden of domestic violence and ruthless competition from global markets. More than two decades into the new, post–Congress Party era, these trends are evident, but they do not threaten a collapse of the Indian nation-state.

Students of India have been slow to understand this evolution because during much of it the European model of the nation-state was unquestioningly accepted as the only model for newly decolonized nations to follow. Predictions of a gloomy future for India abounded. Members of the Indian elite expressed the first fears in 1957 when the Congress Party reorganized Indian states on the basis of linguistic ethnicity. Many observers were afraid that this would be a prelude to disintegration. India already faced an insurgency in Nagaland, while in Tamil Nadu the Dravida Munnetra Kazhagam (DMK) was openly demanding independence from India. In 1960, in his book *India: The Most Dangerous Decades,* Selig Harrison Jr. suggested that India might disintegrate with the death of Jawaharlal Nehru.[1] Harrison's doubts were echoed more emphatically in 1966 by Neville Maxwell, then the India correspondent for *The Times* of London, in a two-part article titled "India's Disintegrating Democracy."[2] Through the next four decades, such doubts regularly reared their heads as India stumbled from one ethnic insurgency, drought, or foreign exchange crisis to the next.

They gained added strength as the world witnessed the success of the East Asian tiger economies whose authoritarian "neo-Confucian" governments achieved electrifying rates of growth by using state power to systematically crush internal dissent and effect economic change. Doubts and fears about India's future gained added currency as comparisons were made between India's development and the meteoric rise of China. Yet it was only when the Congress Party finally lost its dominance in 1989 that these misgivings coalesced into a full-blown theory of impending state failure. That this coincided with India's most severe foreign exchange crisis was offered as clinching proof of the validity of the skeptics' arguments.

The common strand connecting all of these doubts was the belief that nation-building was impossible without a strong state. The Congress Party shared this belief at the outset. That is why the Constitution gave the center such strong executive powers that constitutional theorists such as K. C. Wheare dubbed India a "Quasi-federal State."[3] These fears stemmed from an awareness that India was an artificial creation of the British held together by the immense influence of the Congress Party, which had led India to independence, and of Prime Minister Jawaharlal Nehru. Worries about what would happen to India gained a sharp new lease on life after Nehru's death, when the Congress Party's share of the vote fell to just above 40 percent in the 1967 elections and the party lost power for the first time in six large state assemblies. These reverses gave rise to the fear that with the weakening of central authority, India's ethnicity-based states would start to pull apart. That they did not do so and that there was instead a steady consolidation of Indian nationhood require us to reexamine the basic premise upon which skeptics have based their arguments.

Western analysts have been slow to understand India's evolution because for them and for subscribers to that perspective within India, the European model of the nation-state was the only viable model for new nations to follow. Paul Brass, for instance, claims that India is a quasi-authoritarian state in the guise of a democracy, as does Ayesha Jalal.[4] But the creeping authoritarianism they detect is a product of the growing weakness of the state, not of its strength. Even scholars such as Stephen Cohen and George Tanham, who admire India's democratic record, cite India's lack of strategic thinking and haphazard acquisition of arms to prove that India is incapable of accumulating, much less projecting, the hard power that is an essential element of a successful modern state.[5]

What many critics were reluctant to acknowledge at the time was that the unitary nation-state was not the only model of viable statehood in history. India's founding leaders perceived nationhood to be a "flexible envelope" capable of accommodating cultural diversity within a multilayered state. They did not seek to impose a singular identity upon its entire people. They did not therefore regard the periodic outbreak of local challenges to national authority as threats to the nation's existence. In addressing this issue, as Cohen has done in his writings on the rise of India, the critics overlooked the organic connection between the way the Indian state handled its domestic issues and the way it projected its interests abroad.[6] In other words, India's external policy carried a heavy impress of the need to forge a unique national identity around which the diverse nationalities of India could coalesce.[7]

As explained in Chapter 2, India has used the strategy of interlocking balances to achieve domestic integration while deploying relational control in areas neighboring its borders to protect itself. In the pursuit of this strategy, India's central governments have readily accommodated ethnic nationalism in the interior parts of the country, such as Tamil Nadu, Andhra Pradesh, and Maharashtra. Demands there for autonomy do not raise the specter of secession. In border states such as Kashmir, Punjab, and Nagaland, the perceptions are different. Here the central governments have feared for India's national security and the cross-border linkages many ethnic nationalities have made. They have therefore adopted a harder stance. But their ultimate purpose for the most part has been to use coercion to the extent needed to persuade the leaders of the secessionist movements to give Indian democracy a chance to meet their demands.

By contrast, the European nation-state has developed around a paradigm of conquest, followed by a forced consolidation of conquered territories and an imposition of cultural homogeneity on its inhabitants. Although the formation of this nation-state began well before the rise of industrial capitalism, it attained its full-blown modern shape as a direct result of attempts to cope with the conflicts that capitalism unleashed in society. The key additional features this historical development introduced were hard borders, first intended to keep the manufactures of other countries out and then to prevent immigration so as to keep the gains from industrialization within national boundaries and allow wage rates to rise. A strong state was needed to guard the frontiers, project the state's power abroad in order to secure raw materials and markets, manage the internal conflicts generated by economic change, and ensure that the revenues needed to perform these functions were extracted from the people.

The post-1947 Indian state never fit into this model, not even in the heyday of Nehruvian rule. Despite the government's best efforts, India's borders have remained porous. Far from imposing cultural homogeneity, India has made a virtue out of diversity, and instead of stamping out ethnic identities, it has sought to co-opt them into the nation-building project. Rather than creating a unitary relationship between the state and the individual, India has tolerated, and even encouraged, the existence of a layered relationship between the individual and various tiers of the state where loyalty to caste, community, and religious affiliation coexist with loyalty to distinctive levels of authority (the special constitutional status of Indian Kashmir and Nagaland and the separate personal law for Indian Muslims are cases in point). In the European paradigm, the presence of insurrection is a sign of failure. In India, it is frequently a prelude to accommodation and democratic absorption.[8]

Western democracy, which was born as an antidote to economic conflict within the state, empowers the individual. Indian democracy empowers caste and ethnic groups. In the process, individuals at the bottom of each such group have frequently remained disempowered. The acceleration of growth after 1991, which has been accompanied by a widening gap between the rich and the poor, has made the disempowerment of the poor more acute. This is the main reason for the skeptics' not wholly unfounded criticism of the hollowness of India's democracy. India's cultural, and now economic, heterogeneity therefore remains the single most important cause of the skeptics' doubts about the country's future. For the very notion of heterogeneity implies a lack of control and suggests that a nation that actively tolerates it is at constant risk of falling apart.

What the critics often ignore is that the European nation-state in its fully developed form is barely 150 years old and the bells of its demise may have already begun to toll. In the European Union (EU) and the Association of Southeast Asian Nations, member nation-states have begun to look for an alternative that is better suited to the age of economic globalization. The very base of the skeptics' pessimism about India's future—the belief that a nation-state with a strong center is an essential prerequisite for success—is eroding with each advance in globalization.

India owes its stability to never having emulated the European nation-state. Far from a disadvantage, India's ethnicity-based federalism endows it with the flexibility to cope with dissent through accommodation, compromise, and co-optation. When the state fails to accommodate, ethnic communities frequently resort to violence and even insurgency.

As Chapter 2 describes at length, this model was not a product of conscious design. On the contrary, it grew out of a general understanding among nationalist leaders of India's history. From the Mauryan dynasty to the Mughal Empire, Indian states have always been constructed upon three pillars: universal ideology, regional autonomy, and a layering of authority in established administrative order. What India's leaders accomplished in the first, crucial decade of independence was to resurrect this form of state in a modern guise. The three changes they made were to replace a loosely bound authoritarian system with an ethnicity-based federal democracy, soft and porous boundaries with hard ones, and conscripted armies with a professional standing army. Seen from the outside, these three attributes may have given India a superficial resemblance to the European nation-state; in truth they served to clothe a far older model of the state in modern garb.

The period of Congress Party dominance therefore needs to be viewed against this broad historical background. As explained in detail in Chapters 2 and 3, the era of dominant-party democracy was a period of transition from the colonial Indian state to a modern incarnation of the historical Indian state. It was the Congress Party, under Mahatma Gandhi, that first offered the consolidation and preservation of ethnic identities, and it did so as far back as in the 1920s. India's entire freedom movement was therefore based upon the implicit promise of ethnic empowerment. Even the strength of the center during the period of Congress Party dominance was based upon fulfillment of that promise in 1957. When we take all this into consideration, the weakening and ultimate fading away of the Congress Party's dominance were not merely inevitable; indeed, they were necessary for the Indian state to attain its full maturity.

Coalition Governments as Game Changers

As the preceding chapters demonstrate, India's coalition governments have performed far better on every score than the Congress Party governments of Indira and Rajiv Gandhi, which presided over Indian politics for most of the years between 1966 and 1989. The end of Congress Party dominance in 1989 did not lead to a decline, much less to a collapse, of the central state as many had expected. In the realm of politics, coalition governments dealt successfully with the four most potent challenges to the Indian state: from backward castes and Dalits, from Hindu nationalists, from ethnic separatists supported by Pakistan's intelligence agencies, and from India's rising middle classes.

Coalition governments developed new methods of forging consensus, especially in economic policy, through a division of ministerial portfolios at the center and a greater devolution of power to the states. They also revived and enlarged the functions of institutions for coordinating center-state policies that had been foreseen in the Constitution but had lain dormant during the days of Congress Party dominance. Forming stable coalitions forced regional parties that were partners in government to dovetail their agendas and policies with those of the national government. For the first time in India's history, local leaders were compelled to understand the national and international consequences of their actions and develop responses to cope with global markets.[9] The Bharatiya Janata Party (BJP) thus moderated its anti-Muslim stance once it became a government, DMK leaders worried about the impact of a World Trade Organization dispensation on tea growers in their state, and state chief ministers routinely went abroad looking for foreign direct investment (FDI) in their states. Greater diffusion of power downward complicated the achievement of consensus on reform and policy, but as the enormous transformation effected since 1989 indicates, coalition rule as it evolved and stabilized at the apex learned to address them through consensus.[10]

The Economy

In the realm of economics, the coalition governments successfully resolved the three conflicts that had saddled India with one of the slowest growth rates in the world: conflicts between the state and market, between small and large capital, and between Indian and foreign capital. The coalition governments redefined the role of private and public capital and sought partnerships with private domestic and foreign capital to build India's infrastructure and export industries. This policy was in marked contrast to that prevalent during the years of the command economy when private capital was regarded with suspicion and hostility. The coalition governments accomplished this, moreover, in a step-by-step manner that allowed India to make the transition from a command to a market economy with remarkably little pain. Indeed, the supposed weakness of the state after 1991 proved a boon because it allowed first the Narasimha Rao and then the Inder Gujral and Atal Bihari Vajpayee governments to resist frenetic exhortations by well-meaning neoliberal economists, including those of the World Bank and the International Monetary Fund, to adopt the shock therapy mode of policy change that led to disaster in Russia and most of Eastern Europe.

The pace of economic reform, however, remained slow and erratic. Reform occurred in piecemeal increments and was frequently reversed in deference to public and political opposition. Since 1991, however, coalition reforms have transformed the economy and unleashed impressive entrepreneurial energies that placed India, between 2003 and 2010, among the fastest-growing economies in the world.

Foreign Policy

As for foreign affairs, it was the rise of coalition governments, and a consequent lightening of the baggage of past policies and commitments, that enabled India to give up Nehruvian idealism in favor of an increasingly hardheaded realism. The clearest evidence of this was the decision of the Singh, Gujral, and Vajpayee governments to continue with the development of nuclear weapons that Rajiv Gandhi had resumed in 1988 after a fourteen-year hiatus. The quest for nuclear weapons was eventually consummated during the tenure of the Vajpayee government in May 1998. The same practical realism led to India siding with the West against Iran on the board of the International Atomic Energy Agency in October 2005 and to the signing of the Indo-US nuclear agreement in 2008. It was also during the coalition era that India finally shook off its preoccupation with its immediate neighborhood, South Asia, and began to explore a wider role in the post–Cold War international order. This was the genesis of India's extended neighborhood and look east policies, which have brought it to center stage in global affairs.

Defense and Strategic Policy

Lastly, every coalition government continued Rajiv Gandhi's thrust to modernize India's conventional defense forces. This task was undertaken with new doctrines and missions in mind and included the development of the Cold Start doctrine for responding to attacks. This doctrine was seemingly abandoned, but the Indian military continued to put in place essential parts of the tactical requirement to launch a punishing foray into Pakistan envisaged in Cold Start. India built up its navy not only to defend its far-flung Andaman and Nicobar Islands territories but also to participate in the protection of international sea-lanes and trade routes. The striking feature of these diverse initiatives was the continuity of core objectives: to protect India's strategic autonomy and to build the strength to enhance India's international standing.

Throughout the years that India has taken to come to terms with coalition rule, there has remained a core of strategic policies (i.e., pushing economic reforms, friendly ties to the United States, projecting power in the extended neighborhood) passed down from one government to the next. Indeed, coalition rule displays an identifiable rhythm. The core party weakens a few months before elections as individual coalition partners begin to reassess their electoral prospects and determine whether to remain within the ruling coalition or forge an alternative alliance. But first-past-the-post conditions more often than not force them into alliances and seat adjustments to ensure their electoral chances in the polls. Thus far the Congress Party and the BJP have served as the core parties while the constellation of supporting regional parties around them has changed from one election to the next. This has adversely affected the balance of power within the ruling coalition and the pace of reforms, as amply evident in the policy paralyses that gripped the United Progressive Alliance (UPA) between 2010 and 2012. The Janata Party has tried to become a core party but so far it has not succeeded in providing a stable foundation for an alternative coalition. Both the National Front and the United Front governments failed to complete their terms in office.

Another consequence of the widening political competition is the striking contrast between the behavior of political leaders when they are in opposition and their behavior when they come to power. Skeptics have viewed this contrast with a measure of cynicism and chosen to see in it the hollowness of Indian democracy. Critics on the left, in particular, have viewed it as the definitive proof of a newly minted economic elitism.

Even though there is a measure of truth in these observations, they fail to explain the durability and stability of the consensus beneath the battles between the core parties and their allies. Indeed, on economic and foreign policy the differences between the Congress Party and the BJP are arguably less about the substance of policies than about their pace and modalities. The missing element, the one that critics always ignore, is the shared urge among India's population to build a strong and modern country. This urge springs from the realization that India's ethnicity-based federation has created both a cultural homeland for every Indian within his or her own state and a much larger field of endeavor in the country as a whole, in which he or she can strive to achieve cherished goals.

That more than 300 million people have migrated from one state to another in search of jobs proves that economic horizons have expanded just as opportunities have increased.[11] With fewer and fewer exceptions, these are not the desperately poor who are being pushed out of the villages by hunger and lack of employment, but those who are consciously seeking a new life within the modern sector of the growing economy. The phenomenal growth of second cities and small towns throughout India is proof of the rapidity of this transition.[12] The fall in the popularity of the left and the BJP, reflected by the sharp decline in their share of the vote in the May 2009 general elections, can be traced back in considerable part to the growing impatience of people who have their eyes set on growth.

The sudden onset of global recession, which resulted in a 25 percent fall in exports in the last quarter of 2009, was the first severe test of India's newfound economic strength. India came through with only a momentary slowdown in growth. By the second quarter of 2009–2010, its growth rate had once again risen to nearly 8 percent. Equally important was the quality of its recovery. Not only had India come out of the economic recession as rapidly as China, but it also had done so in a more sustainable manner because China's stimulus package increased the demand for steel, cement, chemicals and plastics, engineering goods, instrumentation, and computer software. All these were produced in large plants located in China's urban areas. The overall effect was to further increase the already large income gap between urban and rural areas.

In contrast, even though the Indian government's decision to spend on welfare for the poor has been criticized as being a populist measure to secure votes, and critics have lamented that India did not avail itself of a golden chance to rectify the country's infrastructure deficit when the threat of inflation was minimal, it cannot be denied that India's stimulus option has led to a substantial improvement in the purchasing power of the poor. The government distributed the bulk of the stimulus money in (1) a farm loan waiver scheme that benefited millions of debt-ridden farmers who had lost access to banks and been reduced to borrowing from moneylenders at exorbitant rates of interest; (2) a 144 percent increase in disbursements under the National Rural Employment Guarantee Scheme; (3) targeted programs for rural health, education, and infrastructure development; and (4) a strengthened public distribution system for providing subsidized food to those living below the poverty line.[13] It is true that intermediaries siphoned off much of these funds through bribes and kickbacks, but progress was made raising incomes even in the economically backward state of Bihar.

The large-scale subsidies did, however, create new problems: they widened the fiscal deficit and slowed economic growth. What made this more difficult in 2012, as opposed to earlier decades, was that the poor were no longer quiescent and the middle classes were even more assertive in the defense of their interests. Nevertheless, it is to the credit of the Manmohan Singh government that it managed to shake off the paralysis and in September 2012 proposed a whole slew of economic legislations—dealing with foreign direct investment in retail trade and insurance as well as cuts in diesel subsidies—to revive the economy and restore economic growth. Singh, however, failed to follow through on these measures. The next few years will test the capacity of India's coalitions to build a consensus around the next measures of changes required to stay on the path of growth.

What all this reveals is that India's coalition governments—whatever their composition and compulsions—have been strong enough to advance the country's interests abroad and respond to rising popular expectations at home. To onlookers, the gradualism, the stop-and-go nature of change so characteristic of India's transformation, has obscured the extent to which the coalition governments are capable of envisioning India as a great power and creating new institutions and laws, rules, and regulations to achieve that status—in other words, to meet Eric Ringman's first two criteria for measuring India's potential as an international power. As explained in Chapter 1, these criteria serve us better than conventional measures of power used in the recent works of scholars such as Baldev Raj Nayar and T. V. Paul and Stephen Cohen. The emergence of stable coalition rule following ten years of unstable governments underscores the extent

to which Indian leaders were successful in evolving the new rules for
the coalition "game." In fact, the coalition governments demonstrated
a far greater capacity to integrate the aspirations of castes, classes,
and ethnic communities than the governments of Indira and Rajiv
Gandhi. What is more, the coalition governments were no less adept
at conflict resolution than the previous Congress Party governments
had been.

Challenges Ahead

India has weathered the end of dominant-party democracy with
remarkable ease. But even as old challenges have been surmounted,
new ones have emerged. The new multiparty coalitional democracy
India has evolved faces at least four broad challenges: growing conflicts over land, social issues arising from land expropriation, changing voter behavior, and intensifying party competition.

For six decades after independence, the Indian government took
for granted the availability of land for the creation of roads, power
stations, steel and aluminum plants, and mines. It was able to do so
because it relied upon laws passed by the British in 1894 that
allowed traditional land users to be expropriated with only a pittance
for compensation. So long as the government could claim that the
land was being acquired for a public purpose from which the people
would benefit, the opposition to the expropriation remained muted.

In earlier decades, evicted farmers and forest dwellers sought
relief from the courts. This delayed but did not boil over into a political challenge to the state. But once the state began to acquire land to
hand over to private investors, the exploitative nature of the expropriation could no longer be hidden. A direct consequence has been
the resurgence of Naxalism: armed resistance headed by former
members of the radical left in Bengal and Andhra Pradesh.[14]

Today, by the central government's own assessment, 83 out of
India's 546 districts are "most seriously affected" by Naxalite
unrest.[15] These make up one-seventh of the total land area of the
country. Located in the forest and mineral-rich east-central belt of
India, they contain most of the iron ore, coal, bauxite, uranium, several rare earths, and other precious ores of the country. In these districts the writ of the state and central governments runs only fitfully.
As a result, the concessionaires of mining rights have been able to

exploit them. With mines declining owing to violence, India is importing a rising part of the coal consumed by its power plants even though it has the fourth-largest coal reserves in the world. Current plans for construction of two giant steel plants are at a standstill, and private power generation companies have been unable to set up 35,000 megawatts of plant capacity because of the lack of coal. It is abundantly clear that without somehow making those who own land or obtain their livelihood from it partners and permanent beneficiaries from its development, India risks its industrialization coming to a halt.

So far, the government has been unable to respond constructively to the social issues raised by the appropriation of land. The Congress Party–led government of Prime Minister Manmohan Singh is aware of the challenge. As far back as 2007, he warned that the Maoist threat in Central India was the greatest challenge the country faced. But the only response that the government was prepared to contemplate at that time was to use force.

It is only when this proved entirely ineffective, and in fact strengthened the hold of the Maoists on the disturbed areas, that his government was able to return to a search for a political solution. One indication of the change was a drastic revision of an amendment to a land acquisition bill that had been tabled in 2007. The revised bill, which was tabled four years later in 2011, acknowledged the need to make those who lost their land and livelihoods cosharers in the future stream of benefits that the land would generate. But even that bill was watered down to the point where it lost its main purpose, which was to prevent the alienation of land by corrupt politicians and bureaucrats who had claimed it for development but used it for speculation and profit.

Indeed, one single amendment that the members of the Lok Sabha insisted upon before passing the bill was that land that had been acquired for a project that failed to take off would not be returned to the original owners and users but kept in a land bank to be used for future projects. This one clause reopened the gates for speculation in land that the original version of the bill had sought to close. The bill finally passed through both the houses of Parliament in August 2013. The reason for the stiff resistance to the 2011 version of the bill was the organic connection between electoral finance and speculation in land. The 2013 version of the bill does not tackle this unhealthy connection between these two problems. Until this connection is broken by other reforms, corruption and expropriation are likely to remain integral parts of Indian democracy.

Electoral finance also lies at the root of the growing disenchantment of the Indian public with the country's democratic system. Public protests erupted in the closing months of 2010 with the uncovering of a huge scam in the award of contracts for the commonwealth games that India had hosted; these protests matured into a full-fledged challenge to the crony capitalism and clientelist system that India had become by 2011. Whether it was the capture and private sale of iron ore mines or of coal-mining concessions, one central dilemma was at the core: India's growth had accelerated, development required land, land was scarce, and so permissions to exploit it commanded a price. But that land had to be taken away from someone who was already in possession of it, so intensified expropriation became the other face of accelerated development.

Another set of challenges has arisen from changing voter behavior, a diminishing importance of identity politics, and a growing public mobilization around issues of governance and equity. In the halcyon days of Congress Party dominance, India aspired to be a developmental democracy and combine equity with individual freedom. Nehru's model of a mixed economy unabashedly aimed at speeding up growth in order to make up for the time lost under colonial rule. That the purpose was the general good of the whole of Indian society was never in doubt. But intensifying political competition and the state's monopoly over resources turned what had been intended as a developmental into a clientelist democracy in which votes are traded for material and other promises that may not promote national development. One effect of this was to divorce economic from political competition. Democracy increasingly dealt with only the latter. In the economy, a crony, clientelist relationship developed between those who wielded power to grant permissions and those who sought them to further their own economic interests. This increasingly left the poor out of the reckoning.

The conflict between the winners and losers from development remained muted during the prereform days of slow economic growth, but it surfaced rapidly after the state retreated from the market, leaving investment almost completely to private enterprise. The resulting sharpening of economic conflict is leading to a change in the expectations of the electorate. More and more voters are deciding their vote not on the basis of caste and creed, but on the basis of what the aspirants to power are promising to deliver in terms of a better future.

The visible sign of this change was a weakening of the anti-incumbency vote. This began in a few state governments but spread to the center in 2009. The first state was Gujarat. In spite of severe communal disturbances in 2002 that drew nationwide condemnation and contributed to the fall of the National Democratic Alliance (NDA) government in 2004, Gujarat has reelected BJP governments to power in all four state assembly elections since 1995 and reelected the BJP and Narendra Modi in the December 2012 elections. The reason is the state's double-digit growth since the mid-1990s and the widespread perceptions that the BJP and Modi government's policies were the reasons for the state's prosperity. In the ensuing years, a widening circle of other state governments have also benefited from better economic delivery to their people. These include Delhi under the Congress Party, Madhya Pradesh under the BJP, Orissa under the Biju Janata Dal, and Bihar under a BJP–Samata Party coalition headed by the latter.

The voters' growing tendency to reward performance became visible in the general elections of April–May 2009 when the Congress Party overcame the much-dreaded anti-incumbency factor, winning 206 seats against the 145 seats it had won in 2004.[16] This victory did not come altogether as a surprise. The country had enjoyed five years of nearly 9 percent annual growth, and there was also a noticeable shift away from a politics of hate. Within days of the terrorist attack on Mumbai on November 26, 2008, the Congress Party won the Delhi state elections in the teeth of a hyperpatriotic campaign waged by the BJP. Bihar is another example of a change in voter behavior: in the first days of 2010, Bihar surprised the country by reporting an 11.03 percent annual growth rate from 2005 to 2009 and has reelected the incumbent state government repeatedly as a reward for its performance.[17]

The most powerful indication of change in voting behavior, however, came when millions gathered in peaceful demonstrations in 400 cities in April 2011 to support a drive against corruption led by Anna Hazare, a political activist from the state of Maharashtra. The public protest forced the UPA government to refashion a bill to create a Lok Pal (national ombudsman) to investigate charges of corruption in government. The anticorruption movement transcended the usual divisions of caste, class, and religion.[18]

Taken together, these tendencies herald a tectonic change in voter behavior. The driving force behind the change is the voters' quest for security and predictability in their lives. This quest has been apparent in rural areas for some time. One indicator is a steady decline in the agricultural labor force. Its main cause is the decision of more and more families to pull their children out of the fields and send them to school—preferably to English medium schools, where the language of instruction is English, often at considerable expense.[19] Behind the quest for security is the erosion of the Hindu family "under the twin pressures of rising aspirations and stagnant or slow-growing incomes. It has forced the urban and rural poor to confront a terrifying new question: who will look after us when we are too old to work? Safeguarding the future has therefore become a matter of supreme importance."[20]

These changes in voter behavior are so recent that a definitive analysis of their causes is still some way off. One probable cause seems to be the steady and rapid increase in the interstate movement of labor in search of employment, which was mentioned earlier. Data collected by Praveen Visaria and Lila Visaria and cited by Ram Bhagat, among others, show that this migrant workforce doubled to nearly 303 million between 1971 and 2001.[21] With the acceleration of economic growth since then, the numbers of internal migrants in search of work have undoubtedly increased significantly. According to a report published by the International Organization of Migration in 2012, the number of rural migrants stands at about 309 million.[22] The return flow of remittances from these workers to their families has improved their standard of living and sparked a desire for a better life that is an essential precondition for economic growth and a demand for accountability in the state.

The decline of divisive, identity-based politics and the rising demand for performance and accountability are in their early stages in the Indian democracy. The direction of change, however, has become increasingly visible and is a profound tribute to the success of India's ethnonational federal democracy. Two generations of Indians have now lived under it, and even though rebellions and demands for further adjustment have not subsided, a vast majority of young Indians in particular have come to accept a dualistic concept of their relationship with the state: their ethnic identity is safe in their home state, while the whole of India is their field of economic opportunity. This is as true of the migrant worker from Bihar as of the medical school applicant from Guwahati or Kohima.[23]

The steady shift of power from the center to the states is also giving rise to intensifying party competition. This has had the most profound effect on the decisionmaking and policy implementation capacities of the coalition governments. In contrast to previous decades, state-level actors and parties increasingly dominate both these areas. The turnaround in Bihar and voter behavior in Gujarat also point to the shift in power away from the government in New Delhi to state-level political clusters. This became evident in the inability of the second UPA government to move forward with economic liberalization in retail trade and insurance, in its failure to pass the land acquisition and rehabilitation bill, and in its having to backtrack on several decisions it had made to control budget deficits. When the margin of parliamentary majority is thin, as it was in 2012, ruling parties usually refrain from making hard decisions that displease their powerful coalition partners.

The coalition governments are governed by a pattern of ebb and flow: relative centralization of power at the apex followed by a steady erosion in the second half of its term as the schedule of state elections (held every two years) alters the arithmetic of parliamentary majority. Even when parties that support a coalition have been reelected in the state (leaving the coalition majority intact), the extent of their success has redefined the equation of power within the ruling coalition. The 2011 elections in Uttar Pradesh and West Bengal did precisely this. Although the winner of the electoral contest in Uttar Pradesh, the Samajwadi Party (SP), was a part of the UPA coalition, its massive victory narrowed the Congress Party's room for maneuver. The Congress Party's other difficult ally was the Trinamul Congress (TMC) in West Bengal led by Mamta Banerjee.

Banerjee was chief among the coalition allies to force Prime Minister Singh to withdraw the introduction of FDI in retail trade in 2010. She again objected to the appointment of Dinesh Trivedi, the new railway minister, who had introduced hikes in rail fares as a way to raise capital to modernize the railroads and rolling stock. Banerjee blocked the hikes and demanded Trivedi's immediate replacement with a candidate of her choice, Mukul Roy. Caught between the devil and the deep blue sea—loss of TMC support or postponement of badly needed infrastructure reforms—Manmohan Singh acquiesced, replaced the railway minister, and rolled back the price hikes. A rupture between the Congress Party and the TMC came with the opening of India's retail market to big multinationals such as IKEA and Walmart in September 2012. The government held firm, but only with a wafer-thin majority in Parliament, which had all but paralyzed it.

The damaging consequences of an immobilized government were evident in the UPA's slow response to the eruption of ethnic violence in Assam in 2012, as well as to a power blackout that hit all of North India on July 30, 2012, affecting more than 600 million people. The national power grid that supplied electricity to several large states in North India had failed.[24] The three-person inquiry commission appointed by Minister of Power Sushil Kumar Shinde pointed to, among other things, the overdrawing of electricity by the agro-rich states of Punjab, Haryana, and Uttar Pradesh, which had completely disregarded quotas allotted to them. What is more, their state governments were confident that the weak central government of Prime Minister Singh would do nothing to bring them to heel.

Commentators in media and print blamed the UPA's policy lapses on the peculiar separation of power and authority within the government in which Sonia Gandhi, the Congress Party president, set the agenda while Prime Minister Singh was reduced to fending at the margins. Even if both power and responsibility were to be vested in the prime minister's office in the future, forging a consensus and retaining control over the national agenda will continue to plague India's coalition governments.

Rising Civil Society: A Double-Edged Sword

The task of forging a consensus is made more difficult by rising activism and massive popular protests around issues of equity and governance. Although these are signs of a healthy and maturing democracy, popular mobilization is not without danger, particularly when the civil society organizations behind it begin to take over the functions of Parliament and the courts. This is what happened when a faction of the anticorruption movement led by Arvind Kejriwal convened public meetings in New Delhi to accuse sitting cabinet ministers and political personalities of gross corruption. The public anger was understandable, but the process was fraught with danger for India's democracy.

The rise in civil society underwent three principal phases over the ensuing years until it arrived at the current dangerous phase of attempting to render elected institutions redundant. The first was public interest litigation (PIL). The second was passage of and increasing recourse to the Right to Information (RTI) Act. The third was an increasingly skillful use of the media to hold officials accountable for corruption and gross abuses of power and to force the state to make corrections. But by 2013, the steam had run out of Arvind Kejriwal's dramatics and crowds began to lose interest.

PIL, the first phase, developed in the 1980s through what was akin to a juristic revolution, spearheaded by two justices of the Supreme Court of India, P. N. Bhagwati and V. R. Krishna Iyer. Before their intervention, the courts entertained pleas for redress only from aggrieved parties, but Bhagwati and Iyer set a series of precedents that allowed any citizen, consumer, or social action group to approach the highest court to seek legal remedies in cases where the interests of the general public or a section of the public were at stake.[25] Over the years, PIL has become a catalyst in compelling the central and state governments to deliver on promises mandated by law and to give directives designed to avert threats to the general public from the exercise of rights by private interests and corporations. Some of the notable successes of PIL have been the conversion of public transport buses in the larger cities from gasoline and diesel to the much cleaner natural gas, the cleaning of the Yamuna River in Delhi, the protection of the famed Taj Mahal in Agra through the compulsory relocation of brick kilns and other factories producing noxious effluents, and a similar relocation of hazardous industries in Delhi. The courts have entered the conflict over agricultural land acquisition by the state. In July 2011, the Supreme Court ordered that the Greater Noida Industrial Development Authority return land to villagers in greater Noida, an area only a few miles from official Delhi.[26] It further ruled that the Salwa Jadum, a special police force that had been created to counter the Naxalite insurgency and that had become notorious for brutality and human rights abuses, must be disarmed and disbanded.

Most of these public interest litigations were triggered by information obtained by the media and civil society organizations under the 2005 Right to Information Act. The act, which initiated the second phase in the emergence of civil society, has created a veritable low-key revolution that is redefining the state-society relationship in India. The RTI requires the central and state governments to furnish information demanded by the public except in a few cases where doing so could impinge upon national security or a legislative process still being shaped. In the short time since the act has come into force, more and more nongovernmental organizations have used it to compel government officials to implement the law, to expose corruption, and, perhaps most important of all, to inform the public of the murky pasts of legislators. Among their main successes so far have been forcing the disclosure of the assets and the criminal records of candidates for Parliament and state legislatures and tracking the performance of high-profile social programs such as the National Rural Employment Guarantee Scheme. Nevertheless, many brave whistleblowers have been victimized and even murdered for their part in exposing corruption and other crimes by politicos or agents of the government. The UPA government therefore passed the Public Interest Disclosure and Protection to Persons Making the Disclosure Act (2010), which empowers the Central Vigilance Commission to penalize people who expose the identity of whistleblowers.

Civil society movements entered the third phase with the establishment in 2010 of the anticorruption drive organized under Anna Hazare. The movement took the nation by storm as it exposed a series of scams in high places. In 2011 and 2012, between the anticorruption activists and the press, close to twenty-five scams came to light. In 2012 alone, over forty scams were exposed. The total estimated costs to the national exchequer ran into billions. The social activists and civil society organization led by India Against Corruption (IAC) occupied center stage throughout 2010 to 2012. Anna Hazare's close associate and the ideologue of the anticorruption movement Arvind Kejriwal fashioned new tactics to keep attention focused on what he called the people's movement outside the formal structures of government and political parties. "Mr. Kejriwal has shaken the political class with his confident allegations of corruption against some of the nation's most powerful figures, often holding apparent documentary evidence in both hands," writes Manu Joseph of the *New York Times*. Joseph goes on to say,

> Mr. Kejriwal, by general opinion, is a new kind of Indian politician. But in fact he is operating in the realm of journalism. Journalism is the art not merely of telling a story, but also of finding permissible vehicles for telling that story. By holding Mr. Kejriwal up as a revolutionary public figure, Indian journalism has devised such a vehicle. The stories that journalists cannot tell—or cannot tell the way they wish out of fear of libel suits or their promoters' fear of politicians—are now told through coverage of Mr. Kejriwal's accusations, which may have some holes in them but retain enough substance to set off a brisk news cycle.[27]

In late 2012, led by Kejriwal, the movement morphed into a political party in anticipation of the 2014 national elections. The change from a movement to a party is, however, fraught with serious danger because the new party, in its eagerness to win elections, can easily become tarnished with the same brush that tarnishes all political parties in India. IAC has nevertheless performed a yeoman's service in mobilizing the public behind legislative measures such as the creation of national and state-level ombudsman offices to oversee complaints of corruption in public office.

By all accounts, social activists have been the catalysts in pushing for landmark welfare legislation since the UPA came to power in 2004: the Right to Education Act; the Food Security Act; the Mahatma Gandhi National Rural Employment Guarantee Act; the Right to Information Act; the Land Acquisition, Rehabilitation, and Resettlement Act; and the Lok Pal bill. The greatest impact of the RTI was felt in Indian Kashmir, where ordinary citizens mobilized massive demonstrations against the corrupt and inefficient government of Chief Minister Umar Abudullah and exposed human rights abuses by Indian security forces. In the case of Indian Kashmir, the RTI is a double-edged sword. It can help separate the popular demand for a separate state of Kashmir from that for a clean and honest government. But it can also deepen popular alienation and escalate violence. Each has profound implications for India's domestic and foreign policy.

A Rising India and the International Balance of Power

Will an India constrained by all these challenges become a significant player in international politics and the global economy? A short answer is yes provided India regains the economic momentum it lost in 2011. This in turn depends on the capacity of India's elected elites to forge a sustained national consensus over the reform agenda. In the realm of international policy, however, the Indian government enjoys a degree of latitude not available to it in domestic policy because there is a national consensus of sorts on the broad contours of India's foreign policy goals. A majority in India's policy community want India to be a great power. They agree that China, a formidable rival if not an enemy, should be counteracted and that Pakistan,

India's traditional enemy, must be neutralized or at least prevented from destabilizing India. A majority also agree that India should forge close economic and defense ties with the United States without compromising its policy of independence, build an extensive network of ties with emerging markets and Southeast Asian countries, gain influence in the extended neighborhood, and build up India's soft power assets through stronger trade and cultural ties. Policymakers differ on the nature of the threat China and Pakistan pose and the extent to which India should cooperate with and support the United States. On the broad goals of long-term policy, however—guarding India's strategic autonomy, exercising strategic restraint, and building up hard and soft power—there is significant consensus within the political community.

India's nation-building is still a work in progress. But against universal skepticism, India has emerged as a cohesive and increasingly integrated nation-state with a steadily growing power to affect outcomes beyond its borders. History has taught us to look askance at the rise of large and potentially powerful states because this has generally presaged a new round of challenges to dominant powers that has frequently ended in conflict. India's rise does not pose this threat even to its neighbors because India has rarely initiated a war.

The United States is currently engaged in creating a plural and balanced security architecture in Asia Pacific, largely to distribute its burden and preempt China's possible domination of this region. India, too, has an interest in promoting plural security architecture partly because it cannot by itself cope with China or the United States and does not wish to acquire weapons and capabilities that may prove financially ruinous. Given this convergence in future agendas, New Delhi's interest lies in supporting Washington in creating a network of loose alignments to counterbalance Beijing. At the same time, the common preoccupations of the United States and India are not limited solely to guarding against a rising China. The two democracies can cooperate on myriad issues, including countering international terrorism, maritime piracy, global pandemics, proliferation of weapons of mass destruction, and climate change. Given India's size and population, no solutions on any of these issues will work without India's participation and support. This is especially true once US troops withdraw from Afghanistan in 2014 and confront the United States with the problem of retaining influence without possessing hard power assets on the ground. India will then be a voice in the shaping of the emerging regional and international order.

But the success of India's strategy faces several obstacles in the extended neighborhood. The US exit from Afghanistan will create a vacuum that may be filled by actors hostile to India, and Pakistan may become increasingly unstable. China has concluded a deal to build two civil nuclear reactors in Pakistan that will make India's national security even more dependent on building counteracting alliances and forging ahead with nuclear weapons development. This might in turn jeopardize whatever plans India has to gain friendly understanding with Pakistan. At this juncture, no one knows what post-US withdrawal from Afghanistan will mean nor can one predict with any certainty the fate of Pakistan's civil democracy. The course of China-Pakistan relations remains similarly unpredictable. These are huge challenges to India's diplomacy and security. India is not, however, a helpless bystander in the drama unfolding in its neighborhood. It has acquired the ability to move diplomatically and influence the emerging equation of power in the region. Friendly Indo-Pakistani relations and normalization in the Indian Kashmir can free India's hand to impart real momentum to its desire for power projection in its extended neighborhood.

Although realpolitik considerations dictate strategic alignments, India's long-term interest lies in promoting a multipolar world order in which no single great power dominates international politics. This is evident in India's refusal to abide by UN Security Council–mandated sanctions against Iran or to join in the West's campaign of regime change in Syria. However, the most unequivocal manifestation of India's advocacy of a multipolar world order is reflected in its active role in the formation of the BRICS (Brazil, Russia, India, China, South Africa) Forum, a five-nation platform for the advocacy of a multipolar world. BRICS is an organization that has no precedent in international relations so far. It is not a political or military alliance; nor is it a customs union. Its members do not all share common boundaries and candidly admit that they have political differences. What unites them is the search for a new international order that is peaceful, multipolar, and based upon a respect for national sovereignty.

The prime goal of BRICS is therefore advocacy—but on behalf of half of the population of the world and by governments that collectively command vast financial resources, large armies, and sophisticated technologies. The formation of BRICS reflects a serious engagement with the issue of how the future global economy should be governed. This vision-cum-advocacy shaped the declaration that emerged from the BRICS Fourth Annual Summit Meeting held in Delhi in March 2012.

India Matters

By the yardsticks set out in this volume to measure potential power, India easily passes the test. India does not dazzle by rapid change but makes slow progress. This has obscured its actual achievements, which have been quite impressive. But India's achievements are of more than purely national importance. They offer an alternative road to nation-building at a time when the European model of the nation-state, with its hard economic and political boundaries, has been eroding at the edges for several decades under the impact of economic globalization. This has already brought down barriers to the movement of capital and, to a slightly lesser extent, to the movement of goods. The need to coordinate economic, cultural, and political aspirations in this new transnational environment has steadily reduced the autonomy of sovereign states.

A new form of federalism is clearly being born. In this, India, which is not unlike the European Union, has a head start. It functions on a very different conception of statehood. For the hundred or more new states that have been created during the past half century, the Indian model is of greater relevance than the European because it bypasses the phase of nation-state formation and goes directly to the postnational phase. In fact, in some ways both the EU and India are postnational states.

In international politics, dangers emanating from state failures can make one nation vital to the security of others. Russia after the disintegration of the Soviet Union, Pakistan, Sudan, Yemen, and Somalia are notable cases in point. That moment has long passed for India. In the twenty-first century, with all its stops and starts, it is India's rise that will make a mark on world events. It will do so not only because of the hard power assets it will accumulate as it becomes affluent but also because of the living example it will provide—in both its achievements and failures—of how to think differently about prosperity, power, and history.

Notes

1. Selig Harrison Jr., *India: The Most Dangerous Decades* (Princeton, NJ: Princeton University Press, 1960).

2. For example, "famine is threatening, the administration is strained and universally believed to be corrupt, the government and the governing party have lost public confidence and belief in themselves as well." These various crises had created an "emotional readiness for the rejection of Parliamentary democracy." The "politically sophisticated Indians" whom Maxwell spoke to expressed "a deep sense of defeat, an alarmed awareness that the future is not only dark but profoundly uncertain." *The Guardian*'s assessment of India disagreed: "Indian democracy is now for the first time coming fully alive." All quoted in Ramachandra Guha, "Verdicts on India," *Hindu Magazine,* July 17, 2005, http://www.hindu.com/mag/2005/07/17/stories/20050717 00140300.htm.

3. K. C. Wheare, *Federal Government* (Oxford: Oxford University Press, 1963), 77.

4. Paul Brass has concentrated largely on the question of how ethnic nationalism has shaped the structure of factional politics within and outside established political parties in India and how that structure has reproduced the Hindu-Muslim divide since 1947. He argues that genuine democracy was only possible if a large degree of local autonomy was granted to India's culturally distinctive communities. But the imperatives of competitive politics led to quasi-authoritarian practices that were dangerous for India's survival as a state and democracy. See his *Forms of Collective Violence: Riots, Pogroms, and Genocide in Modern India* (Gurgaon, India: Three Essays Collective, 2006); and *The Production of Hindu-Muslim Violence in Contemporary India* (Seattle: University of Washington Press, 2003). Ayesha Jalal, *Democracy and Authoritarianism in South Asia: A Comparative and Historical Perspective* (Cambridge: Cambridge University Press, 1995).

5. Stephen Cohen and Sunil Dasgupta, *Arming Without Aiming: India's Military Modernization* (Washington, DC: Brookings Institution Press, 2010); George Tanham, "Indian Strategic Thought: An Interpretive Essay" (Santa Monica, CA: Rand, 1992).

6. Stephen Cohen, *India: Emerging Power* (Washington, DC: Brookings Institution Press, 2001), 103.

7. Several recent writings have explicitly made national identity a basis for analyzing India's foreign policy. See, for example, Tobias F. Englemeier, *Nation-Building and Foreign Policy in India: An Identity-Strategy Conflict* (Cambridge: Cambridge University Press, 2009).

8. See Charles Tilly, "War Making and State Making as Organized Crime," in *Bringing the State Back In,* ed. Peter Evans, Dietrich Rueschemeyer, and Theda Skocpol (Cambridge: Cambridge University Press, 1985), 174–175. My brief description of state making omits many

variations in the European experience, but the purpose here is to expose the contrast between the two experiences of state formation.

9. Rob Jenkins suggests that, although central states can and do influence foreign economic policy, the complicated and sometimes contrary agendas of state politicians, national politicians, and bureaucracy limit that influence. Rafiq Dossani and Srinidhi Vijaykumar, in contrast, argue persuasively that, even though state-provincial-level parties that are part of the ruling coalition may be constrained by the need to keep the coalition intact, opposition parties can exert significant influence on foreign policy, particularly in border states such as Tamil Nadu, Assam, the Northeast states, and Kashmir. These states have influenced decisions by controlling migration of foreign nationals and goods across the border. Rob Jenkins, *Democratic Politics and Economic Reforms in India* (Cambridge: Cambridge University Press, 1999), 119–172. See Rafiq Dossani and Srinidhi Vijaykumar, "Indian Federalism and the Conduct of Foreign Policy in Border States: State Participation and Central Accommodation Since 1990," *Stanford Journal of International Relations* 7, no. 1 (Winter 2006), http://sjir.stanford.edu/7.1.07 _dossani.html.

10. There was, of course, an obverse side to rule by consensus, that is, rule by threatening to break away from the coalition and jeopardizing the ruling majority. For example, opposition from left-wing parties threatened to leave the coalition and bring down the first UPA coalition government over the Indo-US nuclear agreement, and more recently the Trinamul Congress and Mamta Banerjee withdrew from the Manmohan Singh–led UPA in 2012 in protest over the decision to increase gas prices and introduce FDI in retail trade.

11. Several left-leaning economists question this figure and suggest that the methodology used to arrive at this number of interstate migration may be flawed. Prabhat Patnaik, a leading left economist, expresses serious reservations about the published numbers of migrants in Ram Bhagat, "Internal Migration in India: Are the Underclass More Mobile?" paper presented at the Twenty-Sixth Annual General Population Conference, Marrakech, Morocco, September 27, 2009, http://iussp2009.princeton.edu/papers/90927. But he acknowledges that his objections are based not on any systematic study of either the methodology or the data. Author's conversation with Prabhat Patnaik at the Conference on South Asia, New York University, New York, New York, February 16, 2013.

12. Avijit Ghosh, "Small Towns Big Leap," *Times of India,* December 4, 2010, http://www.timescrest.com/coverstory/small-towns-big-leap-4186.

13. For details, see the February 16, 2009, budget speech of Finance Minister Pranab Mukherjee, http://indiabudget.nic.in/ub2009-10/afs.htm.

14. The word Naxalism originates from the armed peasant uprising in the village of Naxalbari in West Bengal in the late 1960s. The uprising, led by the Communist Party of India (Marxist), was crushed by the Indian government but has resurfaced, in the tribal regions of central India, again led by radical leaders inspired by Maoism.

15. This number has fluctuated over the years. In 2009, the number of affected districts was 180. These came down in 2011 to 83. See Ministry of Home Affairs, Government of India, "Naxal Hit Areas," cited in http://www.satp.org/satporgtp/countries/india/maoist/documents/papers/DATA_%20Extent_Naxal_Violence.pdf (accessed February 13, 2013).

16. In the other states, the Congress Party did well principally because its main rivals, the BJP and some of the larger regional parties, fared a lot worse than they had in 2004. However, with only some exceptions, these voters did not cast their lot with the Congress Party; instead, they voted for smaller, hitherto unknown regional and local parties—a sure sign of growing disenchantment with the traditional mode of politics in the country.

17. In Madhya Pradesh, Delhi, and Gujarat, voters have returned the same party to power three times. In Bihar, Nitish Kumar's victory in 2005 was a revolt that cut across caste lines. The voters punished the political parties for misgovernance. The 2009 elections demonstrated the weakening, if not the disappearance, of the anti-incumbency factor in Andhra Pradesh, Tamil Nadu, Bihar, and Orissa. Similarly, Narendra Modi and the BJP were reelected in Gujarat in four consecutive elections since 2001. He is still the chief minister in Gujarat.

18. The UPA coalition government responded to the anticorruption protests by harnessing its digital identity card scheme (Aadhar) to deliver for the first time twenty-nine categories of subsidies (largely pension and scholarships) in direct cash transfers to the accounts of recipients. Cash transfers are meant to eliminate the middlemen all along the current delivery system.

19. Montek Singh Ahluwalia led the Planning Commission's Task Force on Unemployment in 2004. To provide anecdotal evidence, I was told by a rickshaw puller in Bharatpur, Haryana (during the winter months of 2007), that he was saving money from his day's toil (he worked from 6 a.m. to 11 at night) to send his child to an English medium school in the hope that his son would never have to face the uncertainties and humiliations that he himself encountered daily. Many working poor are doing the same across India.

20. Prem Shankar Jha, "The Pie in Smaller Sizes," *Tehelka* 23, no. 6 (June 13, 2009), http://www.tehelka.com/the-pie-in-smaller-slices/.

21. Bhagat, "Internal Migration," Table 1.

22. "Overview of Internal Migration in India," United Nations Children's Fund, New York, March 12, 2012, http://www.unicef.org/india/1_Overview_(03-12-2012).pdf.

23. Balbir Punj, "Death by Marx, Mandal," *Asian Age,* January 8, 2010. The data are from state government reports. The effects of this shift are being felt in the economy as well. Bihar is an outstanding illustration of the change. The state's economy had been a casualty of internecine caste wars for more than three decades, and as a result, economic development and plan allocations went unused year after year for more than a decade. The sea change that Chief Minister Nitish Kumar brought in governance can be highlighted by one statistic: in four years, from 2005 to 2009, his govern-

ment spent $8 billion on development. By contrast, his predecessor had spent about half of that over a spell of fifteen years.

24. Jim Yadley, "2nd Day of Power Failures Cripples Wide Swath of India," *New York Times,* July 31, 2012, http://www.nytimes.com/2012/08/01 /world/asia/power-outages-hit-600-million-in-india.html?pagewanted=all.

25. PIL is controversial, and its abuse is beginning to draw increasing attention. On the whole, however, it has advanced the cause of democracy by enhancing transparency and accountability in government. An important use of public interest litigation is to expose and scrutinize hidden or misleading information, including the cost of potential social programs (which the state and corporate entities on occasion have reasons to exaggerate or hide). During droughts in Rajasthan and Orissa in 2001, PIL cases exposed, in the words of Varun Gauri, "the extent of unreleased government grain stocks . . . and that state governments could in fact afford to widen the statutory food and nutrition programs—including the midday meals scheme in schools—notwithstanding official denials to the contrary. In the Delhi vehicular pollution debate, the Delhi Health Minister claimed that air pollution did not increase the risks of heart or lung disease, the Delhi government said that the timely installation of compressed natural gas (CNG) stations would be impossible, the Ministry of Petroleum and Natural Gas argued that CNG bus conversion would not be sustainable in the long run, producers of commercial vehicles stated that the conversion to CNG was not economically cost-effective, and others argued that CNG is explosive." But the court insisted that the government deliver without delay on what it had promised. See Varun Gauri, "Public Interest Litigation in India: Time for an Audit" (Philadelphia: Center for the Advanced Study of India, November 9, 2009), http://casi.ssc.upenn.edu/iit/gauri.

26. "SC Orders Return of Land to Greater Noida Villagers," *Business Standard,* July 7, 2011, http://www.business-standard.com/india/news/sc -orders-returnland-to-greater-noida-villagers/441876/.

27. Manu Joseph, "Messenger and Message Under One Cap," *New York Times,* October 24, 2012, http://www.nytimes.com/2012/10/25/world/asia /25iht-letter25.html?_r=0.

Acronyms

AAPI	American Association of Physicians from India
ADC	Autonomous District Council
AIADMK	All India Anna Dravida Munnetra Kazhagam
AIDS	acquired immune deficiency syndrome
ASEAN	Association of Southeast Asian Nations
ATM	anti-tank missile
AWACS	airborne warning and control system
BIMSTEC	Bay of Bengal Initiative for Multi-Sectoral Technical and Economic Cooperation
BJP	Bharatiya Janata Party
BRICS	Brazil, Russia, India, China, South Africa
BSP	Bahujan Samaj Party
CPI	Communist Party of India
CPI(M)	Communist Party of India (Marxist)
CS	Cold Start
CTBT	Comprehensive Test Ban Treaty
DAC	Defence Acquisition Council
DMK	Dravida Munnetra Kazhagam
EU	European Union
FARP	Field Artillery Rationalisation Plan
FDI	foreign direct investment
FRBMA	Fiscal Responsibility and Budgetary Management Act
GDP	gross domestic product

GNP	gross national product
GoM	Group of Ministers
HDI	Human Development Index
HIV	human immunodeficiency virus
IAC	India Against Corruption
IAF	Indian Air Force
IBSA	India, Brazil, South Africa
ICOR	Incremental Capital to Output Ratio
ID	identification
IDS	Integrated Defence Staff
IISS	International Institute of Strategic Studies
IMF	International Monetary Fund
INC	Indian National Congress Party
IPKF	Indian Peacekeeping Force
IR	infrared
ISAS	Institute of South Asian Studies
ISI	Inter-Service Intelligence
IT	information technology
JD	Janata Dal Party
JD(U)	Janata Dal United
LARRA	Land Acquisition Rehabilitation and Resettlement Act
LARRB	Land Acquisition Rehabilitation and Resettlement Bill
LF	Left Front
LoC	Line of Control
LPD	landing platform dock
LTIPP	long-term integrated perspective plan
LTTE	Liberation Tigers of Tamil Eelam
NCMP	National Common Minimum Programme
NDA	National Democratic Alliance
NF	National Front
NGO	nongovernmental organization
NIC	National Intelligence Council
NPR	nonproliferation regime
NPT	Non-Proliferation Treaty
NSG	Nuclear Suppliers Group
NSSO	National Sample Survey Organisation
NSSP	Next Steps in Strategic Partnership
NTI	Nuclear Threat Initiative
OBC	Other Backward Caste
ONGC	Oil and Natural Gas Corporation

PDP	People's Democratic Party
PIL	public interest litigation
PL	Public Law
PLA	People's Liberation Army
PLB	poverty-line basket
PoK	Pakistan-occupied Kashmir
RBI	Reserve Bank of India
RTI	Right to Information (Act)
SAM	surface-to-air missile
SEZ	Special Economic Zone
SIPRI	Stockholm International Peace Research Institute
SP	Samajwadi Party
TDP	Telugu Desam Party
TMC	Trinamul Congress
UF	United Front
UIDAI	Unique Identification Authority of India
ULCRA	Urban Land Ceiling and Regulation Act
UPA	United Progressive Alliance
USAID	US Agency for International Development
USINPAC	US India Political Action Committee
USTR	US Trade Representative
VHP	Vishva Hindu Parishad
VRS	Voluntary Retirement Scheme
WTO	World Trade Organization

Bibliography

Ahluwalia, Bhupinder Kumar, and Shashi Ahluwalia. *Netaji and Gandhi.* New Delhi: Indian Academic Publishers, 1982.

Ahluwalia, Montek Singh. "Economic Reforms in India Since 1991: Has Gradualism Worked?" *Journal of Economic Perspectives* 16, no. 3 (Summer 2002): 67–88.

Appadorai, A. "India's Foreign Policy." *International Affairs* 25, no. 1 (January 1949): 37–47.

Appadorai, A., and M. S. Rajan. *India's Foreign Policy and Relations.* New Delhi: South Asian Publishers, 1985.

Bajpai, G. S. "Ethical Standards on World Issues: Cornerstone of India's Foreign Policy." In *Foreign Policy of India: A Book of Readings,* ed. K. P. Misra. New Delhi: Thomson Press, 1977, 91–96.

Bajpai, Kanti, and Pant Harsh. *India's National Security: A Reader.* New Delhi: Oxford University Press, 2013.

Bajpai, Kanti, and Siddharth Mallavarapu. *International Relations in India: Theorizing the Region and Nation.* Hyderabad, India: Orient Longman, 2005.

Bardhan, Pranab. *Awakening Giants, Feet of Clay: Assessing the Economic Rise of China and India.* Princeton, NJ: Princeton University Press, 2012.

Baruah, Sanjib. "Confronting Constructionism: Ending India's Naga War." *Journal of Peace Research* 40, no. 3 (May 2003): 321–338.

———. *India Against Itself: Assam and the Politics of Nationality.* Philadelphia: University of Pennsylvania Press, 1999.

Bhatt, Chetan. *Hindu Nationalism: Origins, Ideologies, and Modern Myths.* Oxford: Oxford University Press, 2001.

Blackwill, Robert. "U.S.-India Defense Cooperation." *The Hindu,* May 13, 2003. http://www.hinduonnet.com/thehindu/2003/05/13/stories/20030513 01101000.htm.

Bozeman, Adda. "India's Foreign Policy Today: Reflections upon Its Sources." *World Politics* 10, no. 2 (January 1958): 256–274.

Brass, Paul. *Forms of Collective Violence: Riots, Pogroms, and Genocide in Modern India.* Gurgaon, India: Three Essays Collective, 2006.

———. *The Production of Hindu-Muslim Violence in Contemporary India.* Seattle: University of Washington Press, 2003.

Chadda, Maya. *Building Democracy in South Asia.* Boulder: Lynne Rienner, 2001.

———. *Ethnicity, Security, and Separatism in India.* New York: Columbia University Press, 1997.

———. "India in 2011: The State Encounters the People." *Asian Survey* 52, no. 1 (January–February 2012): 114–129.

Chandra, Dinesh. "Golden Quadrilateral Highway Project Completion Advanced by 2003." *Financial Express,* January 9, 2000. http://www.expressindia.com /news/fe/daily/20000109/fec09041.html.

Chatterjee, Partha. *The Nation and Its Fragments: Colonial and Postcolonial Histories.* Princeton, NJ: Princeton University Press, 1993.

Chellaney, Brahma. "Assessing India's Reaction to China's Peaceful Development Doctrine." *NBR Analysis* 18, no. 5 (April 2008): 23–30.

"China's Stimulus Package." *The Economist,* November 12, 2008. http://www .economist.com/blogs/theworldin2009/2008/11/chinas_stimulus_package.

Chopra, P. N., and Prabha Chopra. *Inside Story of Sardar Patel: The Diary of Maniben Patel, 1936–50.* New Delhi: Vision Books, 2002.

Choudhari, Arindam. "Khao Aur Khilao Budget." *Sunday Indian,* July 5, 2009, 23–26.

"Chronology of India's Missile Technology." Indian Officer, October 4, 2007. http://www.indianofficer.com/forums/science-technology-wiki/1778 -chronology-indian-missile-technology.html.

Cohen, Stephen P. *India: Emerging Power.* Washington, DC: Brookings Institution Press, 2001.

Cohen, Stephen P., and Sunil Dasgupta. *Arming Without Aiming: India's Military Modernization.* Washington, DC: Brookings Institution Press, 2010.

Communist Party of India (Marxist). "National Common Minimum Programme of the Government of India." New Delhi, May 2004.

Corbridge, Stuart, and John Harriss. *Reinventing India: Liberalization, Hindu Nationalism, and Popular Democracy.* Cambridge, UK: Polity Press, 2000.

Das, Gurcharan. "The India Model." *Foreign Affairs* 85, no. 4 (July–August 2006). http://www.foreignaffairs.com/author/gurcharan-das.

———. *India Unbound.* New York: Anchor Books, 2002.

Dasgupta, Ajit Kumar. *A History of Indian Economic Thought.* London: Routledge, 1993.

Dasgupta, Sunil, and Stephen Cohen. "Is India Ending Its Strategic Restraint Doctrine?" *Washington Quarterly* 34, no. 2 (Spring 2011): 163–177.

Devare, Sudhir. *India and Southeast Asia: Towards Security Convergence.* Singapore: Institute of Southeast Asian Studies, University of Singapore, 2006.

Dietmar, Rothermund. *India: Rise of an Asian Giant.* New Haven, CT: Yale University Press, 2009.

———. "Protagonists, Power, and the Third World: Essays on the Changing International System." *Annals of the American Academy of Political and Social Science* 386 (November 1969): 78–88.

Dixit, J. N. *India's Foreign Policy, 1947–2003.* New Delhi: Picus, 2003.

————. "Indo-American Relations." *World Focus* (New Delhi) 20, nos. 12–13 (October–November 1999): 41–42.

Dohrmann, Jona Aravind. "Special Economic Zones in India—An Introduction." *ASIEN* 106 (January 2008): S60–80. http://www.asienkunde.de/articles /a106_asien_aktuell_dohrmann.pdf.

"Don't Go Ahead with Nuclear Deal: CPI(M)." *The Hindu,* August 19, 2007. http://www.hindu.com/2007/08/19/stories/2007081961920100.htm.

Dossani, Rafiq, and Srinidhi Vijaykumar. "Indian Federalism and the Conduct of Foreign Policy in Border States: State Participation and Central Accommodation Since 1990." *Stanford Journal of International Relations* 7, no. 1 (Winter 2006). http://sjir.stanford.edu/7.1.07_dossani.html.

Dutt, R. C. *The Economic History of India.* 2 vols. London: Gollacz, [1901] 1950.

Epstein, Susan, and K. Alan Kronstadt. "Pakistan: U.S. Foreign Assistance." Report No. R41856. Washington, DC: Congressional Research Service, October 4, 2012. http://www.fas.org/sgp/crs/row/R41856.pdf.

Fernandes, Leela. *India's New Middle Classes: Democratic Politics in an Era of Reform.* Minneapolis: University of Minnesota Press, 2006.

Fisher, Margaret W. "India in 1963: A Year of Travail." *Asian Survey* 4, no. 3 (March 1964): 737–745.

Fisher, Margaret W., Leo E. Rose, and Robert A. Huttenback. *Himalayan Battleground: Sino-Indian Rivalry in Ladakh.* New York: Praeger, 1963.

Frankel, Francine, and Harry Harding, eds. *The India-China Relationship: What the United States Needs to Know.* New York: Columbia University Press, 2004.

Friedberg, Aaron L. "Introduction." In *Strategic Asia, 2001–02: Power and Purpose,* ed. Richard J. Ellings and Aaron L. Friedberg. Seattle: National Bureau of Asian Research, 2001, 1–16.

Ganguly, Sumit. *The Origins of War in South Asia: Indo-Pakistani Conflict Since 1947.* Boulder: Westview Press, 1994.

Ganguly, Sumit, and S. Paul Kapur. *India, Pakistan, and the Bomb.* New York: Columbia University Press, 2010.

Ganguly, Sumit, and Rahul Mukherji. *India Since 1980.* New York: Cambridge University Press, 2011.

Gauri, Varun. "Public Interest Litigation in India: Time for an Audit." Philadelphia: Center for the Advanced Study of India, November 9, 2009. http://casi.ssc.upenn.edu/iit/gauri.

Ghosh, Anjali, Chakraborthi Tribid, Majumdar Annindyo, and Chatterjee Shibashis. *India's Foreign Policy.* New Delhi: Pearson Education, 2009.

Ghosh, Avijit. "Small Towns Big Leap." *Times of India,* December 4, 2010. http://www.timescrest.com/coverstory/small-towns-big-leap-4186.

Gilmartin, David. "Rule of Law, Rule of Life: Caste, Democracy, and the Courts in India." *American Historical Review* 115, no. 2 (April 2010): 406–427.

"Global Economic Power List: India Enters Top 5." *Indian Express,* February 26, 2011. http://www.indianexpress.com/news/global-economic-power-list-india -enters-top/755105/.

Gopal, Sarvepalli. *Jawaharlal Nehru: A Biography.* 3 vols. London: Jonathan Cape, 1984.

Gorwala, A. D. *India Without Illusions.* Bombay: New Book Co., 1953.

Government of India. Electricity Act 2003. March 2006. http://www.power min.nic.in/acts_notification/electricity_act2003/preliminary.htm.

Govinda, Radhika. "Re-Inventing Dalit Women's Identity? Dynamics of Social Activism and Electoral Politics in Rural North India." *Contemporary South Asia* 16, no. 4 (December 2008): 427–440.

Guha, Ramachandra. *India After Gandhi: The History of the World's Largest Democracy*. London: Macmillan, 2007.

———. "Verdicts on India." *Hindu Magazine*, July 17, 2005. http://www.the hindu.com/thehindu/mag/2005/07/17/stories/2005071700140300.htm.

Guha, Ranajit. *Elementary Aspects of Peasant Insurgency in Colonial India*. Delhi: Oxford University Press, 1983.

Guha, Ranajit, ed. *A Subaltern Reader, 1986–1995*. Minneapolis: University of Minnesota Press, 1997.

Gupta, S. P. "India Vision 2020." New Delhi: Planning Commission, Government of India, December 2002. Habib, Irfan. *The Agrarian System of Mughal India*. New York: Asia Publishing House, 1963.

Habib, Irfan, ed. *Akbar and His India*. New Delhi: Oxford University Press, 2010.

Hagerty, Devin. "India's Regional Security Doctrine." *Asian Survey* 31, no. 4 (April 1991): 351–363.

Hardgrave, Robert, Jr., and Stanley Kochanek. *India: Government and Politics in a Developing Nation*. Boston: Thomson Press, 2008.

Harrison, Selig, Jr. *India: The Most Dangerous Decades*. Princeton, NJ: Princeton University Press, 1960.

Hasan, Munir. *South Asia: Emerging Issues*. Hyderabad, India: ICFAI University Press, 2006.

Heehs, Peter. *Nationalism, Terrorism, Communalism: Essays in Modern Indian History*. New York: Oxford University Press, 1998.

Heimsath, Charles, and Surjit Mansingh. *A Diplomatic History*. Bombay: Allied Publishers, 1971.

Hoge, James, Jr. "A Global Power Shift in the Making." *Foreign Affairs* 83, no. 4 (July–August 2004): 2–7.

Holt, Sarah. *Aid, Peace Building, and the Resurgence of War: Buying Time in Sri Lanka*. Basingstoke, UK: Palgrave, 2011.

Husain, Haqqani. *Pakistan: Between Mosque and Military*. Washington, DC: Carnegie Endowment for International Peace, 2005.

"India's Demographic Moment." *Strategy + Business*, Autumn 2009. http://www .strategy-business.com/article/09305?pg=all.

International Institute for Strategic Studies. *The Military Balance 2012*. London: Routledge, 2012. http://www.iiss.org/publications/military-balance/the -military-balance-2012/.

Isaacs, Harold. *Scratches on Our Minds: American Views of China and India*. Armonk, NY: M. E. Sharpe, 1980.

Jalal, Ayesha. *Democracy and Authoritarianism in South Asia: A Comparative and Historical Perspective*. Cambridge: Cambridge University Press, 1995.

Jha, Prem Shankar. *Crouching Dragon, Hidden Tiger: Can China and India Dominate the West?* Berkeley, CA: Soft Skull Press, 2010.

———. *In the Eye of the Cyclone: The Crisis in Indian Democracy*. New Delhi: Penguin, 1993.

———. *Origins of the Dispute: Kashmir 1947*. Rev. ed. London: Pluto Press, 2003.

———. *Perilous Road to Market: Political Economy of Reform in Russia, India, and China*. London: Pluto Press, 2002.

————. *The Twilight of the Nation State*. London: Pluto Press, 2006.

Jones, Kenneth. *Socio-Religious Reform Movements in British India*. Cambridge: Cambridge University Press, 1990.

Jones, Rodney. "Conventional Military Imbalance and Strategic Stability in South Asia." March 2005. http://www.policyarchitects.org/pdf/Conventional _imbalance_RJones.pdf.

Kamath, P. M. *India China Relations: An Agenda for Asian Century*. New Delhi: Gyan Publishing House, 2011.

Kamdar, Mira. "Forget the Israel Lobby. The Hill's Next Big Player Is Made in India." *Washington Post,* September 30, 2007.

————. *Planet India: The Turbulent Rise of the Largest Democracy and the Future of the World*. New York: Scribner, 2008.

Kaplan, Robert. "Center Stage for the Twenty-First Century: Power Plays in the Indian Ocean." *Foreign Affairs* 88, no. 2 (March–April 2009): 1–7.

Kapur, Ashok. "Eclipsed Moon and Rising Sun." In *Security Beyond Survival: Essays for K. Subrahmanyam,* ed. P. R. Kumar Swami. New Delhi: Sage, 2004, 52–82.

————. *India and the South Asian Strategic Triangle*. New York: Routledge, 2011.

Kaviraj, Sudipta. *The Dynamics of State Formation: India and Europe Compared*. Delhi: Sage, 1997.

Khalidi, Omar. *Khaki and Ethnic Violence in India: Army, Police, and Paramilitary Forces During Communal Riots*. Gurgaon, India: Three Essays Collective, 2010.

Khalilzad, Zalmay, and Ian Lesser, eds. *Sources of Conflict in the 21st Century: Regional Futures and U.S. Strategy*. Santa Monica, CA: RAND, 1998.

Khilnani, Sunil. *The Idea of India*. New York: Farrar, Straus and Giroux, 1997.

Kinnvall, Catarina, and Ted Svensson. "Hindu Nationalism, Diaspora Politics, and Nation-Building in India." *Australian Journal of International Affairs* 64, no. 3 (June 2010): 274–292.

Kochanek, Stanley. "India's Changing Role in the United Nations." *Pacific Affairs* 53, no. 1 (Spring 1980): 48–68.

Kohli, Atul. *Democracy and Discontent: India's Growing Crisis of Governability*. Cambridge: Cambridge University Press, 1990.

————. "Politics of Economic Growth in India, 1980–2005, Part I and II." *Economic and Political Weekly* 41, no. 14 (April 8–14, 2006): 1361–1370.

Kohli, Harinder S., and Anil Sood, eds. *India 2039: An Affluent Society in One Generation*. New Delhi: Sage, 2010.

Kosambi, D. D. *The Culture and Civilization of Ancient India in Historical Outline*. New Delhi: Vikas Publications, 1994.

Kothari, Rajni. *Politics of India*. Boston: Little, Brown, 1970.

————. "Tradition and Modernity Revisited." *Government and Opposition* 3, no. 3 (Summer 1968): 273–293.

Kronstadt, K. Alan. "U.S.-India Bilateral Agreements and 'Global Partnership.'" Report No. RL33072. Washington, DC: Congressional Research Service, April 6, 2006.

Kulke, Marmann, and Dietmar Rothermund. *A History of India*. 4th ed. New York: Routledge, 2004.

Ladwig, Walter, III. "A Cold Start for Hot Wars? The Indian Army's New Limited War Doctrine." *International Security* 32, no. 3 (Winter 2007–2008): 158–190.

————. "India and Military Power Projection: Will the Land of Gandhi Become a Conventional Great Power?" *Asian Survey* 50, no. 6 (November–December 2010): 1162–1183.

Lal, Vinay. "Subaltern Studies and Its Critics: Debates over Indian History." *History and Theory* 40, no. 1 (February 2001): 135–148.

Leadmark: The Navy's Strategy for 2020. Ottawa, Canada: Directorate of Maritime Strategy, 2001. http://www.navy.dnd.ca/leadmark/doc/appendix_D_e.asp.

Lelyveld, David. "Burning Up the Dharmashatras: Group Identity and Social Justice in the Thought of B. R. Ambedkar." New York: Columbia University, April 14, 1990. http://www.columbia.edu/itc/mealac/pritchett/00 ambedkar/timeline/graphics/txt_lelyveld_ambedkar.pdf.

Leng, Shao Chuan. "India and China." *Far Eastern Survey* 21, no. 8 (May 21, 1952): 73–78.

LePoer, Barbara Leitch. "India-U.S. Relations." Report No. IB93097. Washington, DC: Congressional Research Service, December 31, 2001. http://fpc .state.gov/documents/organization/7930.pdf.

Levoy, Peter. "Pakistan's Foreign Relations." In *South Asia in World Politics,* ed. Devin Hagerty. Lanham, MD: Rowman and Littlefield, 2005, 49–70.

Ludden, David. *India and South Asia: A Short History*. London: Oneworld Publications, 2002.

MacDonald, Juli. "Rethinking India's and Pakistan's Regional Intent." *NBR Analysis* 14, no. 4 (November 2003): 5–26.

Mahajan, Ashwani. "Dilemma of the Poverty Line." Shvoong.com, January 1, 2010. http://www.shvoong.com/business-management/1960075-dilemma -poverty-line/.

Mallavarapu, Siddharth. "Democracy Promotion Circa 2010: An Indian Perspective." *Contemporary Politics* 16, no. 1 (March 2010): 49–61.

Mansingh, Surjit. "India and the US: A Closer Strategic Partnership?" *Economic and Political Weekly* (Mumbai) 40, nos. 22–23 (May 28–June 10, 2005): 2221–2226.

Mathur, Jagannath Swaroop. *Industrial Civilization and Gandhian Economics*. Allahabad, India: Pustakayan, 1971.

Maxwell, Neville. *India's China War*. London: Jonathan Cape, 1970.

————. "Jawaharlal Nehru: The Pride and Principle." *Foreign Affairs* 52, no. 3 (April 1974): 633–643.

McDuie-Ra, Duncan. "Vision 2020 or Re-Vision 1958: The Contradictory Politics of Counter-Insurgency in India's Regional Engagement." *Contemporary South Asia* 17, no. 3 (September 2009): 313–330.

Mellor, John W., ed. *India: A Rising Middle Power*. Boulder: Westview Press, 1979.

Menon, Admiral Raja, and Rajiv Kumar. *The Long View from Delhi: To Define the Indian Grand Strategy for Foreign Policy*. New Delhi: Academic Foundation, 2010.

Menon, Rajan. "India and the Soviet Union: A New Stage of Relations?" *Asian Survey* 18, no. 7 (July 1978): 731–750.

Menon, V. P. *The Story of the Integration of the Indian States*. New York: Macmillan, 1956.

Mishra, Kamal Kishore. *Police Administration in Ancient India*. New Delhi: Mittal Publications, 1987.

Mishra, Pankaj. "The Myth of the New India." *New York Times,* July 6, 2006.

Mitchell, Lisa. *Language, Emotion, and Politics in South India: The Making of a Mother Tongue*. Bloomington: Indiana University Press, 2009.

Mitra, Subrata K. "Adversarial Politics and Policy Continuity: The UPA, NDA, and the Resilience of Democracy in India." *Contemporary South Asia* 19, no. 2 (June 2011): 173–187.

Mohan, C. Raja. *Crossing the Rubicon: The Shaping of India's New Foreign Policy*. New Delhi: Viking, 2003.

———. "India's Nuclear Navy: Catching Up with China." ISAS Insights No. 78. Singapore: Institute of South Asian Studies, National University of Singapore, 2009.

———. *Samudra Manthan: Sino-Indian Rivalry in the Indo-Pacific*. Washington, DC: Brookings Institution Press, 2012.

———. "Themes from India's Big Power Diplomacy." ISAS Insights No. 117. Singapore: Institute of South Asian Studies, National University of Singapore, January 26, 2011.

Mukherjee, Rahul. "India's Aborted Liberalization—1966." *Pacific Affairs* 73, no. 3 (Autumn 2000): 375–392.

Musharraf, Pervez. *In the Line of Fire*. New York: Free Press, 2006.

Mushirul, Hasan. "Partition Narratives." *Social Scientist* 30, nos. 7–8 (July–August 2002): 24–53.

Myint-U, Thant. *Where China Meets India: Burma and the New Crossroads of Asia*. New York: Farrar, Straus and Giroux, 2011.

Naipaul, V. S. *An Area of Darkness*. New York: Vintage Books, 2002.

Nair, Neeti. *Changing Homelands: Hindu Politics and the Partition of India*. Cambridge, MA: Harvard University Press, 2011.

Nanda, B. R. *India's Foreign Policy: The Nehru Years*. Honolulu: University of Hawaii Press, 1976.

National Intelligence Council. "Global Trends 2015: A Dialogue About the Future with Nongovernment Experts." Washington, DC: Central Intelligence Agency, 2000.

———. "Global Trends 2025: A Transformed World," November 2008. http://www.dni.gov/index.php/about/organization/national-intelligence-council-global-trends.

Nayar, Baldev Raj. "The Limits of Economic Nationalism in India: Economic Reforms Under the BJP-Led Government, 1998–1999." *Asian Survey* 40, no. 5 (September–October 2000): 792–815.

———. "When Did the Hindu Rate of Growth End?" *Economic and Political Weekly* 41, no. 19 (May 13–19, 2006): 1885–1890.

Nayar, Baldev Raj, and T. V. Paul. *India in the World Order: Searching for Major-Power Status*. Cambridge: Cambridge University Press, 2004.

Nayyar, K. K. "Indo-Russian Strategic Cooperation." In *New Trends in Indo-Russian Relations,* ed. V. D. Chopra. New Delhi: Kalpaz, 2003, 77–83.

Nehru, Jawaharlal. *Discovery of India*. Centenary ed. Delhi: Oxford University Press, 1989.

Ogden, Chris. "Norms, Indian Foreign Policy, and the 1998–2004 National Democratic Alliance." *Round Table* 99, no. 408 (June 2010): 303–315.

Ollapally, Deepa, and Rajesh Rajagopalan. "The Pragmatic Challenge to Indian Foreign Policy." *Washington Quarterly* 34, no. 2 (Spring 2011): 145–162.

Padmanabhan, Anil. "Fuel Price Decontrol: History Repeating Itself?" Livemint.com (*Wall Street Journal*), February 7, 2010. http://www.livemint.com/2010/02/07230959/Fuel-price-decontrol-history.html.

Palit, Amitendu. "Growth of Special Economic Zones (SEZs) in India: Issues and Perspectives." *Journal of Infrastructure Development* 1, no. 2 (December 2009): 133–152.

Panagariya, Arvind. *India: The Emerging Giant*. New Delhi: Oxford University Press, 2008.

———. "Pro-Market Reforms and Growth." *Economic Times,* June 28, 2006. http://www.columbia.edu/~ap2231/ET/et91_June28-06.htm.

Pandey, Bishwa Mohan. *Historiography of India's Partition: An Analysis of Imperialist Writings*. New Delhi: Atlantic Publishers, 2003.

Pandey, Gyanendra. *Routine Violence: Nations, Fragments, Histories*. Stanford, CA: Stanford University Press, 2006.

———. "Subaltern Studies as Postcolonial Criticism." *American Historical Review* 99, no. 5 (December 1994): 1475–1490.

Pandian, M. S. S. "Notes on the Transformation of 'Dravidian' Ideology: Tamilnadu, c. 1900–1940." *Social Scientist* 22, nos. 5–6 (May–June 1994): 84–104.

Panikkar, K. M. "Middle Ground Between America and Russia: An Indian View." *Foreign Affairs* 32, no. 2 (January 1954): 259–270.

Pant, Harsh V. *Indian Policy in a Unipolar World*. London: Routledge, 2009.

Parajulee, Ramjee. *Democratic Transition in Nepal*. Lanham, MD: Rowman and Littlefield, 2000.

Paranjape, Makarand. *Altered Destinations: Self, Society, and Nation in India*. London: Anthem Press, 2009.

"Progress Toward Regional Nonproliferation in South Asia." Washington, DC: Congressional Research Service, February 8, 1994. http://www.fas.org/irp/threat/940216-327448.htm.

Prouty, Winston L. "The United States Versus Unneutral Neutrality." Speech to the US Senate, September 19, 1961. *Congressional Record,* vol. 107, 87th Congress, 19015–19028.

Punj, Balbir. "Death by Marx, Mandal." *Asian Age,* January 8, 2010.

Raghavan, Srinath. *War and Peace in Modern India*. New York: Palgrave Macmillan, 2010.

Rajan, M. S. "Indo-Soviet Friendship Treaty and India's Non-Alignment Policy." *Australian Journal of International Affairs* 26, no. 2 (August 1972): 204–215.

Rajghatta, Chidananda. "Desis in D.C." *Times of India,* December 19, 2009. http://www.garamchai.com/ObamaAdminNRIs.htm.

Rajiv, Sikri. *Challenge and Strategy: Rethinking India's Foreign Policy*. New Delhi: Sage, 2009.

Rana, A. *The Imperatives of Non-Alignment: A Conceptual Study of India's Foreign Policy Strategy in the Nehru Period*. New Delhi: Macmillan, 1976.

Rao, M. Govinda, and Nirvikar Singh. "The Political Economy of India's Fiscal Federal System and Its Reform." August 2006. http://www.escholarship.org/uc/item/3xf1752z?display=all.

Retzlaff, Ralph J. "India: A Year of Stability and Change." *Asian Survey* 3, no. 2 (February 1963): 96–106.

Richard, John F. *The Mughal Empire*. Cambridge: Cambridge University Press, 1993.

Ringman, Eric. "Empowerment Among Nations: A Sociological Perspective on Power in International Politics." In *Power in World Politics,* ed. Felix Berenskoetter and M. J. Williams. New York: Routledge, 2007, 189–203.

Rosen, George. *Democracy and Economic Change in India.* Los Angeles: University of California Press, 1966.

Rotter, Andrew. *Comrades at Odds: The U.S. and India.* Ithaca, NY: Cornell University Press, 2000.

Russett, Alan D. "On Understanding India's Foreign Policy." *International Studies* 4, no. 2 (April 1962): 212–240.

Sagar, Jagdish. "Power Distribution Reforms in Delhi." April 2010. www.idfc .com/pdf/.../Delhi-Distribution-Reforms-Draft-Report.pdf.

Sahay, Anjali. *Indian Diaspora in the United States.* Hyderabad: Orient Black-Swan, 2011.

"Sangh Parivar Assails Govt's Economic Policy." *Times of India,* September 1, 1999. http://articles.timesofindia.indiatimes.com/2002-08-04/patna/27322 167_1_sangh-parivar-sjm-bms.

Sarkar, Sumit. *Writing Social History.* New York: Oxford University Press, 1999.

"SC Orders Return of Land to Greater Noida Villagers." *Business Standard,* July 7, 2011. http://www.business-standard.com/india/news/sc-orders-returnland -to-greater-noida-villagers/441876/.

Schofield, Victoria. *Kashmir in Conflict: India, Pakistan, and the Unending War.* New York: I. B. Tauris, 2000.

Scott, David. "The Great Power 'Great Game' Between India and China: 'The Logic of Geography.'" *Geopolitics* 13, no. 1 (Spring 2008): 1–26.

Sen, Amartya. "Human Rights and Asian Values." Sixteenth Morgenthau Lecture on Ethics and Foreign Policy. Carnegie Council on Ethics and International Affairs, New York, 1997. http://www.cceia.org/media/254_sen.pdf.

Sharma, Ashok. "Farm Loan Waiver: Timely Relief but Doubts Remain." *Financial Express,* March 10, 2008. http://www.financialexpress.com/news/farm -loan-waiver-timely-relief-but-doubts-remain/282223/.

Sheehan, Vincent. "The Case for India." *Foreign Affairs* 30, no. 1 (October 1951): 77–90.

Shreedharan, E. "The Growth and Sectoral Composition of India's Middle Class: Its Impact on the Politics of Economic Liberalization." *India Review* 3, no. 4 (October 2004): 405–428.

Shukla, Vatsala. *India's Foreign Policy in the New Millennium: The Role of Power.* New Delhi: Atlantic Publishers, 2005.

Singh, Anoop. "Policy Environment and Regulatory Reforms for Private and Foreign Investment in Developing Countries: A Case of the Indian Power Sector." Discussion Paper No. 64. Asian Development Bank, Manila. April 2007.

Singh, Harinder. *Establishing India's Military Readiness: Concerns and Strategy.* Monograph No. 5. New Delhi: Institute of Defence Studies and Analyses, November 2011.

Singh, Jaswant. *Defending India.* London: Macmillan, 1999.

Singh, M. P., and Rekha Saxena. *Indian Politics: Contemporary Issues and Concerns.* New Delhi: Prentice Hall, 2008.

Sirohi, Seema. "Raised to the Power of N." *Outlook* (Delhi), September 22, 2008. http://www.outlookindia.com/article.aspx?238447.

Sisson, Richard, and Leo Rose. *War and Secession: Pakistan, India, and the Creation of Bangladesh.* Berkeley: University of California Press, 1990.

Subrahmanyam, K. "Commentary: Narisimha Rao and the Bomb." *Strategic Analysis* 28, no. 4 (October–December 2004): 593–595.

Subramanian, Arvind. "The Evolution of Institutions in India and Its Relationship with Economic Growth." April 2007. http://www.iie.com/publications/papers/subramanian0407b.pdf.

Tahir-Kheli, Shrin. *India, Pakistan, and the United States: Breaking with the Past.* New York: Council on Foreign Relations, 1997.

Talbott, Strobe. *Engaging India: Diplomacy, Democracy, and the Bomb.* Washington, DC: Brookings Institution Press, 2004.

Tanham, George. "Indian Strategic Culture." *Washington Quarterly* 15, no. 1 (Winter 1992): 129–142.

Thachil, Tariq, and Ronald Herring. "Poor Choices: De-Alignment, Development, and Dalit/Adivasi Voting Patterns in Indian States." *Contemporary South Asia* 16, no. 4 (December 2008): 441–464.

Thapar, Romila. *Cultural Pasts: Essays in Early Indian History.* New York: Oxford University Press, 2001.

———. *A History of India.* Vol. 1. London: Penguin, 1966.

Tharoor, Shashi. *Nehru: The Invention of India.* New York: Arcade, 2003.

Thorner, Daniel, and Alice Thorner. *Land and Labour in India.* Bombay: Asia Publishing House, 1962.

Tipton, Frank. *The Rise of Asia: Economics, Society, and Politics in Contemporary Asia.* Hampshire, UK: Macmillan, 1998.

Toney, Ellison. "Enron's Eight-Year Power Struggle in India." *Asia Times* online, January 18, 2001. http://www.atimes.com/reports/ca13ai01.html.

Tripathi, Salil. "BJP vs History." *Asian Wall Street Journal,* March 20, 2001. http://www.saliltripathi.com/articles/Mar2001AsianWallStreetJournalEurope.html.

Union Budget and Economic Survey, 1993–1994. New Delhi: Ministry of Finance, Government of India, 1994. http://indiabudget.nic.in/es1993-94/1%20General%20Review.pdf.

Union Budget and Economic Survey, 2008–2009. New Delhi: Ministry of Finance, 2009. http://indiabudget.nic.in/es2008-09/chapt2009/chap12.pdf.

Upadhyay, R. "Globalization Versus Swadeshi." Paper No. 134. Noida, India: South Asia Analysis Group, July 8, 2000. http://www.southasiaanalysis.org/%5Cpapers2%5Cpaper134.html.

Upadhyaya, Prakash Chandra. "The Politics of Indian Secularism." *Modern Asian Studies* 26, no. 4 (October 1992): 815–853.

Vanaik, Achin. *The Furies of Indian Communalism: Religion, Modernity, and Secularization.* London: Verso Books, 1997.

"Why Did India Reform?" Rediff.com, February 24, 2004. http://www.rediff.com/money/2004/feb/24guest1.htm

Wilson, Dominic, and Roopa Purushothaman. "Dreaming with BRICs: The Path to 2050." Goldman Sachs Global Economics Paper No. 99, October 1, 2003. http://www2.goldmansachs.com/our-thinking/brics/brics-reports-pdfs/brics-dream.pdf.

Yahya, Kalimpour, ed. *Images of the U.S. Around the World.* Albany: State University of New York Press, 1999.

Yardley, Jim. "Violence in Tibet as Monks Clash with Police." *New York Times,* March 15, 2008. http://www.nytimes.com/2008/03/15/world/asia/15tibet.html?pagewanted=all.

Index

About the Book

Why is India's rise on the world stage so controversial? How can a state that is losing authority to its regions at the same time grow in international importance? Exploring an apparent paradox, Maya Chadda shows how culture, politics, wealth, and policy have combined to forge a distinctive Indian path to power, both nationally and internationally.

Maya Chadda is professor of political science at William Patterson University of New Jersey. Her numerous publications include *Building Democracy in South Asia: India, Nepal, and Pakistan* and *Ethnicity, Security, and Separatism in South Asia.*